Balinese Food

The Traditional Cuisine
& Food Culture
of Bali

Balinese Food

The Traditional Cuisine
& Food Culture
of Bali

Vivienne Kruger

TUTTLE Publishing

Tokyo | Rutland, Vermont | Singapore

Published by Tuttle Publishing, an imprint of Periplus Editions (HK) Ltd

www.tuttlepublishing.com

Copyright © 2014 Vivienne Kruger
Photos © Vivienne Kruger, except for the following:
Front cover main photo: © irman/istockphoto.com; Front cover inset: © KellyOla/istockphoto.com;
Color insert pages 1 top: © magicinfoto/Shutterstock.com; 1 middle: © Henry Stockton/Shutterstock.com;
3 top, middle, bottom: © www.murnis.com and © www.jonathaninbali.com; 7 middle: © Gail Palethorpe/
Shutterstock.com; 9 top: © Marat Dupri/Shutterstock.com; 13 middle: © Redchanka/Shutterstock.com

Library of Congress Cataloging-in-Publication Data
Kruger, Vivienne L., 1950-
 Balinese food : the traditional cuisine & food culture of Bali / Vivienne Kruger, Ph.D.
    pages cm
 Includes index.
   ISBN 978-0-8048-4450-5 (pbk.)
1. Cooking, Balinese. 2. Food habits--Indonesia--Bali (Province) 3. Bali Island (Indonesia)--Social life
and customs. I. Title.
 TX724.5.I5K78 2014
 641.59598'62--dc23

                            2013040457

ISBN: 978-0-8048-4450-5

Distributed by
North America, Latin America & Europe
Tuttle Publishing, 364 Innovation Drive, North Clarendon, VT 05759-9436 USA
Tel: 1 (802) 773-8930; Fax: 1 (802) 773-6993
info@tuttlepublishing.com; www.tuttlepublishing.com

Japan
Tuttle Publishing, Yaekari Building, 3rd Floor, 5-4-12 Osaki, Shinagawa-ku, Tokyo 141-0032
Tel: (81) 3 5437-0171; Fax: (81) 3 5437-0755
sales@tuttle.co.jp; www.tuttle.co.jp

Asia Pacific
Berkeley Books Pte Ltd, 61 Tai Seng Avenue, #02-12, Singapore 534167
Tel: (65) 6280-1330; Fax: (65) 6280-6290
inquiries@periplus.com.sg; www.periplus.com

Indonesia
PT Java Books Indonesia, Kawasan Industri Pulogadung, Jl. Rawa Gelam IV No. 9, Jakarta 13930
Tel: (62) 21 4682-1088; Fax: (62) 21 461-0206
crm@periplus.co.id; www.periplus.com

Printed in Singapore   1401MP

16 15 14   10 9 8 7 6 5 4 3 2 1

TUTTLE PUBLISHING® is a registered trademark of Tuttle Publishing, a division of Periplus Editions (HK) Ltd.

contents

Dedication and Thanks

THIS BOOK IS DEDICATED to the extraordinarily beautiful young Bali-Hindu goddess Saraswati. Seated atop a pure white multi-layered lotus flower with her loyal white swan mount at her feet, Saraswati is the revered goddess of literature, wisdom, science, music and the arts. She is worshipped by everyone interested in knowledge and learning, especially students, teachers, scholars and scientists.

I also dedicate *Balinese Food* to my beloved, precious, beautiful Balinese dog—and constant companion—Chessie. With love and protectiveness and loyalty, my sweet Chessalopolis sat right by my side, watching me and guarding me during virtually all of the joyous, creative, multi-year writing, tasting and photo-taking process. Chessie and I lived side by side, body to body and soul to soul with each other; we shared the same karma and the same road towards enlightenment. Very special thanks goes to Starbucks on Jalan Pantai Kuta, Starbucks in the Discovery Mall (Tuban), Starbucks on Orchard Road in Singapore (Plaza Singapura) and in Waikiki, Oahu (Hilton Hawaiian Village), USA. My pretty black and white border collie patiently sat underneath the table at every single Starbucks from our home base in Kuta and Tuban in Bali to Karangahape Road in Auckland, New Zealand, to her favorite place in the world—Waikiki Beach in Hawaii. My little girl watched me write and rewrite every single page of this extreme love affair with the food and food culture of her native island of Bali.

Special gratitude goes to Wayan Sarma, long-time friend and driver from Pelaga village, Sanggingan-Ubud, who patiently accompanied me as I trekked through muddy rice fields to photograph dragonflies on the wing and ducks on the march, and to distant experimental agricultural farms where he sampled Bali's famous *kopi luwak* (civet droppings coffee) for me. Wayan showed me almost every edible food source on Bali, from rice field eels to *wani* fruit, from *taop* nuts to barrel-cured speckled black eggs. We sat together on a wooden bench at the famous Gianyar night market to feast on Bali's classic mixed rice dish, *nasi campur*, and to photograph buckets of blood-blackened Balinese *urutan* sausages. Wayan drove me to ramshackle rural village stalls, known as *warung*, to sample delicious finger bananas, tulip-shaped *kue mangkok* offering cakes and freshly made *jaja gina* rice cakes.

Extra special thanks also goes to another long-time friend and driver in Bali, Gede Kasena from Desa Jinengdalem, Singaraja, who patiently sat with me through endless food conferences and *nasi goreng* (fried rice) lunches in the mountains of Pacung to answer my most persistent questions about Balinese foodstuffs and cooking. With a happy heart, ready smile and spotless soul, Kasena generously enlightened me about Balinese eating culture and village produce, from the countless species of chili peppers to intriguing varieties of edible yard-long beans to ceremonial turtle *lawar*. Blessed with Balinese grace, intelligence and kindness, Kasena was my most important living local dictionary. He knows everything about Bali and this book would not have been possible without him.

Spiritual thanks go to my yoga teacher and friend in Darwin, Australia, Sanjit Das, who patiently explained the constellation of gods, kings and heroes in the ancient Hindu epic, the *Mahabharata*. In the legendary tale of the great warrior Yudisthera rests the ancient nexus between steadfast dogged myth and lunchtime dog satay in *warung* throughout Bali.

Academic acknowledgment is awarded to the elegant state-of-the-art Parliament House Library in Darwin, Australia. As a visiting scholar from the United States, I was accorded innumerable research privileges, kindness and Internet courtesies by head librarian Gaynor Lovett and librarian Suzie Young during the initial stages of this work. The library fortuitously maintained an invaluable Indonesian language resource on their reference shelf: Alan M. Stevens and A. Schmidgall-Tellings, *A Comprehensive Indonesian–English Dictionary* (Ohio University Press, 2004 and 2010 editions).

As a social historian with a Ph.D. in American history from Columbia University in New York, I wanted to produce a meticulously researched and comprehensive storehouse of hard-to-find information on Balinese cuisine, encompassing all aspects of traditional village food found, grown and consumed on the island. I first began to write about Bali in the late 1990s, producing a number of culture articles for *Bali and Beyond* magazine (2000–6). I have special memories of working with my talented editor at Bali and Beyond, Debe Campbell. During these years, I also wrote a large number of reviews of published books about the island of Bali, which still appear on www.amazon.com. I then spent eight years (2005–12) doing field research on the extraordinary foods and peoples of Bali, during which time I lived in Bali for two years. Earlier and shorter versions of the chapters in this book appeared in the *Bali Advertiser* (www. baliadvertiser.biz), Bali's most widely distributed English-language expatriate newspaper in Indonesia after the *Jakarta Post*: 13,000 copies are printed twice each month. I was fortunate enough to be asked to write their monthly food column ("Food of the Gods") for two years, from 2006 to 2008. This was a very fertile breeding ground and test run for my own Balinese cultural cookbook.

I am enormously grateful to a large caste of Balinese cooks and villagers throughout Bali. They guided me well with open hearts and took me inside many cramped compound kitchens during my spice-laced odyssey through the culinary Ring of Fire. Thank you to the hundreds of smiling, giggling, helpful friends everywhere in Bali, among them Mr and Mrs Dolphin (Warung Dolphin), Made Janur and Iloh (Janur Dive Inn), Justine Friedman (owner of the Akar Cafe), Iluh Padmi Antariasih (whose father is a powerful village *balian*), Australians Moira and David (owners of the Dolphin Beach Holiday Apartments), and my loyal friend and massage lady Yoni—all in Lovina on the north coast of Bali. Mr Dolphin was gracious enough to send me many international sms's to answer my emergency questions about local red snapper and mysterious coral reef fish! Endless thanks go to my very good friend Mega Barbara Ngoei from Jakarta; we had the best fun and food parties and food orgies in Lovina in 2009!

Special gratitude goes to another very good friend, since 1993, in Kuta, Eka Noviyantie, originally from Jakarta but resident in Bali since childhood. Eka helped me immeasurably with this amazing food journey, speeding off on her *sepeda motor* (motor scooter) to buy me *nasi jenggo* in the local market and sending me many sms's about my urgent *jaja* and

Balinese roast duck dilemmas! When I am in Bali, Eka accompanies me everywhere—to the fabulous Hard Rock Hotel for Mexican quesadillas and to Matahari Department store for tropical *sandal* shopping. Eka made phone calls all over Bali to help me get formal permission to use the beautiful Balinese recipes in this book. When Beachie (my dog Chessie's mother) died inside McDonald's in 2012, Eka and Kasena drove this precious dog to a veterinarian for a special Balinese cremation ceremony, performed from the heart with love, honor and kindness.

On a plane trip from Bali to Darwin, I was also fortunate to meet Balinese ecologist I Wayan Mudita, who teaches at the Faculty of Agriculture at Nusa Cendana University in Kupang, West Timor. He was kind enough to spend a great deal of time and effort helping me track down some of the most beautiful edible leaves in Bali: *daluman*, *bulan baon* and *salam*.

Additional thanks go to Ni Wayan Murni and Jonathan Copeland in Ubud, who blessed me with many original recipes; Urip Sudiasa and wonderful chef I Wayan Sudirna at the Tanis Villas in Nusa Lembongan; the Puri Lumbung Cottages in Munduk; Cok Oka Derana, a Balinese prince from Guwang, and my little sister Miss Era and her real sister Sri in Seririt, who gave me food, family recipes, cooking demonstrations and insight into the ancient, divine cooking on the spectacular island where the gods live.

Introduction

THIS BOOK ON THE TRADITIONAL CUISINE OF BALI bears witness to Bali's time-honored village cuisine. The legendary beauty of Bali is mirrored in both its creative culinary arts and its food culture. Three million Balinese share the same small green jewel of an island and the same culinary worldview. Together, they embrace a deeply ingrained cultural and spiritual understanding of ancient, divinely ordained foods, food preparation methods, cooking skills and motivations. They also live in complete culinary and philosophical harmony with nature—with the island's lava-enriched soil and with the flora and fauna, mysterious sea life and rare spice gifts that govern their exotic equatorial cuisine. The preparation of Balinese food is steeped in divine rituals and religious perfectionism. We, as curious Westerners, can only gape in awe as we struggle to learn how to eat and make food offerings on the island of the gods. *Balinese Food* breaks new ground in its study of Balinese culture and the extraordinary people of Bali, approached through the unique vehicle of their traditional cooking rites. Curious cooks elsewhere now have an unprecedented opportunity to absorb the anthropological, agricultural and practical village context in which traditional Balinese food is so painstakingly created.

The many faces and pleasures of Balinese food and drink spring to life in *Balinese Food* as it explores the social, cultural, ceremonial and religious implications of taking nourishment eight degrees south of the equator. As a paean to Balinese cooking culture and customs and its contribution to world food, we appreciate each dish in a unique spiritual context and on a grand historical scale. *Balinese Food* is divided into twenty-one chapters, each enriched by two or three easy-to-follow popular Balinese recipes. These step-by-step guides enable readers to re-create the unique food culture of Bali in the comfort of their own home.

Two sections of color photographs enhance each chapter's food themes, recipes and artistically prepared dishes.

Balinese Food celebrates the island's culinary bounty set in the shadow of lava-packed volcanoes. Written from the perspective and worldview of the people of Bali, the book casts first light on the previously unexplored secrets of Bali's virtually unknown cuisine, kitchen layout and apparatus and culinary mindset. Except for the ancient and sacred lontar texts, the Balinese have an oral rather than a written tradition of information preservation and transmission. It is therefore left to Westerners to record and archive Bali's food heritage. Authentic traditional Balinese food is hard to find outside the villages because the secrets of the island's cuisine, along with the preparation of the food itself, is steeped in religious ritual and devout Bali-Hindu belief. Three million peasants by day, three million artists by night, the Balinese carve and etch and paint their food into the rich spiritual shapes and divine colors of fragrant holy temples and imposing royal palaces. They build and they labor and they cook only to please and honor their gods.

CHAPTER ONE

Sacred Ceremonial Cuisine: Food of the Gods

———— ǂ ————

B ALI, THE GREEN JEWEL in the fiery heart of the Indonesian archipelago, is graced with fertile rice fields, rich volcanic soil, flourish-
ing fruit trees, edible wild greens, plentiful fish and a natural supply of
fragrant herbs and spices. Born and bred in equatorial abundance,
Balinese food has evolved into a cuisine full of exotic ingredients, aromas,
flavors and textures. It also plays a pivotal role in Balinese religion,
ritual and society. The Balinese cook in order to eat as well as to honor,
please and serve their gods. They incorporate their traditional values
into their food. To understand Bali's cuisine, one must appreciate the
tripartite role of food as vital human sustenance, sacrificial offering to
both respect the gods and appease the demons, and essential ritual component of Bali-Hindu religious ceremonies. As with everything else on
Bali, food is inextricably intertwined with faith. Behind high family
compound walls and on *bale banjar* (neighborhood meeting halls), entire
communities make ceremonial quantities of colored rice, sweet rice
cakes, meat-filled banana leaf offerings and regulation rows of skewered
chicken satay offerings for the gods, who will absorb the *sari* or essence
of this decorative consecrated feast held on sacred festival grounds. In
the Bali-Hindu religion, the making of ceremonial food and offerings
is, in itself, an act of worshipping and honoring the gods. Traditionally,
the Balinese gain karma by preparing food and offerings for a large ceremony, such as a mass cremation, which normally took one month in
the past and carried with it a one-month gain of good karma.

Balinese food is distinctive among the leading cuisines of the world. Dedicated to the gods, this time-consuming, almost completely manual culinary art is inextricably bound to the island's Bali-Hindu religion, culture and community life. Rituals and ceremonies always escalate into large-scale ceremonial feasts. Bali's most visual, color and taste sensations only appear at major celebrations as the ingredients are costly and an inordinate amount of preparation time is required. Exquisitely embellished ritual foods are prepared for life cycle rituals (ground-touching ceremonies, weddings, tooth filings and cremations), temple anniversaries and important religious holidays like Galungan-Kuningan. The family or community involved contributes materials and labor, and the dishes are cooperatively fabricated in the temple kitchen. Some dishes are prepared as religious offerings while others are to be shared and eaten communally afterwards by co-workers, friends, family and *banjar* (village association or hamlet) members who have helped with the hard labor. Special mini-*rijistaafel* platters with small portions of several foods, crowned with decorative woven bamboo basket covers or *tutup*, are prepared and served to VIP *cokorda* (Balinese royalty) in attendance. In accordance with local custom, meals for the other castes are presented on a *round* platter. Each tray artfully displays such treasures as *nasi kuning* (yellow rice with turmeric, peanut and spiced grated coconut) and vegetarian *lawar* (the traditional preparation of such vegetables as ferns or *paku*, egg and green beans mixed with coconut and spices).

Mass tooth filings may entail two months of preparation and the women of the compound have to prepare daily meals to sustain the armies of workers. Grand ceremonies turn the family kitchen into an ongoing neighborhood food production factory. Banana leaf-wrapped packets of food are also hand-delivered to distant family and friends following any major village ceremony, even in modern, bustling workaday Kuta.

When the Mexican painter, traveler and amateur anthropologist Miguel Covarrubias's seminal work, *Island of Bali*, was published in 1937, it ignited the world's love affair with Bali. Covarrubias's vivid impressions of a pre-modern, pre-tourist Bali included the first Western descriptions of traditional Balinese food and food culture. In his classic text, he described local feasts or *banjar* banquets and ceremonies in Bali in the 1930s: "When the food is ready and the guests are assembled, sitting in long rows, they are served by the leading members of the banjar and their assistants. They circulate among them carrying trays with pyramids of rice and little square palm leaf or banana leaf dishes pinned together with bits of bamboo. These holders contain chopped *lawar* mixtures, *saté lembat*, *babi guling*, *bebek betutu*, and little side dishes of fried winged beans (*botor*), bean sprouts with crushed peanuts, parched grated coconuts dyed yellow with *kunyit* (turmeric), and preserved salted eggs—always accompanied by *tuak*, *arak*, and *brem*."

There is a strict gender division of ritual labor in Bali. The preparation of dishes that require sacrificial meats, from the slaughtering of the animals to the expert grinding of the spices, from the winding of the satays to the mincing of the turtle and pork dishes, is strictly a male responsibility because it is physically strenuous work. Ritual food is traditionally prepared at night as it has to be ready in the morning for ceremonies which often begin at dawn. Scores of men from each household gather at the *bale banjar* armed with large cleaver-like Balinese knives (*belaka*) and cutting boards to perform a sacred procedure known as *mebat* or *ngeracik basa*, the chopping of all the ceremonial ingredients. The spices are presented to them in woven coconut leaf baskets. The teams of men sit crosslegged on the ground on coconut leaf mats in two long rows facing each other, their chopping boards in between. Clad in traditional sarongs and sashes and wearing large antique silver or gold rings embedded with magical stones and potent protective powers, they mix and grind piles of pre-chopped spices. The men energetically smash shallots and garlic cloves, crush spices, scrape galangal and turmeric roots and hand-grate and shred dozens of freshly roasted coconuts for three hours on the evening before a ceremony. The tek-tek-tek sound of their knives on the cutting boards can be heard far away. This sound is an inescapable part of Balinese village life. When the spices are prepared and ready, the men go home for a few hours of sleep and return at 1 a.m. to butcher and prepare the animal meat—a whole sea turtle (*penyu*) in southern Bali, ducks or pigs in other parts of the island. The men boil organ meats to be skewered and grilled and prepare blood soup and pork tartare from 3 to 5 a.m. A jug of *arak* is often passed around to enliven the proceedings. Women are only allowed to wash salad ingredients, fry onions and assist with other basic preparation chores. They also cook the rice, prepare vegetables, make coffee, tea and rice cake refreshments for guests and helpers, and plait hundreds of coconut leaf offerings.

The *megibung* ritual (*megibung* means having a meal together), a cultural feast of epic proportions, is still carried out in Bali, as largely unchanged customary practices continue to take precedence over modernity. The traditional *megibung* food feast originated in the eighteenth century during the time of the Karangasem kingdom in East Bali and is still widely observed in the villages. Beside being a tool of religious ritual and a communal gathering, the purpose of the *megibung* was also to ascertain how many troops were in the kingdom's army at that time. This traditional event is now held in order to build togetherness and reinforce friendship and brotherhood within the community. At the gathering, all participants are considered equal—none is rich or poor and none is educated or uneducated. The *megibung* is carried out at meal times during the laborious group process of organizing and implementing temple ceremonies and during life cycle rituals such as weddings. The early morning (3–6 a.m.) *mebat* procedure is the entrance ticket for the subsequent male only *megibung* feast, which takes place at the *banjar* before every large temple festivity, around 6 a.m. Holy cooking responsibilities are taken very seriously. The *mebat* men conscientiously chop ingredients pre-dawn for all the ceremonial food, special community portions for family members and ritual *banjar* chefs, and the upcoming *megibung* participants.

The distinguishing feature of the *megibung* is that the men eat together from the same big plate (*sela*) and share the same dishes using their hands as utensils. They must consume all the food that is served. This normally consists of an array of traditional Balinese festival dishes (satay, vegetables, *lawar*, rice, etc.) placed in bamboo or banana leaf containers in the center of a group of five to eight (up to a maximum of ten) men seated on the ground on a communal bamboo mat. (One unit of *gibungan* typically consists of eight people sitting around the food.) If a hundred men attend the *megibung*, there will usually be twenty groups. Ancient protocols govern conduct during the *megibung* gathering. No one may try to start ahead of another and each participant takes his portion from in front of where he sits. The oldest participant is appointed the group coordinator. On the agreement of the participants, the coordinator invites the members to start and then determines when the gathering will be completed, usually when all the members have been satisfied. The coordinator also selects the next side dish to be added to the food tray. Generally, the first side dish served, equivalent to the first course, is selected from less tasty foods such as star fruit leaf, *lawar* and *komoh*, a thick soup made from chopped pork, fresh chicken or pig blood, and a little bit of water. *Komoh* only can be found in some areas in western and northern Bali when people celebrate Penampahan Galungan, one of Hindu Bali's most auspicious days. When the side dishes run short or the participants get bored with them, it is time to serve more mouth-watering dishes, such as satay or meat.

The entire village comes together to facilitate Bali's communal feasts. A grand ceremony may entail days or even weeks of cooking to prepare enough food for 700 or more people, necessitating the slaughter of several small pigs and the purchase of 110 pounds of spices! Each village or area has its own male ritual cooking specialist who directs and inspects the work. There is tremendous local variation and theological competition in the preparation of traditional ritual foods intended for the gods. When men from different regencies, villages or even adjacent *banjar* prepare ceremonial foods together, methodological differences and debates arise over such minutiae and practices as the correct order in which to add and mix the spices, vegetables, coconut and other *lawar* ingredients. When it comes to preparing ritual banquet food, the men are the ceremonial chefs and it is the men alone who can prepare the great festival dishes of roast sucking pig and sea turtle, the cooking of which requires the skilled, secret magical arts of famous specialists. Certain prosperous *banjar* have earned reputations for their superlative cooking, and their "famous cooks" are always in great demand island-wide to officiate at feasts. Locals eagerly anticipate the arrival of well-known ritual cooks to direct the preparation of epicurean masterpieces like *saté lembat*, *babi guling* and *lawar*. Keepers of the knowledge and philosophy of traditional religious cuisine, Bali's men jealously guard these age-old secrets of sacred ritual cooking, only passing on the techniques and traditions to their own sons when they reach age sixteen.

Lawar (which means thinly sliced) is Bali's most famous festival masterpiece. This style of cooking uses many different materials and combinations of fresh, shaved and roasted coconut, seasoned coconut milk, egg omelette, shredded young jackfruit or fern tips, young beans, starfruit leaves, black, white, fresh green and long pepper, fried chilies, spice paste, shrimp paste, kaffir lime, palm sugar, green papaya, garlic, salt, shallots, finely chopped pork meat, skin, stomach lining, entrails and cartilage, fresh congealed pig's blood (set aside after slaughtering or available in small plastic bags in the market), and the closely minced cooked innards of sacrificial animals, all of which are mixed together by hand to produce the different types of *lawar*. This complex, time-consuming, highly perishable ritual dish is served with crisp pork crackling at all large family rituals or temple ceremonies on Bali. It is the first mandatory plan in any ritual cooking activity. The excess of all the rest pales in comparison to the religious requirements placed on the creation of *lawar*. Many different kinds and ritually significant colors of traditional *lawar* accompany Balinese feasts to represent the eight sacred cardinal points and directions, each of which symbolizes a different aspect of god with and its associated color. The Balinese make an entire suite—a minimum of five different kinds—of *lawar* dishes for a festival. Only a ritual food specialist or the oldest, most ceremonially seasoned men are allowed to combine the color-coded components. A coveted complication is the need to add fresh raw pig blood to the *lawar*. The abundance of spices is believed to prevent and protect against trichinosis from the consumption of raw pork.

Lawar is usually named according to its color, as in *lawar merah* (red *lawar*) and *lawar putih* (white *lawar*). Red *lawar*, symbolizing Lord Brahma and the southerly direction, must always contain blood and skinned raw meat. Turtle or pork strips mixed with slivers of young papaya, mango or coconut, spices, uncooked animal blood and pounded raw entrails yield red *lawar*. If fresh raw pig blood is added to the *lawar*, the *lawar* has a pink or red color. Alternately, the Balinese will dry the blood on a table for thirty minutes, cut it up into blocks or pieces, fry it and then add it to the *lawar*. The *lawar* will be black in color if it contains this dried, fried pig's blood. In Gianyar regency, more vegetables are added to red *lawar* than in other regencies (long beans, in particular, are prominent in chicken *lawar*). *Lawar* can also be named according to its ingredients. *Lawar* mixed with pork is called *lawar babi* (pork *lawar*) and *lawar* which contains young jackfruit is called *lawar nangka*. White *lawar* is largely made of coconut meat. It contains raw meat but no blood and represents the north. Yellow *lawar*, representing the east, is a mixture of red and white lawar. Green *lawar*, representing Lord Wisnu and the westerly direction, is made of peanut leaf or peanuts, *belimbing* (starfruit) cloves or diced long green beans, spices, coconut milk and boiled meat. Multicolored *lawar*, representing Lord Siwa and the center, is a mixture of all the other four colors. A common ingredient in all five types of *lawar* is roasted coconut.

Ngelawar (*lawar* making) is a frequent activity on Bali. Formerly, traditional Balinese *lawar* was only made in conjunction with Galungan feast days, temple anniversaries and customary or religious ceremonies. *Lawar* can now be made any time, especially to commemorate Indonesia's national day or for festivities to welcome the New Year. In Tabanan regency, *ngelawar* is commonly performed by young teenage boys in rural communities. They spontaneously buy an amount of meat, and since it is not a religious event, the exact type of meat and the kind of menu that is required is more flexible. Financed by high priests, lucky hamlets will slaughter a pig and employ it to make Bali's favorite pork *lawar* delicacy. The meat is also processed into other types of *lawar*, grilled dishes, satay and local specialties. The young men make auspicious cones of rice, Manila duck *lawar*, grilled fish, young banana trunk soup and assorted fresh cakes (*jaja*). Seated face to face *megibung* style on bamboo mats, the boys are dressed in temple attire as they chop the ingredients into slivers with traditional cleavers on tree trunk cutting boards. Endless rows of smoking satays on thin sticks will also be fanned and grilled on braziers on the ground to cheer up the workers. This traditional food festival also celebrates the anniversary of the founding of the village youth club. Staged at the local hamlet hall, the joyous annual December event, replete with family atmosphere, celebrates the end of the old year and welcomes in the new one. Traditional Balinese dances are performed and the rice cone is ceremonially cut.

Specialty *lawar* abounds in Bali. The exotic hallmark of *lawar embung*, a traditional recipe from Tabanan, is sliced fresh young bamboo mixed with peanuts, peanut leaf and meat. Today's increasingly urbanized Balinese, however, no longer relish eating bamboo (*embung*) and recall the difficulties of cutting down the tree and slicing it, and thus *lawar embung* is a village rarity nowadays. Apart from ceremonies, various kinds of *lawar*, including jackfruit, can be sampled at local *babi guling warung*. Spicy red hot *padamare lawar* is a combination of many kinds of *lawar* together (*padam* means to put out a fire; it also means fiery red or scarlet). This very heavily peppered *lawar* recreates the historical taste of original Balinese food, uncorrupted by the introduction of chilies in the sixteenth century and other culinary concessions to the modern age. Negara regency boasts its own Balinese recipe for chicken *lawar* in which young coconut is the core ingredient.

To process the coconut, villagers pour out the water, scrape the soft skin from inside the shell, boil it in water and then press out the excess water by hand. The resulting material is chopped into small pieces and combined with a spice paste mixture (*bumbu*), onions and a small free-range boiled Balinese chicken. The Balinese draw daily on their ancient heritage and religious culinary imagination to create superb dishes geared towards the gods.

Vegetables (*sayur*) are eagerly recruited into festival culinary service. Vegetable and fruit dishes, such as fried winged beans (*botor*), bean sprouts with crushed peanuts and grated coconuts dyed a reverential yellow with turmeric, are an integral part of Bali's festival cuisine. Vegetarian *lawar* is made with ferns, egg and long green beans mixed with grated coconut, shallots, garlic cloves, red chilies, small hot green chilies, kaffir lime, salt and *bumbu* spice paste.

Elaborately executed *bebek betutu* (whole smoked duck), *babi guling* (suckling pig) and *jukut ares* (classic banana tree trunk soup) also feature prominently on the temple-bound menu. The Balinese marshal condiments, oddments, bananas and coconuts to turn almost anything edible into an outstanding village delicacy. The tender harvested core of a young banana palm stem, resembling a crunchy, rounded piece of bamboo with tiny holes, is very thinly sliced and boiled with spices, minced meat (pork or beef), duck (wings, legs and head) or chicken to make *jukut ares*, a substantial aromatic stew composed of young banana tree trunk and meat. Banana pods (the flower buds) can be used instead. (Stems from the mature banana plants are only used as pig food on Bali.) The resulting dish will be called *serosop*. *Ares* (which means the pith of the banana plant) is typically served at large ritual feasts and to family and neighbors who assisted in cooking, making offerings and arranging the ceremonies.

Ceremonial *tum* is cooked daily in many family compounds for Bali's ceremonies. *Tum* are minced parcels of ground pork, duck, chicken, chicken liver (*tum hati ayam*), fish, beef or eel liberally laced with shallots, ginger, garlic, kaffir lime leaves, chilies, turmeric, lesser galangal, *salam* leaves, *sambal* and spice paste. *Tum* starts out similarly to *saté lilit* but it contains no grated coconut or palm sugar. The pasty mixtures are packed into triangular, pleated banana leaf purses or corn husks to create this classic Balinese ritual dish. The purses are sealed with either a sharp banana stick, a sharpened coconut leaf rib used specially for fastening leaf-wrapped packages or, more usually, with a tiny bamboo stick called a *semat*. Shaped to look like a holy mountain peak, they are then steamed. Chicken or fish *tum* is also prepared as an occasional, everyday food for lunch or dinner. Created and conveyed with love, art and reverence for the gods, Bali's temple-bound food offerings are purified by white-robed, bell-ringing high priests, sprinkled with holy water and then carried home to be eaten. Nourishment dances and vacillates between sustenance and sacrifice on an island of the gods perfectly positioned and protected eight degrees south of the equator.

Red Pork Lawar with Blood

LAWAR MERAH (BAHASA INDONESIA), OR LAWAR BARAK (BALINESE)

In this holy covenant between god, man and food, lawar is the undisputed high priest of festival cuisine. Each different lawar dish is impossibly time-consuming and complex in its creation and preparation, offering deeply harmonized layers of texture and flavor in a glorious Balinese presentation. It is sacred work and ritualized worship. The gods cook here for all the world to see.

Recipe courtesy of Cok Oka Derana, Guwang village, Gianyar, Bali, 2008. Cok Oka, a Satria caste prince, works as a bellboy at the Inna Kuta Beach

Hotel, Kuta. His brother, Cok Raka, is a woodcarver-artist and maintains an impressive local art gallery in their home compound in Guwang. A happy, always smiling ambassador of his beloved island, Cok Oka is dedicated to promoting and preserving native Balinese culture, ceremonies and traditions.

11 oz (300 g) good quality pork
11 oz (300 g) pork skin
1 bowl pig's blood
11 oz (300 g) long green beans
½ piece young jackfruit
1¼ lb (600 g) shallots
11 oz (300 g) garlic cloves
½ coconut
small amount of coconut milk with spices (*kalas*)
11 oz (300 g) chilies
½ piece white ginger and ½ piece yellow ginger
½ package very hot small peppers (*merica*)
lemongrass
shrimp paste
¼ tsp lesser galangal
black and white pepper and salt to taste
brown sugar to taste

First, prepare the *bumbu* or spice paste mixture. Peel and slice the shallots, half the garlic cloves and the white ginger, then fry. Complete the *bumbu* mixture with finely minced fried chilies, fried shrimp paste, brown sugar, black pepper, white pepper and salt. Grind all the above ingredients to a fine powder.

Boil the sliced pork skin, young jackfruit and long beans. Use ¾ of the young coconut, grated. Use the rest of the coconut—preferably half a coconut—for *kalas* (coconut milk with spices) for *lawar jukut* (vegetarian *lawar*) or for *lawar putih* (white lawar). Mix the coconut with blood to make it red, then grill (burn) the coconut. Add sugar. Peanut leaf or other vegetables can be added to the pork *lawar* according to preference.

Prepare the pork meat by chopping it into very small particles until smooth. Grill the meat first. Add some *bumbu*, *terasi*, salt, brown sugar, hot chilies and finely sliced pandanus leaves. Mix together. Make the mixture flat and level.

Crackling, sliced pork skin (*kulit babi*)—good color skin.

Fry garlic and add one whole white onion, already sliced.

Grind and add small black and white peppers (*tabia merica*). Mix the result together into a powder—a dry grind. Cut an old (brown) *kelapa* (coconut) in half. Grill (burn) it first. Slice the coconut. Add the burnt coconut.

In order to make the *lawar* the religiously required red color, add the raw blood to the sliced coconut. Use real fresh blood from the pig. The fresh blood becomes hard after only ten minutes. When you want to use the blood for the *lawar*, it must be blended with lemongrass to make it soft again—the consistency of red water. Mix hot coconut oil into the blood, and then mix it together with the meat, sauce and coconut. Add a squeeze of lime for fragrance.

Taste the *lawar* mixture to test the balance of sweet and salt levels. Adjust to taste.

This *lawar* recipe can be used to make *lawar jukut* (vegetarian *lawar*). Simply omit the pork meat, blood, skin and by-products. Add yellow ginger to turn the *lawar* a yellow color and add young burnt taro and peanuts. Add *kalas*, made by mixing coconut milk with *bumbu* (spice paste) and boiling to a temperature of 80 degrees centigrade.

Various other important side dishes are usually prepared as an offshoot of the effort and number of ingredients involved in making *lawar*. A meat version of *kalas* is ordinarily prepared as a spin-off. Boil the *kalas* (coconut milk with spices) with pork meat and mix with long green beans. Delicious pork meat sausages (*urutan*) are always made on the side from the rich extra supply of pork meat available on these ceremonial occasions.

The *lawar* is transferred to a pan. The same recipe can also be prepared as *lawar putih*—white *lawar* without blood.

Serves 4–6.

Jukut Ares

(YOUNG BANANA TREE TRUNK IN SPICY SOUP)

Ares is a Balinese stew made from young banana stalks and chicken or other meats. Banana trunk (the tender heart of the banana tree stem) may admittedly be hard to find, but it's worth enquiring at specialty Asian stores. The flavor of banana trunk is similar to celery.

Ni Wayan Murni is the successful owner and creator of internationally famous Murni's Warung (the first real Western-style restaurant in Ubud, opened in 1974), Murni's Warung Gift Shop, Murni's Houses, the Tamarind Spa in Murni's Houses, Murni's Villas and the treasure-filled Kunang-Kunang

I and Kunang-Kunang II antique shops in Ubud. Murni's prestigious, well-trafficked network of Ubud businesses has attracted many decades worth of annual customers, friends and repeat food-loving clientele. Her extensive, culturally oriented website empire, www.murnis.com, is a leading online resource center for all things Balinese.

Recipe courtesy of Ni Wayan Murni, Murni's Warung, Campuhan-Ubud, Bali, 2006.

10 shallots
2 garlic cloves
10 red chilies
5 hot chilies
4 candlenuts
1 tsp coriander seed
1 tsp cumin seed
½ tsp grated nutmeg
½ tsp lesser galangal
½ tsp white pepper
1½ in (4 cm) lemongrass leaf
1 tsp shrimp paste
1 tsp black pepper
1 tsp salt to taste
3 tsp vegetable oil
4½ lb (2 kg) banana trunk, finely sliced
8 cups chicken stock made from 2 tsp Masoko chicken powder or
　　　2 crumbled chicken stock cubes

Place the spices in a blender and pulse until reduced to a smooth paste or, for a better taste, grind with a mortar and pestle. Add a little water, if necessary.

Fry the paste in vegetable oil for a few minutes, taking care not to scorch it. Add the sliced banana trunk and stir fry until the banana wilts.

Add the chicken stock and gently simmer until the banana trunk is tender. Serves 4–6.

Lawar Capung

(DRAGONFLY LAWAR)

Lawar capung is only prepared and eaten for ceremonies. It is not an everyday village food. It is normally cooked for family ceremonies, not for temple ceremonies, such as a six-month baby ceremony for a son. In Nusa Lembongan, the dragonflies are caught with a net resembling a tennis racket. In Bali, the capung are caught in the sawah (lush rice fields), but in more arid Nusa Lembongan they are found in the cassava or corn fields. The weather varies in different parts of Bali. Nusa Lembongan is dry and hot and the only source of water is rain; there are no rivers, mountains or wet, irrigated rice fields as in Bali. Because there are different conditions, the food is different. The people of Nusa Lembongan only eat capung when the rainy season (musim hujan) is coming or in the rainy season itself when they can get the capung. The men catch them in the morning rather than at night.

Recipe courtesy of I Wayan Sudirna (Ceningan Island), a local Balinese chef at the Tanis Villas Resort, Nusa Lembongan. The village chief in Nusa Ceningan depends on Wayan to prepare the lawar for Balinese wedding parties. Two hundred men will come to a typical Nusa Lembongan wedding with many traveling back from Bali for the event. Wayan makes the food for the men while the women make the offerings for the gods. There is a different menu at wedding parties for single young men and for old married men. The young men will eat chicken curry, chicken nuggets, saté ayam, lamb (kambing) and suckling pig. The old men will eat pork or fish lawar, saté lilit (pork only) and ares. Members of the banjar will cook from 4 a.m. until 9 a.m. The men do the chopping (only the chopping, no grinding) until the ingredients smell and taste very good. The foods are cooked from 1 p.m. to 7 p.m. or until ready. Dinner is usually held from 7 to 10 p.m. The local banjar also asks Wayan to make the required number of satay sticks for ceremonies. Cooking is still very traditional in Nusa Lembongan. In order to cook, the satay sticks rest on two stones suspended over a fire dug in a traditional sandpit. www.tanisvillas.com, December 2011.

- 1 tsp fresh turmeric
- 1 tsp fresh ginger
- 1 tsp fresh galangal
- 4 oz (120 g) shallots

2½ oz (60 g) garlic
2½ oz (60 g) small red chilies
¼ tsp black pepper
1¼ lb (600 g) dragonflies
¾ lb (350 g) young coconut
½ lb (250 g) jackfruit
4 kaffir lime leaves, sliced
Masoko chicken powder
brown sugar

Clean and wash the turmeric, ginger, galangal, shallots, garlic and small red chilies and chop until small. Fry the spices in coconut oil for 5 minutes.

Clean and cut the heads off the dragonflies and grill the bodies until brown.

Grill the whole young coconut on the fire, then hand-grate for 10 minutes.

Boil the jackfruit for 10 minutes, then chop until small. Put the jackfruit, grilled dragonflies and grated coconut into a bowl.

Fry the shallots until crispy along with the sliced kaffir lime leaf, Masoko chicken powder and brown sugar. Add to the bowl of jackfruit, dragonflies and grated coconut. Mix well.

Thread the dragonflies onto a satay stick, ten to a stick.

Serve the *lawar* with yellow rice.

CHAPTER TWO

The Balinese Kitchen: Hearth and Home

———— ✦ ————

Traditional Balinese cuisine is home-based village cooking in contrast to its ceremonial culinary splendor. There is no written history of Balinese food. None of the complex ancient recipes for daily food or for extraordinary festival cuisine are copied down or recorded in cookbooks, nor are they mentioned in the sacred lontar inscriptions (old manuscripts originally written on lontar leaves from the Borassus, the Asian Palmyra palm). Collecting consistent, reproducible recipes from the Balinese is difficult. Like so many other traditions in Bali, cooking techniques and eating habits are passed down verbally by elders to their children and grandchildren who help in the kitchen. However, Indonesia has an old orally transmitted food culture because the pleasure of storytelling is entwined with the pleasure and effort of cooking and eating. Indonesians generally, including the Balinese, weave food tales into culinary myths and legends as they pass on the communal food ways of the group or village. Nourishment is a family secret and everything is learned from the old folks in the compound, including relatives and neighbors. Before the modern food era, people relied for guidance about what to eat on their national or ethnic or regional cultures. Balinese food culture, and the Balinese food environment, still has a great deal to say about what, how, why, when and how much the people of Bali should cook and eat.

Balinese cooking is labor-intensive. Spice pastes are blended in a stone mortar and pestle, meats are very finely minced, vegetables are cut up and progressively reduced to microscopic bits and fibers. The numerous ingredients are invariably mixed by hand, and most foods are double or even multiprocessed, sequentially boiled or steamed and then fried. Preparing Balinese food is a slow, passionate labor of love. From childhood, Balinese know how to slice, chop, mix and grind out recipes with great skill. They observe, learn and master the fine collaborative art of creating monumental spice pastes and *sambal* sauces, the twin culinary symbols of traditional Balinese cuisine. The Balinese do not follow set recipes or weigh, measure and gauge level teaspoons of ingredients. The hand is the standard measurement device in the Balinese kitchen. Wizened old grannies and calm, resolute fathers rule the Balinese kitchen, cooking by taste, hereditary custom, instinct and past experience. With accumulated years of culinary, religious and cultural wisdom, they are great everyday cooks. The pungent food is brought to life with gusto, enjoyment, community bonding and reverence for the task at hand.

Women cook the simple, routine daily meals in Bali, making full use of the array of spices, fruits, grains, fish and vegetables that nature has given them to work with. When humans eat, they use all of their senses (sight, hearing, smell, touch and taste) to judge how delicious a food is. The Balinese exalt and tease and celebrate every last one of their God-given senses while selecting and cooking their nourishment. Bali's early morning markets are the dynamic focal point of local community life and the source of food in every Balinese village. The typical *ibu* (mother) leaves the house at 5 a.m. each morning, just after dawn to go to the market or to a more expensive, more convenient neighborhood *warung*, to buy fresh provisions for the day's meals, offerings and ceremonies. The traditional village market, better known as the *pasar tenten* (*tenten* means wake up), remains a strong institution even in the midst of ever-encroaching modern supermarkets. The price of articles at village or traditional markets is much cheaper than at supermarkets, contingent, of course, on the good bargaining and social skills of the shopper. Although their stock is less complete, village markets can provide daily consumer goods. The Balinese also rely on local markets for necessities for rituals (selected chickens of a particular color, ducks and piglets) not found at modern markets. Another advantage of the daily village market is that it opens very early in the morning (3–5 a.m.). Its goods, still relatively fresh at 10 a.m., are often repurchased mid-morning by brokers to be sold at larger markets. Typical markets are often situated at the T-road junction of the local village. Buyers and sellers, mostly from local hamlets, congregate in a jumble of kiosks and sheds in a compact area. Most of the goods on sale consist of farming and garden commodities produced by the local community. In the front and middle areas, traders array themselves in a row to offer their wares, while in the rear spaces are reserved for the vendors of ducks, chickens and piglets.

Eager to finish shopping before 7 a.m., Balinese women go early when trading is most brisk (the markets sell out of goods and die down by 10 a.m.) to interact with friends, neighbors and regular sellers as they bargain for the day's household necessities. A woman's family will wake up to the comforting, familiar kitchen smells of rice steaming in the *dangdang* pot, smoke from the wood stove fire and chilies frying in oil. Aromatic fresh spices, roasted first in some village households, must also be ground every morning in a mortar and pestle to make a fresh spice paste. The traditional skill and knowledge of how to wield the *batu base* (*cobek*) is carefully passed down from mother to daughter. Indeed, in the past a prospective daughter-in-law's worth was based on her ability to use the mortar and pestle. The wife cooks and completes the entire day's food supply of rice and other dishes and leaves them on a table or inside a cupboard, covered with banana leaf squares, for family members to eat cold whenever they get hungry. There are no set meal times.

Banana leaf squares and wrappers are a necessary part of Balinese kitchen equipment. Like all Southeast Asians, the Balinese have developed sophisticated techniques of utilizing leaves to wrap a host of traditional dishes. Different leaves impart different flavors and aromas to food, and specific leaves are specially pre-prepared before they are used. There are many classic techniques of wrapping food with leaves to produce delicious and artistic edible treasures. The daily food may also be placed in a special basket called a *kerenjang gantung*, which is suspended from the ceiling of the kitchen. A *kereneng* is a bag or pouch made of pandanus leaves or a charcoal basket made of bamboo wickerwork, and a *keranjang* is a rough basket. *Gantung* means to hang or suspend, and *antung-antung* is a hanging suspended holder for a *kris* or for kitchen utensils. In modern Denpasar kitchens, food is placed on the kitchen table covered by a pretty pink or red plastic net basket called a *tutup makan* (food cover).

Young bamboo nodes and tubes as well as empty coconut shells are also used as food molds, storage vessels and food packaging. They also serve as containers for cooking food over fires and grills. The *bungbung* is a cylindrical tube made from cut bamboo, and is used to cook fish, chicken or pork, in fact any meat-based dish. Only young bamboo is used as old bamboo is too dry and can catch fire. Meat cooked in a *bungbung* has a unique taste and smell as it absorbs the scent of the bamboo. A complement of spices is added to the meat, put in one end of the tube with a little water so it will boil and the *bungbung* is closed with a leaf to keep the water inside. The size of the bamboo tube depends on the amount of meat being cooked. Usually, one segment of bamboo, 30 to 45 cm in length, is used. If there is a lot of meat, two segments may be used. A small fire is built and the bamboo tube placed on the ground, leaf-covered end upward, leaning on a slant against the wooden frame placed above the fire. The *bungbung* cannot be put directly in the fire because it will burn. As the meat cooks, it becomes "melting soft" because the water inside cannot escape. This is ancient pressure-cooking, Balinese village style! The cooking time depends on the fire. If the fire is good, one hour is enough, though typical cooking time using a *bungbung* is one to two hours. The Balinese will only do this for special occasions like Galungan or Kuningan when they have a lot of meat. The *bungbung* is not used for daily cooking as people are too busy and the method is complicated.

Nasi (steamed rice) *campur* (mixture) is the basic thrice daily meal on Bali. The Balinese eat the same food for each meal as the wife only cooks once a day. Food also varies very little from one day to the next. Bali's ubiquitous plate of steamed white rice is inseparable from its cuisine. Bali's rice-based culinary culture requires that fresh rice be cooked every single morning. Rice left overnight is deemed to be fit only as animal food. The women cook both ceremonial and ordinary household food with great care, at a low cooking heat, with attention to detail and inner joy. This reflects their essentially reverential culture: they always cook everything as if they are making offerings for the temple and for the gods. Cooking and culture are inseparably bound together on Bali;

food preparation is intricately tied to Balinese religious beliefs and traditional village life. Cockfighting, marriage rituals, creation ceremonies and tooth filings are never far from the chef's mind in the Balinese kitchen. The spectacular pageantry of edible temple offerings takes birth in even the simplest of rural Balinese kitchens.

The Balinese show their respect and gratitude for this god-given abundance by sharing their food with and honoring the household spirits. After the morning pot of rice is cooked, symbolic portions of the newly prepared food are first presented to the pantheon of gods, the deified ancestors, and both the good and evil spirits before being consumed by the family. A few grains of rice and salt and tiny pieces of food are placed on a small banana leaf square called a *joten* or *saiban*, and are offered daily to the invisible forces of the cosmos before people are allowed to eat. The *saiban* are put at the portal entry in front.

My great friend in Bali, Kasena, told me that "*joten* (Balinese) is an offering made to the ancestors' spirits. After you cook the day's food, you then offer what you cook—you share to the ancestors before you eat it. *Joten* (a *banten*, or gift to the gods) are put in many places, like the water jar. After you make these offerings, only then you can eat what you cook." Called *nitya* (daily) *yajna* (holy sacrifice), this personal path of worship is always carried out at home. The preparation of *saiban* offerings and regular worship keep the Balinese god-conscious and their home holy. *Saiban*, or *naivaidya*, is performed every day without exception after cooking in the morning. It represents the daily gratitude of the Balinese for the given endowment, and is presented to the Creator before any food is consumed.

Depending on the size of the household, Balinese women prepare a tray full of 30–70 modest daily offerings called *banten* (or *yadnya*) *saiban*, *banten nasi* or *banten sesajen*. Two basic types of folded *banten* banana leaf offering baskets are used in this god-fearing, god-pleasing interval between cooking the food and eating it. *Tangkih* is a one-inch-wide, two-inch-long strip of banana leaf (*daun pisang*) folded over in the center to resemble a bow or a military medal, held together with a *semat*, a tiny, sharp, bamboo stick toothpick. The other similarly sized banana leaf model, *celemik*, appears as a round, three-sided, triangular mini-basket. There are also tiny, flat, one-inch-square banana leaf pieces

containing a few freshly steamed grains of rice alone, or rice partnered
with flowers, a tiny amount of the recently cooked food, and perhaps
coffee. The Balinese also weave small, square, green coconut or banana
leaf offering trays (*ngedjot*) holding a few grains of rice, a flower, salt
and chili pepper, which they set on the ground to placate the evil spirits and negative forces that live there and haunt the house. If the Balinese drink tea, coffee or rice wine, they will also spill a little on the
ground as an offering. These offerings (called *sajeng* or *sajen*) are set
out to appease the bad spirits (*sajeng* comes from the word *ajengan*,
which means food or rice). *Sajeng* offerings are prepared and *arak* or
brem is also spilled on the ground.

The Balinese distribute these diverse, duality-driven domestic offerings to various supernaturally charged household shrines along with
a prayer directed heavenwards. They place the offerings at particular
locations determined by the priest: on the ground by the entrance gate,
in the altar in the middle of the courtyard, in front of all the buildings
in the compound, at the family temple, on the family shrines, in the
backyard garden, in the sleeping quarters, at the source of water, and
in the kitchen on both cooking ranges, the firewood rack, the mortar
and pestle, the pan or bowl where the rice is kept (dedicated to the rice
goddess Dewi Sri, who has blessed the food with prosperity), the pump,
the well, the cover of the water jar, the cleaning broom, and in the special devotional kitchen areas.

The kitchen always has two small shrines or alters called *sanggah*.
The one hanging on the wall is called a *sanggah paon* (kitchen) for Lord
Brahma, the god of creation and the fire used to cook the rice, represented in the fireplace and oven. The shrine by the well is called a *sanggah sukan* (holy water or spring water) for Lord Wisnu, the god of
preservation and the water resident in a large water jar placed beside
the oven. Food and rice are transformed into edible forms by fire and
water (the five basic elements are air, fire, water, earth and ether) through
the cooking process. The gods must be thanked. Only after this daily
round of religious activities ends is the family allowed to savor breakfast
and rejoice in the gift of food.

In the 1930s, Miguel Covarrubias described the traditional Balinese
kitchen as "a simple roof of coarse thatch supported by four posts, with

a bamboo platform at one end—the kitchen table—and a primitive mud-clay stove at the other." The kitchen or *paon* (meaning "ashes") is still a small, spare, utilitarian room with not much more than the basic wood-fired stove and a chopping bench. Most village kitchens continue to be built outdoors as a freestanding compound building out of traditional mud and red brick with a basic tiled or grass roof. They are also usually dark, blackened and dirty: the ceilings are covered with soot from years of burning traditional cooking fuels such as local wood, bamboo, kerosene and smoky coconut oil. Ritually considered to be one of the least pure areas of the family compound, the kitchen, along with the bathroom, pigsty, compost heap and rubbish dump, is always constructed in the least auspicious, southwest, *kelod*-facing corner of the property closest to the sea. Direction in Bali is reckoned on a *kaja–kelod* axis: *kaja* is mountainward and upward, in the direction of the magic mountain, Gunung Agung, and the gods, while *kelod* is downward and seaward, in the direction of the negative spirits and forces. The rustic Balinese kitchen is not a place in which to relax, entertain, socialize or feed guests. It is a functional production site to cook and prepare food offerings. More modern indoor kitchens within the dwelling or in a room or building within the compound are always characterized by plain, institutional-looking gray concrete walls and angular tiled counters and workspaces.

Basic cooking equipment and installations include a simple open wood-fired, mud-brick stove, and perhaps, in more modern homes, a second two-burner stove called a *kompor*, or a gas cooker to boil water and fry. The *kompor* (Dutch for stove) is powered by *minyak tanah* (motorbike oil), kerosene or petroleum. The *kompor* is also known as a *kompor panci* after the Dutch *panci*, an ordinary metal cooking pot with two handles which sits atop the *kompor*. The *panci* is used to steam rice or make soup. There will also be a large clay container or water basin for water (*gebah*), and a long, low, rectangular tiled chopping bench against the back wall. Over 90 percent of people living in the villages still have antiquated wood-fired stoves, evidenced in the piles of wooden logs in local kitchens. This traditional Balinese oven (*tempat memasak*) has three holes in the top—the Balinese believe that evil fortune will befall anyone who builds a stove with only two holes—and an opening underneath to burn the firewood. Rice is always cooked over the most powerful middle hole, with other dishes cooked on the side.

Producing steamed white rice (*nasi kukus*) is a laborious multi-step process in Bali where rice perfection is de rigueur. It employs an ingenious three-tiered rice steamer known as a *dangdang, kukusan* or *kekeban*. This is an hourglass-shaped gray sheet iron or aluminum pot designed by the Balinese to reflect the symbolic shape of the beloved rice goddess, Dewi Sri. The *dangdang* is filled up to the waist with water and placed on top of an iron brazier (*kran*). A large, loosely plaited, cone-shaped bamboo steamer called a *kukusan* or *pengukusan* fits like a funnel down into the mouth of the *dangdang*. To make steamed rice, fresh drinking water, which, as recently as the 1990s had to be carried home daily in an earthenware pot, bucket or empty plastic jug from a nearby spring, is brought to the boil in the *dangdang*. Thoroughly washed rice grains (*beras*) are then placed in the naturally vented cone-shaped bamboo *kukusan*. A special heavy clay bowl with a handle (*kekeban* or *kekeb*) is placed on top of the inverted "Southeast Asian rice farmer coolie hat" to cap the rising heat and steam. The rice is steamed for thirty minutes, transferred into a clay container to soak up a little hot water for twenty minutes, and then returned to the steamer for another thirty minutes. The traditional woven bamboo steaming basket adds a distinctive flavor and aroma to the finished rice. More modern households now use huge blackened pots or have substituted an electric rice cooker. The *dangdang* and *kukusan*, along with various large pots are frequently hung outside on a compound wall or from tree branches in the garden area above the family's assorted collection of battered and burnt thin aluminium pots and pans. There will also be an inevitable plastic rack of brightly colored plastic tubs and mismatched plastic, woven bamboo and metal baskets, bowls and crockery.

Every traditional Balinese cook brandishes large, weighty, hand-crafted axe-like Balinese cleavers (*belaka*) for chopping and special knives for ceremonial food preparation. Used solely to process ritual ingredients, these have carved handles with powerful Hindu symbols etched on the blades. A thick round tree trunk cutting board (*talenan*), a bamboo rice basket (*sok asi*) used to store fresh steamed rice, a clay pot to steam small banana leaf-wrapped bundles of food and perhaps a coffee roasting pan are other essential Balinese utensils. Banana leaf squares or rectangles used for enclosing, rolling and folding food parcels and offerings to be steamed or grilled, are also a part of the kitchen, as are their substitutes, corn husks and vine leaves. There will also be traditional stamping utensils—the *lu* and *lesung*—used for hand pounding and grinding foodstuffs. The *lu* is a long hand-held wooden pole used to physically grind rice, spices, meat (*daging* or flesh) and traditional Balinese village coffee. The *lesung* is a large mortar or bowl made from a hard material, generally stone, with a round hole in its center corresponding to the circumference and size of the *lu*. Recreating ancient agricultural sounds and rhythms, the Balinese put the unprocessed material in the *lesung*, which is placed solidly on the ground, and stand above it with the pole, crushing or pounding the coffee beans or rice into the desired particles or consistency.

Most important of all is the mortar and pestle, an important kitchen tool of varying size and shape common to all Southeast Asian countries. The shallow round stone mortar (*batu base*), wrought from rustic black volcanic rock, and its corresponding pestle are used to crush, combine, bruise and grind dry spices and aromatic seasonings. It is with these implements that exotic spice island treasures are transformed into the fragrant spice and herb pastes so essential for Balinese cooking. To prepare the ground spices, the freshly cut up or whole spices and roots must first be crushed into a coarse paste. Using a mortar to process the spice paste affects the flavor of the dish, as does the physical effort expended while pounding the spices. Patient, powerful, slow movements give the best flavor and texture for the dish. Modern appliances cannot replicate the culinary results and tastes achieved with the traditional mortar and pestle. The Balinese cook also owns a rudimentary wooden, hand-held paddle bristling with rows of small, sharp iron nails called a *parutan sayur* for fine-grating vegetables or a *parutan kelapa* for scraping coconuts to make desserts or for obtaining coconut milk. (Its traditional bamboo predecessor boasted spiky rattan points held together and trimmed with bamboo.) A different type of coconut grater made out of tin with elongated holes framed in wood is used for shredding coconut to the texture required for ceremonial food. A *kukur* (*parut*) is a grater or rasp for grating coconuts (*mengukur* means to grate or rasp the flesh of the coconut using a *parut*).

The Balinese invariably use fresh locally available cooking ingredients and foodstuffs, along with live animals. Food is picked, caught, bought and consumed directly off the vine, tree, hoof, fin and wing. The Balinese have always preferred fresh natural flavors. For this reason, ingredients are bought in small quantities to obtain maximum flavor, spices are bought throughout the week, and seasonal market produce is carried home daily. The Balinese have great respect for the food ingredients that they select and use to complement the inordinate amount of care and attention that goes into producing each dish. Spices are freshly ground and fried, coconut is roasted and grated, vegetables are prepared and cooked separately, and then all are combined and mixed thoroughly with the bare hands. The final cooking method—grilling, smoking or simmering—marries the diverse flavors and aromas into a distinctive, delicious whole. Traditionally, none of the resulting dishes was designed to last long because there was no refrigeration. Leftovers were always fed to the compound dogs and livestock. Because refrigeration is still a recent innovation, there is no custom of saving religious feast foods for the next day. Instead, all leftovers are wrapped in banana leaves and distributed to the neighbors. The Balinese live one day at a time—on every single level.

Refrigeration is slightly more common today but it is still far from universal. The Balinese do not know its function and do not see or understand a need for it. According to long-time custom, most local people still shop at the traditional market every single morning and cook fresh foods and produce from scratch every day, so they do not need a refrigerator to preserve their food and meat. Some more modern Balinese do own refrigerators but they just use them to house offerings and offering components, such as fruits, vegetables, eggs, tofu, *tempe* and flowers. The cooked daily food is still left out unrefrigerated on the kitchen table all day long, and the remains will not be saved and stored overnight in the refrigerator. This is not a leisurely, leftover food culture of recreational eating and extended cold storage. The Balinese do not order takeout food or bring "doggie bag" portions home from restaurants. It goes against the very grain of Balinese food philosophy and practice to cook large meals in large quantities to last for several days of meals and snacks. The Balinese are horrified when you insist that food can be kept until the next day. Nothing is stored or saved or planned as food for tomorrow. No cold New York pizza slice for breakfast, no frozen or reheated food, and no cold chicken are treasured on Bali. Simple food, often in scanty amounts, is cooked fresh every single day, and is always consumed in its entirety on that same day. In the villages, the wondrous, redundant, "curiosity" refrigerator often takes lonely pride of place in the living room because the venerable, small, "traditional Balinese kitchen" is still full of soot, smoke and ash!

Tumis Pakis

(STIR-FRIED FERN TIPS WITH GARLIC, CHILI AND SHRIMP PASTE)

Komang Winaya, head chef at the Puri Lumbung Cottages in Munduk, comments that "It's really different the cooking cultures between Balinese and Westerner. The Balinese cooking culture is on cooking preparation, then they eat all (the dishes) at the same time, while the Western culture is the enjoying the result of cooking: mix with wine, or which dishes come first to suit with certain drinks. We do hope our small hotel can give contribution for food lovers all around the world!" His favorite local creation, "tumis (to stir fry) pakis (fern tips), is just everyday Balinese food dish that can come to each house in Bali."

Recipe courtesy of the beautiful Puri Lumbung Cottages (guests sleep in luxurious renovated Balinese-style two-story rice barns!) in Munduk, in northern Bali, 2011. Special thanks to the extraordinary Balinese chef at the Puri Lumbung (Komang Winaya) and the very helpful, always courteous Yudhi Ishwari. The Balinese cuisine served at the Puri Lumbung's relaxed mountain restaurant in Munduk (with nearby, panoramic views all the way across the sea to East Java!) is authentic Balinese village food. Puri Lumbung Cottages (A Unique and Authentic Hotel), Munduk Village 81152, North Bali—Indonesia. Phone : +62 362 7012887. www.purilumbung.com.

6 bunches fern tips (1.5 kg)
24 shallots, thinly sliced
12 garlic cloves, thinly sliced
6 big seedless red chilies cut in ¼ in (6 mm) widths
6 small red chilies cut into small pieces
¾ cup coconut oil to stir fry

1 cup liquid chicken stock (or made with Masoko powder in 3 tbs water)
1 tsp salt and pepper
1 tsp shrimp paste
6 tomatoes

Cut the fiddlehead fern tips into 2½ inch (6 cm) lengths and wash.

Heat the pan and pour in the oil.

When the oil is hot, fry the sliced garlic, then the sliced shallots, then add the chili and shrimp paste and stir fry for about 2 minutes.

Add the fern tips and pour in the chicken stock. Simmer until soft.

Add salt and pepper to taste.

Tomatoes cut into wedges can be added when the fern tips are nearly cooked. More tomato can be cut into wedges and use as a plate garnish or decoration.

Serves 4–6.

For a vegetarian version, delete the shrimp paste and substitute water for the chicken stock.

Jukut Kacang Panjang Goreng

(STIR-FRIED LONG GREEN BEANS)

Kacang is a generic name for many sorts of pulses, peas and beans. There are many types of kacang (beans) in Bali. Panjang means long (of distance, time or length) and goreng is fried. Kacang panjang itself is a cowpea or long bean (Vigna unguiculata/sinensis/sesquipedalis). Kacang panjang are long green beans on the outside, but when you dry them in the sun, the beans inside turn red. You can fry the kacang beans and eat them as a snack or garnish.

Murni's Warung is ideally located by the old Dutch suspension bridge in Campuan-Ubud, an easy ten-minute stroll from the cultural heart of Ubud. This gorgeous four-level restaurant is beautifully decorated with Murni's exquisite Ganesha statuary, rare stone Buddha antiques and local Balinese artworks, and overlooks an enchanting natural river gorge. Murni's Warung offers a tropical blend of legendary Balinese specialties, outstanding Indonesian classics and superb Western comfort food (and desserts) to thousands of visitors to Bali each year. Here, master restaurateur Murni recreates one of Bali's most popular village compound vegetable dishes.

Recipe Courtesy of Ni Wayan Murni, Murni's Warung, Campuhan-Ubud, April 18, 2011.

2⅔ lb (1.2 kg) long green beans cut into 1¼ in (3 cm) lengths
30 shallots, finely chopped
18 garlic cloves, finely chopped
18 hot chilies, sliced (use more or less chilies according to taste)
2 tbs shrimp paste
2 tbs Masoko chicken powder (or 1 chicken stock cube, crumbled)
small amount of chicken stock to moisten
2 tbs coconut oil
salt and pepper to taste
3 onions, sliced

Heat the oil in a pan and fry all the above ingredients except the green beans, onions and chicken stock until cooked. Use a high heat for 2–3 minutes.

Add the beans and continue to cook until done. Add a little stock if the mixture is too dry.

Fry the onions until crisp and use as a garnish.

Serves 4–6.

Leped Lindung

(PEPES BELUT, EEL ROLLED IN BANANA LEAF)

Leped (Balinese) and Pepes (Bahasa Indonesia) both mean "roll." Lindung is Balinese for "eel" (kopat is Balinese for sea eel), and belut means eel in Bahasa Indonesia.

Eel is a cheap food in Bali and can be procured all year round. Eels are also plentiful and easy to catch in Nusa Lembongan. Fishermen bring them in every day by boat from the sea (lindung refers to swamp eels). In Bali, eels are sourced and caught in the sawah (rice fields). Belut refers to rice field eels or Asian swamp eels. The essential local cooking process is summed up in three easy, magical words: "Grill, steam and roll!" Either a man or a woman can cook this dish for their family. Sea eels are used for this recipe in Nusa Lembongan.

Recipe courtesy of handsome, smiling, I Wayan Sudirna, the very knowledgeable local Balinese chef at the beautifully designed Tanis Villas resort on stunning Mushroom Bay in Nusa Lembongan. The Tanis Villas boasts exquisite tasting jukung-fresh snapper, tuna and squid. The overnight fishing boats arrive on the beach right outside the Tanis between 7 and 8 a.m. every morning, loaded with a catch of wriggling fresh local tuna. The Tanis Villas is the ideal access point for world-class snorkeling expeditions, mangrove forest adventure tours and journeys to unspoiled sister islands Nusa Ceningan and Nusa Penida. It also has close truck or motorbike proximity to idyllic Dream Beach, picturesque seaweed farms and Lembongan village. www.tanisvillas. com, December 2011.

2⅔ lb (1.2 kg) sea eels (10–11 inches/25–28 cm in length)
1 whole young coconut
6 banana leaves for the rolling
1½ oz (40 g) ginger
1 tsp lesser galangal
1½ oz (40 g) turmeric
50 g shallot
40 g garlic
1 tsp salt
1 tsp pepper
½ lb (250 g) small, hot red chilies
kaffir lime leaves

Chop all the Balinese spices until very small and grate the coconut.

Wash the eel, cut off the head and chop into very small, smooth pieces.

Put the eel in a bowl and season with the Balinese spices. Add the grated coconut and mix well.

Roll the mixture in a banana leaf, adding one kaffir lime leaf to each roll. Then, either steam or grill the roll.

If steaming, wrap the eel mixture in only one banana leaf wrapper and place in a traditional Balinese rice steamer (*kukusan*). Steam for 20 minutes. If grilling, wrap the mixture in 2–3 banana leaves for protection and to retain moisture. Place the roll directly on the flames over an active fire, not a grill, built over a traditional sandpit. A stick on which to string the eel is suspended above the fire, balanced on two large side stones. Grill for 25–30 minutes.

Serves 4–6.

CHAPTER THREE

Traditional Village Foods: Cooking in the Compound

HUMAN NOURISHMENT CAN BE DIVIDED into four basic food categories according to source: ocean, air, land and field. The Balinese eat all as they pray to the goddess of rice, Dewi Sri, for the ongoing gift of life-sustaining food for their island. In China, there is a saying that the people will "eat anything with wings except an airplane, and anything with four legs except a table." China's cooks routinely prepare whatever is available locally, whether for upscale Imperial-style banquet halls or open-air street markets and stalls: braised bear paw (the more tender left paw is preferred), snake meat stir-fried with civet cat, deep-fried crispy scorpion, pangolin (an endangered species) stew, roast dog meat and free-range field rat kebabs!

The meats and ingredients may differ but the sentiment is much the same in Bali. A high Brahman priest told resident cultural observer Miguel Covarrubias in the 1930s that the Balinese are only prohibited from eating "human flesh, tigers, monkeys, dogs, crocodiles, mice, snakes, frogs, certain poisonous fish, leeches, stinging insects, crows, eagles, owls, and birds with moustaches." Covarrubias also noted that while the Balinese eat chicken, duck, pork and, more rarely, beef and buffalo, they are fond of "stranger foods" like dragonflies (*capung*), crickets, flying ants and bee larvae.

Common threads run through all of Balinese cuisine but different regional styles and usable food resources are found in every corner of the island. Traditional Balinese foods include such natural elements as dragonflies, baby bees, coconut tree larvae, grilled young bamboo, young bamboo soup, young tree trunk soup, sweet and sour frog, rice field eels in banana leaf, fried rice field snails, *nasi sela* (rice mixed with sweet potato), *nasi jagung* (rice mixed with corn) and rock-hard *taop* nuts. Such delicacies leave an indelible impression on young Balinese children who crave them in adulthood, especially during prolonged absences from their traditional villages.

In western Bali, in particular, informal village foods continue to thrive. Dragonflies are a favorite delicacy although they are difficult and time-consuming to catch as they are continually on the wing, landing only briefly on rice stalks. Children hunt dragonflies in the fields using long poles called *kayu panjang* (*kayu* is wood or tree and *panjang* long), the ends smeared with sticky sap as a trap. They pull the wings off, pierce the dragonfly bodies live on a stick, roast and eat them. At home, the bodies are grilled or deep-fried in coconut oil with spices and vegetables.

The villagers of Tengkudak in Tabanan regency, near Mt Batukaru, like everything emanating from the rice fields, from grasshoppers to dragonflies, eels and live baby bees. These villagers also have their own "dragonfly with cassava" recipe called *Rempeyek* (cracker) *capung* (drag-onfly). The dragonflies are captured in the rice fields using a three-tiered device. A long, firm coconut leaf spine is inserted into a bamboo tube handle and sticky sap collected from a jackfruit or frangipani tree is smeared on the tip. The flying prey become irrevocably fixed to the sap of the magical hunting wand when they touch it. Many more practical Balinese sidestep the hard-to-make bamboo handle and substitute a large easy-to-obtain banana leaf spine instead. They attach the coconut leaf spine to the top of the banana leaf spine with sticky sap, thus attaining the desired sky-level height to catch dragonflies on the wing. The banana leaf handle is simply thrown away afterwards. Utilizing only the bodies, not the wings, the requisitioned dragonflies are crushed using a stone mortar (*batu base*) and pestle, while their co-ingredient, cassava, is scraped with a hand-held traditional *parutan* (grater). The desiccated dragonflies and grated cassava are mixed with garlic, chili, lesser galan-gal and seasoning into a soft paste and then fried like a wafer-thin *kripik* (cracker) until dry, or coaxed into a thick, round fritter. Once the wings are removed, Ubud's dragonflies get the cordon bleu treatment usually reserved for fish, as *pesan capung*, grilled dragonfly in a banana leaf roll with spices. Dragonfly soup (*kuah capung*) is another popular culinary tradition. The wings are removed and the bodies boiled in water with spices and fresh turmeric leaf for added flavor. In northern Bali, Lovina's dragonflies are simply served grilled with raw *sambal matah*.

In western Bali, baby bees (*nyawan*) are often cooked with coarsely grated or shredded coffee leaves (*jejeruk nyawan dan don kopi*). To produce this dish, bee hives, located in trees or under house roofs, are raided and the honeycomb sheltering live, stingless baby bees is sold in the market or sold by door-to-door street vendors. The entire honeycomb containing still-living bees is boiled whole in hot water for ten minutes, by which time the bees will be well done. The young coffee leaves are boiled separately as they have a bitter taste. The water is discarded and the coffee leaves wrung out and left to dry, after which they are sliced. A *sambal* sauce is then made of sliced onions, garlic and chili fried in coconut oil. Coconut milk is then boiled for five minutes before the *sambal* is mixed into it. Lastly, the shredded baby bees, sliced coffee leaves, salt and MSG are mixed together. The natural honeycomb is later eaten separately.

The villagers of western Balinese are also fond of coconut tree larvae, which tastes like milk. They chop down a rotting coconut tree, split open the trunk and look for white larvae (*ancruk*) inside to be either eaten plain or boiled with chili and salt as a *sambal*.

Grilled fresh bamboo, called *embung* (young) *tiing* (bamboo) *tabah* (a specific bamboo species) *metambus* (Balinese for grilled), is another natural food supplement. A short young bamboo tree is harvested and cut down near the bottom of the trunk, up to 30 cm high where the bamboo is tender and sweet. The intact conical tube is then grilled on top of a wood fire until blackened. When done, the outer bamboo bark is removed and the interior is sliced and mixed with coconut oil, grilled chilies and salt to produce a taste resembling gourmet mushrooms. In Lovina, *jukut embung* (young bamboo soup) is a common village food. The young bamboo stalk is cut, chopped and boiled for 10–15 minutes with *bumbu* (spices), *sambal* sauce and salt, and eaten like soup.

Western Balinese also whip up a stupendous Balinese-style sweet-and-sour frog dish called *katak bumbu kesuna cekuh* (garlic-ginger spice paste), hopping straight from the wet rice fields (*sawah*) into the frying pan to be fried in oil until crisp. The frogs (*katak* in Balinese, *kodok* in Indonesian) are first twisted by the neck until dead and the skin removed and discarded. The frogs are mixed with turmeric, lesser galangal, garlic, chili, brown sugar and tamarind that have been fried together in oil to impart a sweet-sour tinge to the amphibious culinary dish.

Bali's island-wide rivers, lakes, canals and rice paddies give birth to small eels reconfigured as marinated minced eel in banana leaf and fried rice field eels, commonly served in every *warung*. Eels (*lindung*) are plentiful in the flooded, newly planted rice fields. Submerged and hidden during the day in three-foot-deep burrows in the mud, at night they come near the surface to swim and look for food. Local men go to the rice fields to fish by kerosene lantern light, catching them by the hundreds with only a hook attached to a plastic string sweetened with bait from the same muddy fields. Farmers are grateful for the removal of the eels as the creatures' subterranean digging leads to leakage of the precious irrigation water. Eels are a more rare, seasonal food in drier northern Bali. Here, they are only available and easy to catch in the *sawah* during the rainy season. River crabs, crayfish, prawns, snakes, legions of busy insects and indigenous local snails are also gathered and reincarnated into a variety of Balinese delicacies.

Succulent golden rice field snails (*kakul*), a locust-like threat to the rice crop as they can devour the stalks and leaves en masse, constitute an inexpensive and nutritious food resource, as do their common green garden cousins. Rice farmers search for the snails in their paddy fields at night or before weeding the plants during their daily work routine. The snails are subsequently vended live in plastic bags in every tiny village *warung* in Bali. Living snails can remain intact in plastic for three days. The *warung* lady takes the unsold snails out of their packages at the end of the day, puts them in water overnight and repackages them in the next morning. The fleshy univalves are made into satay and green papaya soup with vegetables in a dish called *gedang* (papaya) *mekuah* (put sauce or broth) *misi* (with) *kakul* (snails). Balinese snails also crawl their way into steamed snail with grated coconut and spices, *jukut kakul* (snails with vegetables), boiled snail curry with spices, grilled snail, fried snail and snail soup with coconut milk. A recipe for snail in coconut milk soup requires 500 g of medium size snails and 100 ml of coconut milk as the basic ingredients. A bouquet of spices (chilies large and small, garlic cloves, shallots, turmeric, greater galangal, ginger and candlenut) is ground and then stir-fried in oil. Snails, *salam* leaves, lemongrass and salt are added to the pan, briefly simmered in water, and the pièce de résistance—coconut milk—is stirred in until it reaches boiling temperature to produce a classic Balinese *kampung* specialty.

Another Balinese snail-based delicacy is *palem kakul* (*palem* is Dutch for palm tree). The ingredients comprise 200 gm of boiled snail flesh, ¼ grated coconut, 1 tbs palm sugar, various spices (6 cloves shallot, 3 cloves garlic, 2 small chilies, 1 large chili, 1 tsp salt, 1 slice turmeric root, 1 slice galangal, 1 tsp pepper powder, ½ tsp coriander) and banana leaves for the wrappings. *Palem* can also be made with crab or prawn. To prepare the dish, the snail flesh is first washed, then cut into smaller pieces. Salt is sprinkled on the snails to remove the mucous before they are washed again. The shallots, garlic, chilies, turmeric and galangal are finely ground or pounded. The grated coconut is then mixed with the snail meat, ground spices, salt, pepper, coriander and palm sugar. Tablespoons of this magical batter are then spooned into each banana leaf wrapper, folded and sealed, and the packets steamed for thirty minutes.

True rustic Balinese peasant fare is born not just out of equatorial volcanic abundance but also economic struggle and an agricultural existence which often borders on bare subsistence or real hunger level. In times of mass want or hardship, such as during the communist political upheavals of the 1960s or natural disasters like the 1963 eruption of Gunung Agung, the Balinese give up their beloved steamed white rice for cheaper rice studded with tough yellow corn (*nasi jagung*) or rice diluted with pieces of peeled and cubed sweet potato (*nasi sela*) to make it stretch further. (As a poignant legacy of the poverty of "Great Depression," *nasi sela* is still sold in the Ubud market.)

A native Balinese tree (*pohon taop*), which has large, hard, oval leaves, produces an inedible thorny yellow fruit resembling a small jackfruit. The *taop* tree has attractive leaves four feet long and two inches wide, some entire and some deeply lobed on the same tree. The bright yellow fruit is 7–8 inches long, covered with curved soft spines an inch long. About forty seeds are arranged around a core, and each is surrounded by a soft white aril composed of many fine fibers. The Balinese open the fruit, discard the white-fleshed interior and harvest the nuts, in competition with rummaging local tree squirrels. The extremely hard peanut-like nuts (*batun taop*) must be smoked over a wood fire or baked before being eaten as a snack. This is a food that the Balinese historically resort to in times of famine. Cashew trees, which grow in very dry soil, are only found in the eastern part of Bali, such as the dry, parched slopes of Gunung Agung, Bali's most sacred mountain.

Traditional fail-safe Balinese rice field foods continue to be sourced and cooked in house compounds but they are not as popular or as crucial today because so much more food is now available in the villages. As recently as the 1980s, there would only be one *warung* in each village carrying a very limited range of goods, but now there are many small Balinese-run *warung* and food is available everywhere. This is a very recent miracle for the Balinese people. In fact, there is comparatively so much food now in Bali that there is no need to cook at home. If the Balinese have money, they can simply go to a *warung* and buy whatever they want. Tourism-related income has also changed Bali's food supply, dietary expectations and cooking possibilities. With fewer Balinese solely reliant on hard-scrabble family rice farming, the young generation can aspire to grilled chicken with rice rather than tree larvae and dragonfly soup. Natural calamities, however, have locked some isolated pockets of the rural Balinese into chronic food emergency. The eruption of Mt Agung reduced the quality of the soil and changed the course of the rivers that ran near several mountain villages. Since then, the people have not been able to grow either rice or most kinds of vegetables. Many have to subsist on leaves or what fruit they can grow, as well as *ketela* (cassava), a root vegetable offering very little nourishment. They also tend a few straggling coffee and cocoa trees and some *salak* and jackfruit as subsidiary, low-income cash crops.

The Balinese love meat, but pork, beef and chicken are still very expensive food commodities on the island and are mainly reserved for special ritual occasions. The Balinese usually feast on pork during most ceremonial festivities, the preferred "food of the gods." The Balinese normally consume very little meat in everyday life, usually adding a few tiny morsels of chicken or fish to their rice. Well-born, first caste, high-status Brahman priests (all *pedanda* are from the top caste) are not allowed to eat meat (cow, bulls or pork) and they also cannot consume food from street sellers or in the market, drink alcohol, or taste consecrated food offerings destined for the gods. (The *pedanda* are also not allowed to eat the offerings once a temple ceremony finishes, thus ordinary folk always bring the offerings home to eat.) According to I Made Arnila, a lay priest (*pemangku*) in Lovina, in order to become a high priest, a religious candidate must go through an education process and learn the mantras. As a novitiate, he already has some dietary restrictions: he must meditate and fast (*puasa* in Bahasa Indonesia) for forty days and forty nights. This meditation and fasting period (no eating and no drinking) takes place right before the ceremony to become a *pedanda*. Once ordained, a *pedanda* can "only eat vegetarian food: vegetables (*sayur*), rice (*nasi*), and water. It is not possible to eat *ikan*, *telur*, *sapi*, *babi*, *ayam*, *bebek*-no! No Masoko (a popular chicken bouillon flavoring). No coffee, tea or milk—only water." Dietary rules for *pedanda* are often subject to modern interpretation and debate. Some Balinese insist that *pedanda* only eat duck meat or be vegetarian. The *pemangku* (lay priests) also cannot eat beef (not all are vegetarian, but they are supposed to be). Secular Brahman and Satria caste Balinese are also forbidden to eat beef (beef is never served at a religious ceremony). *Wesia* (warrior-merchant class aristocrats) and the majority Sudra caste commoners are allowed to eat beef or buffalo but also traditionally choose not to do so.

Numerous animals rummage around or are penned up in the family compound but they are not ordinarily eaten. Cows are more valuable kept alive to plough the rice fields, chickens lay eggs for food and offerings, while pigs are allowed to appreciate in worth, size and girth as future market-bound mercantile investments and ritual food offerings. The Bringkit market in Mengwi district, which operates every Wednesday and Sunday, is Bali's large central livestock market. Farmers from all over the island travel here to sell their live cattle, pigs, ducks and chickens. Lack of home refrigeration militates against the slaughter of large household animals like cows and pigs by single families or even small family groups. Any animal butchered for food must be small enough for a family to consume in its entirety in one sitting as meat spoils quickly in the heat. Goats are rarely raised domestically because they destroy and overgraze plants and flowers growing around the house. Goat satay is in high demand, however. *Saté kambing* (goat or lamb) on skewers is normally served with a spicy hot peanut sauce. The Balinese also like to frequent village *warung* and *kaki lima* (push cart vendors) for a steaming plate of *soto kambing* (goat soup) or *kambing mekuah* (goat or lamb stew in sauce or gravy). *Kuah* is a sauce, broth or gravy, usually over rice, and *mekuah* is to do or put, to add the gravy to it. Curries (*gulé* or *gulai*) and curried food is popular for quick, convenient meals. *Gulé* is Balinese for a spicy soup (*gulai ayam* is chicken curry, *gulai kambing* is goat or lamb curry). Goats are raised as secondary family home businesses, penned up inside humble tofu factories in Seririt, tethered around drying beachside salt pans in Amed and concealed in bamboo squatter compounds inside Bali Barat National Park.

Balinese food springs out of an intensely religious, intensely poor country and economy. The Balinese are opportunistic eaters. Because they live so close to the hunger line, they take advantage of all possible food sources in their environment and do not waste any part of any animal or creature. They eat what they can find. Traditionally, whenever a village fisherman hauls a turtle out of the water or an egg-laying female is found on the sand, the Balinese will eat it. Other native protein sources include scaled anteater (*klesih*), large lizards (*alu*), wild boar, rice paddy birds—from the *glatik* to the tiny *petingan* (scaly-breasted Munia)—and porcupines (*landak*), disguised as a gamey flavored dark meat curry cooked with tamarind. The people of Nusa Lembongan favor large *alu* (monitor lizards) which run very fast and are difficult to catch; both quick and clever, they climb up the local coconut trees! Once the men catch them, they fry the lizard in oil and mix it with coconut. The oil is kept afterwards to treat wounds. The Balinese also like to hunt, shooting with rifles long-tailed squirrels readily located near their favorite food supply, Bali's majestic stands of tall coconut trees. Flying foxes (fruit bats) are another indigenous food. The bats are shot or captured with nets. Squirrels and bats, however, do not appear in the traditional markets. Food fondness, satisfaction and loyalty transcend status. When the rich pay premium prices for an expensive meal, they enjoy it. Poor people equally enjoy and crave their humble plate of plump white *ketupat* rice chunks with tiny sticks of thinly threaded *saté kambing*.

Dog meat is eaten in most villages throughout Bali. Dogs are privately killed, cooked and consumed at home. If a family wants to eat dog, the husband goes out to the street and selects a stray. He knows which ones belong to neighbors and will avoid these. He hits and kills the dog with a wooden stick, puts it in a plastic bag and carries it home to be cooked. These numerous village dogs often wind up on skewers in small, hidden "RW" (pronounced "airway") stalls (*dog satay warung*) in the illicit back lanes of Denpasar. Here, the flesh, which is believed to have medicinal benefit, is discreetly served to homesick ethnic migrants from North Sumatra (Batak), North Sulawesi (Manado) and Timor where black dogs, in particular, are deemed a regional delicacy. Dogs, in fact, are on the chalkboard menu throughout Indonesia. Some Balinese dogs are caught, confined in wooden-slatted crates and exported by overland truck to nearby Java to be eaten. When beaten to death prior to cooking, men consider these dogs to be an aphrodisiac. In traditional Chinese food and medicine cosmology, dog meat is considered a "hot" element, and therefore Chinese martial arts practitioners in Bali will also seek out and eat dog.

Dog meat is not offered or displayed in the traditional Balinese village markets. It is only sold at the specialized *dog satay warung*. Satay RW food stalls are very popular in Bali, with those in Singaraja and Seririt, right beside the main road, opening at 8 a.m. Some stands now even advertise themselves publicly along the main roads of Sanur, Gianyar, Bangli and Denpasar. Here, RW stands for *rawon* (a dark-colored black beef soup from Surabaya) or *gule* (*gule* is curry or spicy soup in the Balinese language). People will come here every day to eat dog. The main methods of serving and cooking dog are grilled satay with rice and *anjing* (dog) soup with rice. Dog meat is also spit-roasted (*guling*) like goat. The preferred part of the dog's body is the underside. The breast is used for *saté anjing*. When sizing up the dinner potential of an intended dog victim, the Balinese stand under a nearby *ketapang* tree and estimate the number of satay sticks that the dog will provide. Small or lean dogs are less of a target.

Many dogs all over Bali fall prey to the meat trade and end up as satay. The RW stalls obtain dog meat by paying people to bring in their own unwanted pets or by capturing stray dogs from the villages. The

Balinese are usually paid Rp.50,000–80,000 for selling one dog victim to an RW stall satay seller, although these *warung* can often find stray dogs and compound pets for as little as Rp.35,000 per animal. Poor families will sell their pets to the dog catcher for as little as Rp.10,000 if the dog has become a nuisance or can no longer be cared for. Some Balinese have turned dog-kidnapping into a major source of income since dogs stolen from neighbors or caught for free on the street represent a 100 percent source of profit. (More affluent Balinese keep imported Rottweilers, Labradors, Dalmatians and other pedigreed breeds as fashionable status symbol house pets but these are too expensive to eat!) RW vendors cannot always obtain the requisite canines. If dog is available, they hang out a *buka* (open) store sign, if not, a *tutup* (closed) sign signals customers that the stall is out of supplies.

Dog meat procurers dare not openly steal stray dogs or loose house pets because the owners love them and will kill them if they are caught. More sinister methods have evolved in the form of large-scale persistent rashes of anonymous, nighttime street dog abductions and cullings. Nocturnal dog catchers on motorcycles resort to mass-poisoning beloved pets to obtain saleable meat supplies. Men toss parcels of meat laced with poison to dogs lounging all over the village streets in the early morning hours. They return one to two hours later with a truck to collect the carcasses. Men also catch stray dogs in Denpasar by motorbike: one man drives while another sits on the back. They prey on dogs sleeping in the street and toss a lasso made of metal attached to a straight bamboo stick around their necks. The meat of the sad, sorry snatched victims is soon sold in Denpasar as hot smoking satay.

Cruelty, karma and cuisine go hand in hand for dogs in Bali. Dogs are disliked, disrespected and eaten in Bali because of a "primitive belief" that is still in wide circulation: if a human being is bad (a thief, for example), he will come back in his next lifetime as a dog (the dog "made a mistake" as a human). It is considered a terrible reincarnation to be reborn as a dog (they are evil souls): the *buta kalas* (negative or evil spirits or demons) are believed to be embodied in the local dogs. To make this a self-fulfilling prophecy, Balinese men customarily rub very hot red chilies onto the gums of young puppies from birth to make them angry and train them to be aggressive. Dogs are also very common targets of personal revenge. If your neighbor does not like you, or he thinks you are doing black magic against him, or your dog is noisy, he will poison your dog. He tosses poisoned *bakso* meat balls into your house yard, which the dog eats and dies. In deep contrast, the Balinese do not kill, cook or eat *cucing* (cat). If they accidentally run over a cat on the road, they will stop and make a ceremony for the cat. If they hit a cat and there is no ceremony, it will bring bad luck.

Fortunately, the Balinese usually sustain themselves with other food besides dogs. They also feast on ample amounts of steamed white rice, stir-fried leaves and greens (*kangkung*) and long green beans (*kacang panjang*), small portions of fish such as *teri* (anchovy) or *pindang* (sardines), chicken simmered with spices, tofu (*tahu*), *tempe*, edible tubers like *ubi* (sweet potato) and *keladi* (taro or calladium), *krupuk* (crackers), peanuts, super-hot chili *sambal* and *jaja* (sweet, sticky rice cakes). Personal nourishment habits follow each generation of Balinese into the afterlife. Many individuals are temporarily buried in the cemetery shortly after death to await an auspicious day and sufficient family funds, sometimes for years, for a mass cremation ceremony. Relatives visit the deceased remains regularly and bring offerings for the grave composed of all his favorite foods as well as mandatory rice, coffee, tea and fruit, enabling his spirit to enjoy a tailored, butler service feast.

The living, however, eat all of their meals by themselves, quickly, privately, alone and undisturbed. Family members carry their food-laden banana leaf "plate" to a corner, turn their back to the others and eat in happy silence. They choose a quiet spot near the kitchen or gravitate towards an unoccupied open-air pavilion in their compound to either stand, balance on a plastic stool, perch on a large green coconut, sit on the floor or squat over the ground. Family dining is not a social custom in Bali. It is not traditional for household members to sit down to eat, talk and socialize over food. Meals are only shared during cooperative ritual food preparation activities, on special festive occasions and at ceremonies. This is partly a result of the way the Balinese prepare their food. Armed with a traditional Asian complement of leaves, roots, herbs and spices, the wife cooks only once a day, in the early morning, and leaves all of the food on the table under upturned bowls or netted covers. Family members help themselves as they please during the day whenever they are hungry. Rice was traditionally eaten cold but modern rice cookers now keep the rice hot and moist during the day. The Balinese also prefer to eat in silence because they believe that talking will kill the spirit of the food. Meals that are prepared by hand are eaten by hand. The children of the gods eat with the fingers of their right hand as the left is used for ablutions and is considered impure. A food-laden banana leaf square or an increasingly popular plastic or ceramic bowl is held in the palm of the left hand. The characteristically small, cut-up pieces of food, portion of white rice and sauce are scooped up with all five fingers together of the right hand. Spoons are only used to service messy dishes. Large banana leaves (*daun pisang*) are Bali's natural chinaware. Sourced from a backyard tree or bought at the village market in long rolled-up pieces, they are used once then donated to the pigs for food.

Ceremonial food functions as social currency, social lubrication and social cement on Bali. It is part of the constant give and take of Balinese community life. Village members frequently assemble at the *banjar* or at the house of a professional offerings worker to make ritual foods and coconut leaf offerings for mass cremations and other family or temple ceremonies. Meals and snacks must be served to sustain and thank them for their work during these preparatory activities which can extend for weeks or months on end, always provided by the village association or the host family. This is the real Balinese food born and bred in ancient ancestral compound and village temple culture—hidden, manufactured and consumed behind high, invisible family compound walls. Workers feast communally on a home-cooked spicy, generous groaning board of steamed rice, fragrant tofu dishes, jackfruit curry, soups, leafy cooked vegetables, marinated tiny fish and throat-stopping *sambal*. Balinese cuisine thrives on the yin–yang contrast between such ordinary compound food and auspicious temple food. With ongoing economic growth, however, traditional festival foods are increasingly crossing over onto everyday menus.

During family celebrations such as ground touching, tooth filing or wedding ceremonies, women from the local *banjar* arrive in steady streams at the family compound bearing gifts of essential basic commodities, such as sugar, rice, coffee and bananas. Sugar, coffee and rice ("the traditional gift") are proffered on all special ceremonial occasions, whether visiting the family of someone who has just died or compensating the *balian* (traditional healer) for medical-spiritual treatments. Coffee, sweet tea and fresh *jaja* rice cakes must be made or bought and served to these visiting guests. Before they leave, the family also fills their empty *keben* with sacred satay sticks, steamed rice and *lawar* as a parting dowry. Friends and neighbors thank each other with the critical food items of life. The custom on Bali is to bring a gift and return home with a value-added reciprocal assortment of ceremonial haute cuisine.

Bubur Kacang Hijau (Ijo)

(GREEN PEA PORRIDGE)

Although the Balinese make bubur kacang hijau as a common family food, it is considered an expensive dish. The cost of a one pound bag of tiny green peas (Kacang Hijau Finna) for this recipe was Rp.19,723, prohibitive for most Balinese, more so since kacang hijau grows in Bali and is actually a small type of local peanut. Half a coconut cost Rp.2,300, a tube of Balinese palm sugar Rp.5,440 and five bananas from a roadside warung stall (Rp.5,000). The Balinese will make bubur kacang hijau for family members when they come home for Galungan. Bubur kacang hijau is not really a ceremonial food but is cooked for birthdays, anniversaries, to celebrate something or on special occasions for the family. We enjoyed a "special edition": people also cook and eat it as a snack.

Recipe courtesy of the beautiful young Miss Era. Miss Era created absolute food magic out of one battered, burnt aluminum pot and a small petrol-fueled kompor stove. The joy of cooking began at 3.20 p.m. one hot rainy afternoon at Era's house in Seririt, northern Bali, May 2011. Era's sister Sri had to go out on a motorbike and purchase more lengis (petrol) to fire up the small kompor stove for our porridge boiling party. Era first learned to cook by watching her mother prepare food at home as she was growing up in their small, traditional rural village (Tirtasari) near Lovina in northern Bali. She is a natural-born cook and does everything by instinct, personal taste and family experience. Era cooks with love, laughter and kindness, which makes the food doubly sweet, doubly nourishing and doubly appreciated by everyone round her. Address: Kadek Era (Kadek Debisugianto), Desa Patemon, Dusun Kawan, Kecamatan Seririt, Kabupaten, Buleleng Propensi, Bali.

½ coconut
1 lb (500 g) green peas (*kacang hijau*)
2 pandanus leaves
2 tubes (1½ lb/640 g) brown palm sugar (*gula merah bulat*)
2 pieces fresh ginger each 1¼ inches (3 cm)
1 tbs sea salt

Cut the coconut into sections, and scrape the brown skin off.

Boil the water (4 x 3½-inch-tall glasses).

Pour three glasses of water into a bowl to clean half of the green peas. Pour away the water.

Bring the water to the boil, put the peas in the pot and stir. Boil for about 40 minutes.

Grate the peeled white coconut pieces using a *parutan*.

Add two glasses of water to the bowl of grated coconut.

Squeeze the shredded coconut by hand over a plastic sieve to press out the liquid coconut water (*santen*) into the bowl below. Discard the coconut shreds.

Add 1½ glasses more water to the boiling peas and bring back to a boil.

Test if the peas are done by squeezing a few. Add more water if still hard.

Add one of the brown palm sugar chunks and more water.

Add the remaining palm sugar.

Add the *pandan* leaves, salt and cut-up pieces of fresh ginger.

Serve the *bubur kacang hijau* in bowls while still hot.

Kolak Biu (Kolak Pisang)

(BANANAS WITH COCONUT MILK AND BROWN SUGAR)

Kolak pisang (banana kolak) is a very popular Balinese dessert. It is rich, sweet, delicious, nourishing and a heart-warming golden yellow in color. Kolak is fruit (usually banana) cooked with coconut milk and brown sugar. It is normally eaten as an afternoon snack. The Balinese also often refer to kolak biu as "banana mayo." It is very good for the soul. Era's sister Sri adds: "For Balinese person it is not real like dessert, but for sure that not for meal every day. We only consume when we together with whole family. It's same like celebrating togetherness with whole family." Sri proudly described the desserts in advance: "Those Balinese cake is real with Balinese ingredients."

Recipe courtesy of the gentle Miss Era, who will always remain an unspoiled local village girl from the small, quiet, bucolic village of Banyuatis in northern Bali. Our sweet banana-boiling escapade continued at 4.40 p.m. on the same hot, rainy afternoon in Era's small, basic, open-walled house in Seririt, northern Bali. Marvel, her three-year-old son, loved this very special, food party treat.

1 tube palm sugar, 2¼ in (5.5 cm) x 1½ in (3.75 cm)
5 big thick bananas (*biu gadang*)
4 pandanus leaves
1 fresh whole coconut, grated and squeezed
¾ inch (2 cm) fresh raw ginger
1 tsp salt

Bring three big glasses of water to the boil, then add the palm sugar tube.

Tie the four pandanus leaves in a knot and add to the boiling water.

Slice the five bananas on the diagonal into thick pieces.

Cut the coconut into half and then into quarters (four pieces). Peel, grate and squeeze it to produce cocnut milk.

Cut up the fresh ginger and add to the pot with the salt.

Continue to boil the palm sugar until it turns a golden syrup color.

Then add the coconut milk.

Add the banana slices and simmer until cooked.

Ladle into serving bowls while hot and sprinkle with some of the grated coconut.

Serves 4–6.

Capung Goreng
(FRIED DRAGONFLY)

Dragonflies are a very traditional, popular, age-old rural village food in Bali. Catching dragonflies in the rice fields as a boy is a cherished childhood memory for many Balinese men. In Karangasem Regency, the people also eat Bali balang, a different insect—using the same recipe.

Recipe courtesy of chef I Wayan Sudirna, Tanis Villas, Nusa Lembongan, www.tanisvillas.com, December 2011.

30 dragonflies (5 per portion)
12 red bird's eye chilies
6 garlic cloves
12 shallots
6 kaffir limes
sea salt
white sugar
coconut oil

Catch the dragonflies in the cassava or corn fields.

Wash the dragonflies and remove the heads.

Fry the dragonflies in coconut oil for three minutes.

To make the sauce, slice the chilies, garlic and shallots. Stir fry together until brown.

Add the dragonflies to the pan and season with salt and kaffir lime juice squeezed into the pan.

Add the white sugar and check for sweetness.

Serve with white rice and vegetables on the side.

Serves 4–6.

CHAPTER FOUR

Snacking on Bali: Warung, Markets and Banana Leaf Wrappers

———— ≠ ————

As an outside observer in Bali in the 1930s, Miguel Covarrubias was quick to notice that the Balinese were "continually eating at odd hours and in odd places, buying strange looking foods at public eating booths, in the market, at the crossroads, and particularly at temple festivals when the food vendors did a gold rush business in chopped mixtures, peanuts, and bright pink drinks." Dining out in restaurants is neither a social custom nor a financial possibility in Bali, except for large group family dinners on Galungan or Saraswati Day. The Balinese are renowned snackers, though, and avidly consume small hot and cold snacks, sweets and drinks every day at cheap, convenient neighborhood *warung*, market stalls and mobile canteens. Snacks makes up one-third of the average daily food intake. Eating large meals is not common in Bali but the people still manage to consume impressive quantities over the course of a day.

Balinese seem to eat around the clock. Wherever villagers gather to chat, watch cockfights, perform obligatory group *banjar* work responsibilities, attend *banjar* meetings, wash, pray or celebrate religious occasions, snacks and *warung* enter the social equation. Children can always be found munching on some type of snack in every housing compound on the island. *Warung* range from temporary tarpaulin-roofed makeshift bamboo lean-tos to established open-air roadside food stalls. Patched together out of bamboo and oddments of timber, they usually offer a long hard wooden bench in front for customers. Permanent *warung* have electricity and running water; refrigeration is non-existent. Casual *warung* operators simply set themselves up at sunset on empty land in a parking lot or outside a closed shopfront to form a busy and popular night market. Men stop here after a morning in the rice fields for snacks, strong sugary Balinese coffee, a *kretek* cigarette, a triangular banana leaf packet of chewy beef *tum* and conversation.

The mysterious aromas of Indonesia's multifaceted ethnic cuisine spill out of streetside market stalls and small homegrown *warung* all across Bali. The *warung* is the place to find the real cuisine of everyday Indonesians and Balinese. It is equipped with small glass soda bottles and straws, plastic dispensers with waxy tissue paper, a television set, jars filled with mysterious bland cakes and sweets, and a glass display case holding vegetables, instant noodle packets and unidentifiable tidbits of *tempe*, pork or salted fish. With the wide availability of stationary roadside or streetside *warung* and *warung* food, many busy locals eat very cheap, quick meals here for the same price as eating at home. Because of the absence of refrigeration, most of the food is fried in oil. *Nasi goreng* (fried rice) is ubiquitous. The fried rice dishes and their counterpart, fried noodles (*bakmi goreng*), normally contain tiny off cuts of meat and cooked scrambled egg. *Sayur hijau* (green vegetables) and *sop jagung* (corn soup) are standard *warung* fare. Some also offer fried soybean cake (*tempe*) or tofu (soybean curd cake) with spicy sauce accompanied by white rice. Specialty *warung* up the food ante with fried or baked chicken, goat, fish or suckling pig. The majority of the dishes are extremely spicy and loaded with fresh chilies and are accompanied by an even more scorching *sambal* (chili sauce) on the side.

Old-fashioned village market place stalls are snacking paradise. Cackling, wrinkled grandmas wearing coiled towels on their heads for carrying heavy loads enthusiastically sell small individually home-cooked steamed Balinese rice cakes (*jaja*) laden with palm sugar syrup. Other sellers in batik sarongs and long-sleeved lace *kebaya*, raised in these markets with their mothers since childhood, still dispense family recipe black rice pudding, soft *bubur* porridges and boiling hot, nourishing *kolak biu*, sunny cooked bananas christened with palm sugar and roasted coconut milk. Every third day is a large rotating market day throughout

Bali. Vendors from all over the island introduce diversified home-cooked taste sensations and regional specialties to supplement the regular local markets. Flimsy grass hut *kubu-kubu lalang*-style food stalls set themselves up at the end of each year in the Puputan Badung Square in Denpasar to sell Balinese foods during an annual entertainment fair. The popular local dishes include seaweed, *tipat cantok*, *serombotan*, porridge with *urab-uraban* vegetables (*uraban* is a jumble, indicating a salad of mixed rather than just one vegetable), *daluman* drinks, fresh cakes like *laklak* and white sticky rice served on a banana leaf wrapper. All of the foods sell out by 11 a.m. even on rainy days!

Bakso sellers are an integral part of the street culture and street life of both Indonesia and Bali. These spoon-tapping, bowl-clanging food peddlers (*tukang bakso*) nudge brightly painted, rickety mobile carts from compound door to compound door in the late afternoon selling *bakso*. Their colorful push cart contraptions, colloquially called *kaki lima* (*kaki* meaning leg, *lima* meaning five) consist of two bicycle wheels, a back stand and the two feet of the cook! A popular Balinese favorite, *bakso* is a clear mild soup usually containing round meatballs or boiled chicken, glass noodles, shredded cabbage, rice cakes, hot chilies and herbs. The soup is served out of a pot kept hot over a burner. Vendors bring their own plates and cutlery, but as there is no running water plates are casually washed in a plastic bucket. Other rotating vendors tempt excited school children to come outside for roast chicken with strong *sambal*, small *bungkus* rice packets and individually made and mashed orders of minced, scented secrets encased in brilliant green banana leaves.

Each mobile restaurant seller makes a specific food-associated sound as he walks or pedals along to let customers know exactly which snack is trundling up their village street. The *mie ayam* (chicken noodle soup) seller hits a wooden stick against a hollow, reverberating bamboo tube ("tek-tek"). The always welcome *bakso* man pings the side of a soup bowl or tinkles a glass with a spoon. The late afternoon steamed rice cake (*kué putu*) merchant toots a bicycle horn. Families look forward to his sweet corn skin wrapped traditional *jaja*. The coconut ice cream cone purveyor rings a small ding-a-ling bell, and the *rujak* (a spicy, sweet and sour fruit salad) hawker squeezes a diminutive horn. Loyal Balinese patrons rush through their carved split household gates, bowls in hand! Mobile food orchestras produce a cacophony of these characteristic snacking sounds (taps, rings, tinkles, toots, whistles, horns and chimes), the unmistakable and familiar resonating trills heard throughout the Indonesian archipelago.

Traveling trolley cooks also congregate outside Bali's larger tri-weekly village markets and at events, fairs and temple festivals, usually in vacant lots or at strategic locations, promoting local foods like tofu in sweet sticky peanut sauce, clear pork ball soup and green mung bean porridge in portable plastic bags. Most street cart food sellers are young, unskilled, otherwise unemployed males from East Java and other neighboring islands. Meatball soup hawkers, young coconut traders and grilled fish purveyors are all local male migrants from outside Bali. Because they obtain working capital easily, they can sell everywhere. *Kaki lima* vendors often live in a compound together with other street hawkers and make their food in the early morning before they set out for a long day of pushcart selling. They typically carry an onboard stove, food supplies, dishes, washing up water and sometimes a dining bench as they take to the road to dish up bowls of noodles, steamed rice coconut treats, tiny satay and *nasi goreng* (fried rice) or *bakmi goreng* (fried noodles). *Bakmi* is a vermicelli-like dish with vegetables, shrimp, shredded meat, etc. *Soto* (soup) *ayam* (chicken) hails from Java but it is available everywhere in Bali that the *kaki lima* men go. It contains cellophane noodles, bean sprouts, scallions, lemon slices, hot chili, egg slices, fried onion bits and sweet soy sauce. Reliable *kaki lima* vendors also feed the thousands of licensed beach sellers roaming the long sandy stretch from Kuta to Seminyak.

Operating from often nothing more than an old bicycle with a wooden board and plastic crate set atop the seat, stationary beach bicycle *warung* are brilliantly equipped to portion out precooked *nasi bungkus* (*nasi campur* to go) in folded conical brown paper packets for Rp.3,000. *Bungkus* means wrapped up in paper or leaves, or a wrapped package (*nasi bungkus* is normally a multi-element rice mixture wrapped in a banana leaf). One determined beach entrepreneur even carries two heavy pink plastic bags all along the *pantai* filled with packets of folded *nasi campur* in brown paper parcels. He easily disposes of them to the communal knots of sleeping-squatting, chattering necklace and manicure ladies who appreciate the convenience of his "walking restaurant."

The busy beach baristas also carry peanuts, swirled *krupuk* sealed in crisp plastic, water in plastic jugs and coffee. They normally stock long hanging strip packets of instant coffee. They snip one off the row with scissors, unravel a plastic cup from a pendulous sleeve and pour in hot water brought from home in ceramic jugs. When they run out of boiling water, they get more from a convenient sister concocting regional specialties at a nearby food stall. Their regular coffee brand attracts customers at Rp.2,000, while special ginseng coffee costs Rp.3,000. A row of permanent beach bars serves ice cold soft drinks and beer to tourists on the white sands across from the Inna Kuta Beach Hotel. Eddy, owner of Eddy's Bar, delivers service with a delighted smile. He greets returning guests with hugs and utter joy, as lost-long family members.

Roving bygone Bali peanut sellers balance a traditional bamboo pole across the back of their shoulders supporting two large V-shaped bamboo slings with tightly packed fiber nets full of brown unshelled peanuts. This shoulder-borne carrying pole with the two baskets is called a *kander* in the Malay language.) Different vendors offer fried peanuts. Customers carry away their piping hot snack wrapped in *kertas bungkus kacang goreng* (special paper used to wrap fried peanuts). A traditional Balinese-style *jagung bakar* (grilled corn) seller squats low over the ground on a rough-hewn hand-made wooden stool. She arrives at 3 p.m. every day and situates herself at the exact same spot on Kuta Beach, by the side of the footpath near the local *warung* market. She brings with her an antiquated, collapsible foot-tall easel-style wood base. It supports a small, battered metal tray under a two-rod grill pan filled with glowing charcoal. The seasoned, weather-wrinkled *ibu* is all set up to do a roaring trade from this primitive contraption well supplied with fresh pale green ears of corn, a spare black plastic bag full of charcoal shavings and a plastic tub of salted butter. She husks yellow cobs of corn and places them on the grill, six at a time, continually fanning the darkening ears with a practiced hand and an old bamboo mat to keep the embers alive. The ears are turned over for three to four minutes and served with a final brush of either salted butter or chili sauce for Rp.5,000 each. Sunset belongs to other two-wheel-and-handle stand corn on the cob cart sellers, usually male migrants from Lombok strung along the water line at lit-up Jimbaran beach. From the sandy southern beaches to busy temple ceremonies, they fan and sell charcoal-grilled browning ears of corn and roasted peanuts by portable kerosene lamplight as the sun descends on the island of the gods.

Warung stalls set up at the local *pasar malam* or at Denpasar's bustling night markets serve simple, fresh, genuine local delicacies at minimal prices in minimal comfort (*nasi goreng* with fried egg is Rp.7,000). *Mie goreng* (hot, fried flat thin noodles) is an Indonesian and Balinese grazing mainstay, similar to *nasi goreng*. Popular snacks include sweet, fluorescent ice drinks; sweet and sour *rujak*; satays; *lawar*; *mie bakso* (meat balls and noodles); *tahu goreng* (deep-fried stuffed beancurd) and salted peanuts. There will always be a market stall selling heavily fried *martabak* (derived from India), a folded-over egg omelette pancake filled with tidbits of vegetables. *Martabak* pancakes are made from a sheet of dough with various added fillings (*martabak telor* is a deep-fried beef, egg and vegetable pancake). *Martabak manis* is a sweet-stuffed pancake.

A vast choice of vividly colored fried rice crackers (*krupuk*) sealed in plastic bags dominates the domestic snack market. *Krupuk* is a generic term for all kinds of baked or deep-fried crackers made from a starch base (various kinds of flour) with seasonings and ground shrimps, fish or other ingredients. *Krupuk udang is* a prawn cracker, *krupuk ikan* a fish cracker and *krupuk sermiyer* a red-colored sago cracker. *Krupuk kacang* is made with rice powder mixed with peanuts and Balinese spices: a little bit hot, people take it home after a ceremony (almost everything is used first as an offering on Bali) and eat it with rice. Standard uncooked *krupuk* (rice flour, water and flavorings) come pre-dried in packages and must be fried before being eaten. Others are cut into slices, dried in the sun and then deep-fried. A very attractive oversized, circular, maze-style rice flour biscuit is swirled by hand instead of sliced into irregular squares or rectangles to produce a lacy white, nest-like cracker. The Sari Rasa brand label on this package of swirling *krupuk* advertises that the crackers are both *gurih* (delicious) and *renyah* (crunchy)! *Krupuk* are generally synonymous with puffy prawn crackers, while *kripik* encompass a range of fried unripe cassava, banana and sweet potato crackers. *Kripik bayam* is an exotic visual garden source of bewilderment: a large, beautiful, multi-edged frilly *bayam* (amaranth) leaf is fried into a lightly battered leaf-shaped, paper thin organic vegetable fritter reminiscent of tempura. *Kripik gendar* are ground rice chips, *kripik singkong* cassava chips and *kripik tempe* thin slices of fried soybean cake. Fried tapioca crackers with embedded peanuts (*rempeyek*) contain additional microscopic slivers of delicious green kaffir lime leaf.

Nasi campur (mixed rice) consists of an ever-changing village smorgasbord of meats, vegetables, tofu, *tempe*, fish and eggs served with Bali's most pleasurable and iconic food—fluffy steamed white rice. The most common meal found throughout the entire Indonesian archipelago, *nasi campur* is both the basic daily meal and the solid snacking backbone of the island of the gods. *Nasi campur's* mandatory white rice base shares a supple banana leaf with smaller pre-prepared companion side dishes like fried chicken, highly spiced pork, preserved salted eggs, a potato, anchovies (*ikan teri*), bean sprouts, steamed vegetables with shredded coconut, *kangkung*, jackfruit curry, sweet crunchy *tempe* (*tempe manis*), tofu fritters and fried peanuts doused with coconut milk gravy. *Nasi campur* Bali is different from *nasi campur Java* as it includes all the Balinese favorites. A homespun Balinese village product, local *nasi campur* is normally finished and dressed with peanuts, *krupuk* and *sambal* garnishes.

There are many types of *nasi campur* in Bali as each village and each *warung* boasts its own specialty. Balinese *nasi campur* typically includes such staple plate presentation ingredients as rice, chicken, egg, satay, *tempe* and vegetables to form a creative harmony from that day's available fresh food materials. Vegetarian *nasi campur* can include curried *tempe*, *jukut nangka* (young jackfruit) and *serejele* (fermented soybeans fried with spices). *Serejele* (*jele* is Balinese for soya) is a specialty of the Blahbatuh area of Gianyar regency. The dish is only popular in Gianyar. You can buy the fermented soybeans in a plastic bag in the market, bring them home and fry them with chili and salt or other spices or eat the beans directly; they have a malty taste. *Serejele* is normally eaten with rice, like a vegetable. *Warung nasi* (rice stall) sellers confidently scoop a large mound of rice out of a big basket and toss on two or three mini-dishes, *sambal* (spicy chili paste) and crisp-fried shallots according to customer preference and pocketbook to create *nasi bungkus* (simplified *nasi campur* packed in a banana leaf to go).

The nexus between food and culture is inescapable. Indigenous, informal traveling village *warung* offer age-old, grassroots, compound kitchen cuisine delivered in a uniquely Balinese-Indonesian way. Older

women stake their territory and their small wooden tables and blackened
pots of food under the village banyan tree, a meeting spot at the center of
town, in the mornings and late afternoons. Here they sell ancient family
versions of steamed white rice, pungent fish, spicy meats, *sambal, bubur
ayam* (home-made chicken porridge) and creamy, soft-boiled rice porridges steeped with barbecued chicken, roasted coconut milk, turmeric,
lemongrass and *salam* leaves. Nomadic *warung* women balance home-
prepared foods, plates and plastic buckets on an upturned table on their
heads as they track the local crowds to village cockfights, temple festivals
and supernatural Barong-Rangda theatrical performances. A traveling
warung woman in Kuta Beach-Tuban bears a heavy glass and wood case
on her head, plying a beachside route offering fried *lumpia* spring rolls.
She uses a knife to cut the *lumpia* rolls into small pieces for individual
customers and then sprinkles very tiny green chilies on each serving.
Her clients are mainly local Balinese and the other beach sellers.

In order to supplement their husband's income, many local village
women carve out a part-time business selling local foods to local people.
They balance an scuffed, slotted plastic tub on their heads with paper-
wrapped triangular packets of *nasi campur* or fried rice, fried fritter
desserts, *krupuk* crackers, slices of watermelon or other fruits, Balinese
jaja cakes (sticky, sweet, rice-based treats) or *rujak*. These ladies can be
seen in all small villages. They will suddenly sashay out of a side lane to
look for likely sales among young boys constructing giant fanged *ogoh-
ogoh* monsters for the pre-Nyepi Day parade. New walking *warung* women
may have to traipse three or four miles a day to sell all their goods until
they establish a set route and a loyal clientele. Locals get to know their
regular *dagang*, traders or vendors who carry their wares. These ladies
often only have to spend a few hours walking until all their food is sold
as drivers, children and passersby stop them. Village customers like to
stay with the proven sellers, where they already know what the food tastes
like and the quality. Enterprising old ladies get permission from entertainment groups to sell soda, beer and mosquito repellent at tourist-
oriented dance performances at Pura Dalem and other temples in and
around Ubud. They know the performance schedule and know when to
come. As they have done for decades, the *ibu* balance their selected goods
on round, dented metal tubs atop their heads for ease and portability.

Denpasar enjoys an even broader range of snacks and opportunities. Sellers from islands throughout the archipelago come to set up food stands on busy eat streets like Jl. Teuku Umar. The cuisine offered depends on the background of the stall owner. Food merchants from Madura run busy nighttime *warung* to peddle popular goat satay to homesick Madurese immigrants. Food sellers from Java outnumber other nationalities in the Denpasar night markets, offering Javanese-style spicy *nasi campur*, while the Chinese cook flat noodle dishes and the Balinese specialize in their native *lawar, ayam betutu* or *babi guling*.

Transmigrated cooks from West Sumatra bring yet another hot and spicy culinary journey with them to Bali. It is said that whenever "three people of West Sumatran origin meet anywhere in the world, a Padang-style restaurant will be set up!" Padang, the provincial capital of West Sumatra, is the birthplace of Indonesia's most popular regional cuisine. In every town and city across the archipelago, there is a *rumah makan Padang* restaurant serving home-cooked Padang food. A large variety of different foods forming a multilevel, stepped pyramid of neatly displayed dishes, is stacked up on shelves in the shop window. The plates are piled high with conical food portions largely containing an array of animal entrail specialties and highly flavored boiled vegetables, such as cabbage. Padang food is the most popular cuisine of the largely Muslim Minang-kabau people of West Sumatra: protein comes from beef, water buffalo, goat, lamb, poultry and fish (not pork). Almost all parts of the animal are used and are sold in Padang restaurants, leavened with rich coconut milk for taste and inflamed with hot chilies. Curry sauces with coconut milk and spices further disguise dishes such as fried beef lung and delicacies made from the ribs, tongue, tail, liver, brain, bone marrow, spleen, intestine, cartilage, foot tendons and skin of the animals.

Customers choose from the dishes displayed in the window, and all food is served family-style with the various selected dishes being brought to the table on small plates, accompanied by hot steamed rice. The price is determined by the number of plates and what is eaten. Tasty beef *rendang*—tender brown meat cooked with coconut oil and coconut milk—is the signature food of the Padang region. *Rendang* reigns supreme among homesick West Sumatran sons separated from their mothers who provision them with a parting gift of portions of classic *rendang*-for-the-road. Slow cooked in a thick, spicy, coconut milk sauce made from shallots, garlic, red chilies, turmeric, ginger, galangal, coriander, kaffir lime leaves, turmeric leaves and lemongrass stalks, this magnificent food can be kept for a long time and becomes better when reheated. Traditional *rendang* has no sauce when it is done. It must be stirred frequently and laboriously while cooking until the sauce is totally absorbed by the meat. Sometimes it is subsequently dried in the sun. Because of the preparation process, the meat is always a dark brown in color. Coconut milk is a widely used element in Padang cooking. Food purveyors in far from home Denpasar reconstruct their classic Sumatran mild coconut milk soup, with its seductive coconut aroma.

Chefs from the Bukittinggi area of Sumatra import their popular local dish, *katupek tek apuak*, the Padang version of *kutupat* rice cooked in coconut leaves. The *ketupat* is cut in pieces and then quickly doused with *gulai nangka* (young jackfruit cooked in coconut milk). The cook skilfully adds cooked vegetables and noodles, finishing the gravy-wet presentation with peanut sauce, fried shallots and pinkish fried Indonesian crackers. Creative Minangkabau culinary masters also hit the night market streets of Bali with *teh talua* (hot tea and blended egg yolk). While the eggs are simmering, they are stirred hard by hand. As the batch becomes bubbly, a hot tea is poured through it, cooking the egg quickly. The result is a sweet, hot, two-colored, two-layered beverage— dark brown tea at the bottom and bubbly white egg on top. A dash of mocha syrup is the crowning touch. Stirred, not shaken, it is the perfect drink to warm up the body during the chilly, rainy *musim hujan* in Bali!

Nasi jenggo, rice mixed with spicy meat, chili sauce, fried noodles, vegetables and dried sweet *tempe* wrapped in a banana leaf, injects additional excitement into the local commercial snack mix. It is a nightly social obsession among locals, young university students and low-income workers on a budget. *Nasi jenggo* was originally introduced to Bali in the 1970s and named after a popular Italian movie, "Django." Movie fans turned a few unprepossessing, pioneering *nasi jenggo* stalls into trendy nightspot hangouts. Hundreds of women now sell *nasi jenggo* at modest food stalls—a simple wooden table, a plastic or bamboo mat to sit on and a kerosene lamp for lighting—from 6 p.m. to 2 a.m. on downtown Denpasar's main streets, concentrated on Jl. Sulawesi in front of the crowded

Kumbasari market. The market itself is very busy every day from 10 p.m. to 2 a.m. as produce arrives from the countryside and vegetable wholesalers offload produce to villagers to bring back and resell in their early morning home markets. People who work at night need simple food and *nasi jenggo* sells for a very affordable Rp.1,500–2,000 in Bali. Before so many competing stalls emerged, the early *nasi jenggo* stalls used to turn over from 500 packages of the delicacy per day to 1,000 on a Saturday night, with the average patron eating two or three servings. The women also sell local beverages like *wedang jahe*, a hot ginger drink. Coffee, tea, soft drinks and beer are also stocked. Customers are often forced to buy an accompanying bottle of beer.

Nasi jenggo is characteristically produced in, and known for, its small portions, typically the size of a handful of food. In actuality, it is a lot bigger than that, about 35–40 percent of the size of *nasi bungkus*. The Balinese and Javanese alike will eat *nasi jenggo* either for breakfast or late at night, from midnight to 7 a.m. They purchase it at local *warung* or a *kaki lima* pushcart. Each *kaki lima* will carry a different type of *nasi jenggo* but all are precooked and prepackaged by larger manufacturers who sell them in bulk to the local *kaki lima* stands. Customers in Kuta can buy *nasi jenggo* closer to home at the nearby Kuta market. They can choose or ask what the day's selection is, but by 8 p.m. most packets are sold out. *Sepeda motor* riders eagerly grab whatever is left and speed off, protected by hot food and good karma instead of a driver's licence! The very modest price ranges from Rp.3,500–5,000 per package. Most Balinese buy three or four to construct a complete meal because they are so small. They can typically contain *ayam betutu*, *lawar*, *ayam*, *babi guling* plus rice, noodles, grated fried coconut (*serunding*) and Indonesia's ubiquitous hot red *sambal* sauce. The wrapping for *nasi jenggo* depends on the seller. Balinese wrap it in banana leaves while more modern Javanese-owned enterprises wrap it in paper.

Creativity is the key to *nasi jenggo*. Each supplier will make it differently and there is variation between Balinese and Javanese producers. *Nasi jenggo* in its purest form resembles an artistic, house-shaped package of pleasure. A double layer of banana leaf squares serves as both outer wrapping and plate, secured with splinter thin *semat* toothpicks. Open the outer leaves to reveal the rice glory inside. The *nasi jenggo* itself is beautifully folded up in another semi-triangular banana leaf bundle with overlapping flaps. Lay the banana leaves out flat as a plate for the *nasi jenggo* construction within. The *nasi jenggo* consists of a triangular dome of white rice stuck against one side of a circular banana leaf piece. The other side of the leaf contains a trendy mixture of hot, blood red *sambal* sauce; thin, wiggly yellow noodles; peanuts, *tempe* slivers, green bok choy shreds, corn kernels; fried coconut *serunding* and tidbits of *ayam*. Eat the *nasi jenggo* with your right hand. Scoop up luscious, fiery fingerfuls and combine it with a generous mouthful of rice for a popular local culinary sensation. Satisfying, fulfilling *nasi jenggo* is a twenty-four hour a day. Indonesian comfort food for the market-going Balinese and Javanese masses in search of a quick, cheap, smaller version of *nasi campur* on the run.

Nasi Campur

(MIXED RICE)

Nasi campur consists of a heaping mound of cooked rice partnered with small quantities of seasonal side dishes. It typically includes creative combinations of banana leaf-wrapped surprise packages, hot curries, fish (teri or pindang), meat, chicken, eggs, peanuts, crisp-fried shallots, fried tempe, tahu (tofu), grated coconut with turmeric and spices and crisp fried crackers (krupuk) enlivened by sea salt and hot chili peppers. The vegetarian part of nasi campur can be any dish, from aromatic jukut kacang panjang goreng (long green beans) to chopped kangkung leaves to vegetables cooked in broth (kuah). Sambal (a typical chili sauce made with salt, fried shallots, shrimp paste, garlic, fiery chopped raw chilies and coconut oil) is prepared daily and put out in a separate bowl as a condiment for the nasi campur. Each person can thus make their food as spicy or as salty as they wish.

The Balinese eat some version of nasi campur almost every single day. It serves as either a snack or a main meal. The combination plate is always composed of white rice and whatever else is fresh, available and cooking in the kitchen that day. A driver will stop off at the renowned night market in Gianyar to enjoy a generous plate of nasi campur after a day of escorting tourists. He may also find time at midday to buy a delicious nasi campur assortment of mixed Balinese favorites at a local warung. Nasi campur is not usually made at home. Most people will go to a warung to eat this surprise orgy of multifarious, spicy odds and ends. The dish will always include satay sticks as an essential, expected and favorite meat splurge. And wherever there are satay sticks, a delicious fresh peanut sauce is sure to follow. The Balinese are experts at creating an eminently simple but perfect easy to create village peanut sauce. All that is required is 11 oz (300 g) of fried peanuts, 3½ oz (90 grams) of long red chilies (cabe Lombok), 2½ oz (60 g) of shallots, 1 oz (30 g) of garlic and ⅔ cup sweet soya sauce (kecap manis). Cut up all the ingredients first, fry all the spices in oil and then blend (or crush them using a mortar and pestle). Fry for ten minutes, and the authentic peanut sauce—forged in the dark, crowded kitchens of paradise—is ready to serve six lucky persons.

Recipe courtesy of the beautiful Pundi-Pundi Restaurant in Ubud, situated in the tall, productive, emerald green rice fields in the heart of the Balinese countryside. The Balinese architecture and natural beauty of these unique surroundings reflects the renowned healing (and eating) environment of Ubud. It is a spiritual experience to sample flavorful nasi campur surrounded by the peace and serenity of Bali's untouched sawah. It is a magnificent and rare privilege to sit outside, facing a pink-flowered lotus pond, while enjoying the Pundi-Pundi's excellent culinary creations. There are five delicious, characteristic Balinese food choices on Pundi-Pundi's extensive menu: crispy duck, bebek betutu, ikan bakar (grilled whole fish) Jimbaran, pepes ikan and nasi campur. Recipe provided by the Pundi-Pundi's executive chef, Nyoman Suartajaya (Karangasem Regency). e-mail: suartajayanyoman@yahoo.co.id Pundi-Pundi Restaurant. Jl. Pengosekan, Ubud. www.pundiubud.com, December 2011.

1 lb (450–500 g) steamed white rice
1¼ lb (600 g) grilled chicken with bone, either plain or spicy
3 boiled eggs
⅔ lb (300 g) chicken or beef for satay
½ lb (250 g) fillet fish (snapper) for grilled minced fish rolled in
    banana leaf (*pepes*)
deep-fried potato or corn fritters (*bergedel*)
sweet *tempe,* sliced (page 70)
⅓ lb (150 g) long beans, sliced on the diagonal
⅓ lb (150 g) white cabbage, chopped
2 oz (60 g) bean sprouts, headed
sambal sauce
shrimp crackers (*krupuk*)

Steam the rice and set aside.

Grill the chicken and cut into suitable sized pieces.

Hard boil the eggs and cut into halves, quarters or slices.

Deep fry the sweet corn or potato fritters using previously boiled corn or mashed potatoes mixed with egg, shallots, chicken, flour and mild spices. Alternately, make minced meat ball patties or crab cakes.

Prepare the mixed vegetables (*urab sayur*) using the beans, white cabbage and bean sprouts.

Grill the minced fish rolled in banana leaf (*pepes*).

Make the satay sauce (page 69) and grill the satay sticks.

Make the *sambal* sauce (below) to put on the egg.

Arrange the various small food items on a round plate in a characteristically Balinese way to resemble a cheerful sundial or a sacred food mandala. Place a mound of white rice in the center, surrounded by an artistically perched chicken piece, half a boiled egg, slices of *tempe*, finely minced *urap* vegetables, *bergedel* fritters, fish *pepes* in a banana leaf, two chicken *satay* sticks and crunchy shrimp crackers (*krupuk*).

Serve warm.

Serves 4–6.

Sambal Tomat

(TOMATO SAUCE FOR NASI CAMPUR)

⅔ lb (300 g) chili
⅓ lb (150 g) shallot
3½ oz (90 g) garlic
2 tbs shrimp paste
4 oz (120 g) tomato

Chop up all the ingredients.

Fry all the ingredients for 10 minutes and then blend.

Crush after cooking.

Serves 4–6.

Achar

(INDONESIAN PICKLE)

Achar is originally an Indonesian dish but it is served in Bali as an accompaniment to both nasi campur and nasi goreng.

1 oz (30 g) carrots, sliced
1 oz (30 g) cucumber, sliced
1 oz (30 g) shallots, cut into cubes
2 tbs vinegar
2 oz (60 g) sugar
3 cups water

Heat the water. Before it reaches the boil, add the vinegar and sugar.

Once the water boils, add the carrots, cucumber and shallots to the pot and boil for a maximum of 10 minutes, mixing the ingredients together until they are barely cooked.

Serves 4–6.

Jackfruit Curry

(KARE NANGKA)

"If you ever find yourself in Bali, you can try these dishes at my restaurant, Murni's Warung, Ubud, or in my guest accommodations, Murni's Houses and Murni's Villas. The recipes are from my village—actually, from my family."
Murni celebrates and acknowledges regional and local variations: "If you go to the next village, the recipe will be different. Such is dining in Bali: Selalu lain tapi selalu enak! Always different, but always delicious!" Selamat makan!
Balinese recipe courtesy of Ni Wayan Murni, Ubud, April 18, 2011.

2⅔ lb (1.2 kg) unripe jackfruit, cubed
6 tbs coconut oil
30 shallots, finely chopped
18 garlic cloves, finely chopped
18 hot chilies, finely sliced

2½ in (6 cm) peeled greater galangal
2½ in (6 cm) peeled lesser galangal
2½ in (6 cm) peeled fresh ginger
2½ in (6 cm) peeled fresh turmeric
6 tsp ground candlenut (as a thickener)
6 tsp chicken powder (or 6 chicken stock cubes, powdered)
6 large coconuts, grated
3 cups coconut milk of the desired thickness, made from 6 large
　　coconuts and 12–15 cups of hot or boiling water
6 tsp shrimp paste
salt and pepper to taste

Grind all the spices into a smooth paste using a traditional Balinese mortar and pestle. Add a little water if necessary.

Heat the coconut oil in a wok and fry the spice paste for a few minutes.

To make the coconut milk (*santen*), grate the flesh of the coconuts into a bowl, add the boiling water, then let stand for thirty minutes. Squeeze the coconut meat by hand until the water turns white and the flesh is dry, to produce thick, creamy coconut milk (first squeeze). Strain before using. Set aside the thick milk. For a thinner coconut milk, add more water to the coconut flesh and re-use the pulp (second squeeze). Mix the result with the thick milk or use by itself for a thin coconut milk. To make an even thinner milk, squeeze the coconut meat a third time. The coconut will yield about six cups of milk, enough for making a curry for six.

Lower the heat/flame, add the coconut milk and cubed jackfruit. Cook gently until the fruit can be pierced with a skewer.

Serve with steamed white rice.

Serves 4–6.

Tempe Manis
(SWEET SOYBEAN)

Tempe manis is a sweet crunchy tempe married to deep-fried peanuts and a secret, wet Balinese combination sauce of fried and simmered village leaves, chilies, sugar and spices. Tempe manis is a typical local Balinese village dish. It is for everyday eating by women in the home and is made fresh each day.

Recipe Courtesy of I Wayan Sudirna, head chef at the Tanis Villas resort in Nusa Lembongan. www.tanisvillas.com, December 2011.

2⅔ lb (1.2 kg) soybean-based block of *tempe*
2⅔ lb (1.2 kg) peanuts
½ lb (250 g) small hot red birds'-eye chilies
13 oz (360 g) big red chili Lombok
13 oz (360 g) shallots
4½ oz (120 g) garlic
6 kaffir lime leaves
5 cups coconut oil
1 tsp sea salt
1 tsp black pepper
1 lb (500 g) palm sugar (*gula merah*)

Cut the block of *tempe* into thin sticks, then fry with the peanuts in the coconut oil for 10 minutes until brown.

Crush the chilies, garlic and shallots in a mortar and pestle, then fry in coconut oil for 3 minutes.

Add the *tempe* and peanuts to the frying pan and cook further.

Season with kaffir lime leaves, salt, pepper and palm sugar.

Serve with white rice or with jackfruit or pumpkin soup.

Serves 4–6.

Kering Tempe

(SPICY CRISP-FRIED SOYBEAN CAKE)

Kering tempe is a very exciting, nutritious, flavorful village specialty. This vegetarian soybean-based protein boost is easy to make and has a delicious crunchy texture (kering means dry or dried out). The core ingredient is Bali's superlative, inexpensive, pale yellow block of fresh tempe—awakened, agitated and brought to life by blazing, fiery, scarlet red chilies and spices.

Recipe Courtesy of I Wayan Sudirna, head chef at the Tanis Villas resort in Nusa Lembongan. www.tanisvillas.com, December 2011.

1 lb (450 g) soybean-based block of *tempe*

15 red bird's eye chilies, seeded and sliced diagonally
3 shallots, peeled and sliced thinly
8 cloves garlic, peeled and cut up
5 oz (150 g) palm sugar
¾ tsp tamarind, soaked in water
1½ pieces fresh galangal root, one inch long
¾ tsp shrimp paste
3 *salam* leaves
sea salt
coconut oil

Cut the *tempe* into small rectangular sticks, deep fry-dry until crisp and brown. Drain and set aside.

Deep fry the red chilies, shallots and garlic and set aside.

Peel the galangal root and crush.

Heat the palm sugar in a pan until melted, then add the galangal, *salam* leaves, shrimp paste, salt, oil and tamarind water.

Continue frying at a low temperature until the sauce thickens and the palm sugar caramelizes.

Add the fried ingredients (*tempe*, onions, red chilies and garlic) to the frypan. Stir until everything is well mixed and well coated.

Serve with steamed white rice (*nasi putih*) or ceremonial *nasi kuning*.

Serves 4–6.

CHAPTER FIVE

The Balinese Bumbu: A Sacred, Powerful Paste

———— ≢ ————

S UGAR, SPICE AND ALL THINGS NICE, that's what Bali is made of. Balinese village cuisine rests on a complex complement of locally available ingredients, seasonings, spices, herbs and condiments. They are not only critical to the production of Bali's hot-blooded cuisine but are what gives Balinese cuisine its intriguingly different flavor. Un-surprisingly, the wooden compartments of the typical Balinese kitchen cupboard harbor a tantalizing array of unusual local leaves, fragrant roots, barks, seeds, pastes and pods.

Most Balinese dishes are built around a *bumbu* (*base* in Balinese), a general term for spices in Indonesian, a perfectly balanced, freshly prepared dry spice paste mixture incorporating a range of seasonings and spices pounded together in carefully calibrated proportions depending on the individual recipe. Ground to a paste in a stone mortar, the *bumbu* is the heart, soul and foundation of the Balinese kitchen. It is not only an amazing amalgam of flavors, it is also a formidable pharmacy for the diner's well-being as many of the ingredients have healing or medicinal properties. Every chef initiates the cooking process by grinding and blending a requisite assortment of spices into a basic *bumbu* with a stone mortar and pestle. Take an early morning tour of the traditional market spice stalls. Smell a golden halo of aromas and examine and admire the adventurous building blocks used to make the *base gede*: shallots, garlic, chilies, ginger root, lemongrass stalks and tubers of bright orange turmeric.

Balinese housewives do not buy the components of the *bumbu* spice mix separately. Instead, they purchase them as one complete package of whole, unground, unchopped ingredients, sold by weight or in a plastic packet for Rp.5,000 in the market. This package of complete spice ingredients is called *bumbu lengkap* in Indonesian, meaning complete in every respect or with everything included, and *base genep* in Balinese. It is also called *base gede* (a "big *bumbu*" of all kinds of spices mixed together). This package of core ingredients includes garlic, shallots, coriander, turmeric, ginger, greater and lesser galangal, lemongrass, black and white peppercorns, onions (*sune* in Balinese), tamarind, red chilies, nutmeg, cloves and candlenuts. In urban Denpasar's Tiara Dewata supermarket, *bumbu lengkap* is packaged in a box-like plastic container lodged in the produce section and contains such whole raw vegetables, shoots and roots as lemongrass, shallots, ginger root, leaves, garlic cloves, turmeric root, candlenut, greater galangal and black pepper to be ground and chopped up at home. *Base genep* is usually supplemented with ingredients such as shrimp paste, coarse sea salt, *salam* leaves, coconut oil and palm sugar, particularly when putting together traditional foods like *lawar* and satay. The extras are usually purchased separately although sellers sometimes include them for free with big orders. In some households and villages, spices are roasted first before they are turned into a spice paste. Spice pastes for beef (*base be sampi*), chicken (*base be siap*), seafood (*base be pasih*), strong meats such as pork and lamb, and vegetables (*base jukut*) feature their own slightly different combinations of aroma, taste and color, and their special secret twists. Thick and moist, spice pastes are prepared in advance in large quantities to be used judiciously in everyday cooking. One refrigerated bowl may last two to three weeks and suffice for ten different recipes.

Bali's traditional culinary arts tease the taste buds and tweak the olfactory glands with fresh ground seasonings, frying red shallots, simmering rank-smelling shrimp paste and the smoky scent of grilling satays. The heady savory smell of Balinese cooking permeates every family compound, alley and rural mountain village. Balinese chefs smell the tips of their spice-laden fingers from time to time to monitor aromatic in-progress spice mixtures; the first "smell check" is done while chopping the ingredients. The Balinese also use their hands to "feel" the food they are fashioning in order to ascertain the quality and texture of special mixtures like *saté lilit*. Taste is the final test. They will use taste to gauge the balance of food cooking and sizzling in the pot to control flavor, consistency and spice levels. If the finished product is too salty, they add extra coconut, and if it is too hot, they add palm sugar. Bali's time, touch, smell and tolerance-tested recipes call for an abundant natural pharmacy of indigenous ingredients, fresh and dried powders and exotic tropical by-products available at bustling local spice markets and food stalls. Completely controlled by women, the dimly lit traditional Balinese market is the pounding bartering heart of local village flavorings and seasonings activity.

Any and all of the following categories and components can be found in the market and come into play in the Balinese kitchen. Hard seeds and nuts (*base wangen*; *wangenan* are herbs) include cardamom (*kapulaga*), sesame seeds (*wijen* or *bijan* in Indonesian, *lenge* in Balinese), nutmeg (*pala*), coriander seeds (*ketumbar*), black and white peppercorns (*merica*), peanuts (*kacang tanah*) and round, cream-colored candlenuts (*kemiri*) used as a thickening agent. Red clove trees and coffee plantations reign supreme and find nurturance in Bali's cooler northern mountain climes. Seasons and spice determine life in villages like Munduk and Pebantenan near Singaraja, ringed by clove, cacao and coffee plantations. For centuries, the legendary isles of the Malukus were the world's only source of nutmeg, mace and cloves, continually fought over by the Spanish, Dutch and Portuguese. Silence reigns in the extensive rice, cocoa and coffee plantations covering the rainforested slopes of Mt Batukaru. Bracketed by high villages, cocoa farms grow cocoabeans (sprouting from tree trunks), which are processed into cocoa powder for hot chocolate, an export product. Many different herbs, spices and fruits grow in the fertile soil of this elevated food forest. Cloves (*cengkeh*) have a recognizable, camphor-like smell and flavor. Rarely used in Balinese cooking, they are instead utilized to make aromatic Indonesian *kretek* cigarettes. Clove trees are common along the roads and in the forests. They thrive in open sunlight and a clear ground surface between trees and need very little work to bring to harvest.

Underground rhizomes and roots star in the ginger family: fresh ginger root (*tingting jahe*), greater galangal, native to Java (*isen* in

Balinese, *laos* in Indonesian), deliciously scented lesser galangal or resurrection lily (*cekuh* in Balinese, *kencur* in Indonesian) and fresh bright orange-yellow turmeric (*kunyit*). Lesser galangal is the reddish-brown root of a palm-like plant (*Kaempferia galanga*) of the ginger family, used as a spice or medicine. The word for ginger comes from the Sanskrit word *singivera*, referring to the antler-like rhizome of the plant. A commonly used cooking spice, ginger is also made into *permen jahe*, a sweet, chewy candied ginger. The most common kind of ginger is pale yellowish white. Plump aromatic fresh ginger is sold in abundance in the traditional markets. Turmeric root (lily family) is regarded as a sacred dye, crucial to the transformation of ceremonial white rice and curries into the color yellow. Turmeric leaves are not ordinarily eaten or used in cooking except as floating flavor enhancers in traditional dragonfly soup. They stand tall with wild torch ginger (*bongkot*), whose edible pink flowers bloom prolifically in Bali's home gardens; the bud is enjoyed raw in *sambal* dishes and rice and is added to curries and soups. A Southeast Asian native, tropical lemongrass (*sereh*) stalks grow in countless compounds as a grass-like plant.

Indonesian cuisine is known for the deliberate combination of contrasting flavors (spicy, sour, sweet, hot) in each of its carefully orchestrated spice-based dishes. The sour flavors feature the juice and often the double leaf of the small, round, knobby-skinned green kaffir lime (*jeruk purut*), finely shredded with kitchen scissors into *sambal*/salad/satay-ready hair-like shreds. The thick leaves of the kaffir lime lend a tangy perfume to Balinese concoctions, while the kaffir lime itself has a clean, sharp citrus bite. Tall tamarind trees dominate dry areas like Singaraja in northern Bali. Their brown suede pods contain large flat seeds and a dark red fruity-sour soft fleshy pulp which is sold in snow-ball shaped blocks for cooking. Locals climb up the branches to retrieve the pods and suck out the sweet-sour innards as a special treat. The Balinese also soak both the seeds (*lunak*) and the pulp in water and strain them into a solution to impart a sour taste to dishes (tamarind or *asam* means sour in Malay). Sweet and salty flavors flaunt two strains of cinnamon: thick, dark brown Sumatra-bred cassia bark and native cinnamon (*kayu manis*). Cinnamon is harvested from two trees of the same species, the cinnamon and the cassia tree. The former, known as true cinnamon, has a less intense aroma than the cassia. Fragrant cinnamon trees surround interior highland villages like Sayan.

The world of spices is complemented by salt, the most important condiment in Bali next to chili peppers. Coarse, flaky sea salt (*garam*) is the only salt used in Balinese cooking. Containing seventy-four different healthy minerals, it is kept in a coconut shell container, called a *tjalon*. Included in every recipe, it is produced in coastal regions like Jimbaran, Yeh Gangga near Tabanan on the southwest coast, Goa Lawah, Kusamba Beach, Tulamben and Amed in eastern Bali. Its popularity has spawned a thriving island-wide coastal cottage industry dedicated to producing table salt from seawater. Salt panning and salt making in Bali are always family enterprises and there are only small producers, no companies or cooperatives. Ten to twenty families work independently to create salt, which is stored in and sold out of their individual homes. Seawater is first hauled out of the sea in pairs of clay pots balanced on an ancient shoulder yoke or in plastic buckets and then up the beach to more elevated sand flats. It is sloshed onto the ground and allowed to evaporate in the sun. The dry salty beach material (sand or mud) is then gathered in bamboo baskets and carried to a storage hut to be leached using seawater and turned into salt water brine. The resulting slushy effluent is fire-heat evaporated and then drip-strained to produce three grades of saleable table salt. In Kusamba and Amed, the leached brine is poured into rows of hollow coconut log troughs set on wooden platforms. Left on the beach to evaporate, the liquid turns into an unprocessed salt slush in the sun. It is then strained through a conical rice steamer basket to yield salt. Distributors come to the coasts to purchase home-made salt by the basketful and take it to the various markets around Bali. It is retailed directly to inland customers in plastic bags.

Dried shrimp paste (*terasi* in Indonesian, *belacan* in Malay) is a rank-smelling, high-protein primary seasoning spawned from pounded, fermented and sun-dried crustaceans or other small fish. With a potent aroma, the red-brown paste is used in small amounts in most sauces. Traditionally, a mixture of fish or shellfish and salt (to inhibit bacterial growth) was left in an earthenware pot in the sun for several months until a clear golden liquid could be drawn from it. The residue was compressed and dried into a very pungent block known as *terasi udang*.

Minute slices of this seasoning are roasted and added to the *bumbu*. Sold "raw" in the market in small brown rectangular patties, *terasi* is fried, grilled or roasted over an open fire, wrapped in foil and kept in an airtight glass jar for several months. *Kecap asin*, a salty soy sauce, is made by inoculating boiled soybeans with Aspergillus oryzae fungus, then exposing them to sunlight and adding anise, *aren* from the areca palm tree and ginger. The flower stalk yields a liquid which can be made into a brown sugar (*gula aren*). *Kecap manis* (thick, sweet soy sauce) is commonly used to both flavor and accompany Balinese food.

The trademark flavor of Balinese cuisine is governed by two separate culinary institutions: the classic *bumbu* (spice paste mixtures) and the use of *sambal* (sauce). *Bumbu* is a general term for spices, flavorings, seasonings and herbs used in cooking. *Sambal* (meaning mixed or more than one ingredient) are super scorching freshly made chili sauces eaten in very small quantities. They are added and mixed into food after it is cooked. These pungent chili preparations are served at every meal as a side condiment in a traditional *kau*, a round coconut shell container, should someone want to make their food tastier. There are hundreds of different *sambal* all over the archipelago. Almost every Balinese and Indonesian dish features its own kind and each family makes it differently. There are unlimited *sambal* combinations utilizing vermilion chilies, purple shallots, garlic cloves, shrimp paste, local leaves, sea salt, sweet soy sauce and oil as the basic building blocks. Fried and cooked together, five of these magical staples become *sambal goreng* (fried chili *sambal*), Bali's most important multifunction seasoning. Used by every family every day, usually for vegetables, *sambal goreng* contains garlic, shallots, shrimp paste, chilies and sea salt. It is prepared by first pounding the chilies and then frying them in oil. The bruising of the chilies allows their natural oil to surface and the heat from the frying allows the chilies to imbue the oil with its flavor. The result is a fiery mouth-warming concoction that is the very essence of local Balinese cuisine.

Fried *sambal terasi* is another renowned condiment made of all-important red chilies, *terasi*, also called *belacan* (shrimp or fish paste) and salt ground together in a traditional *cobek*; lime juice can be added after it is ground. The *cobek* (Balinese) is a shallow earthenware bowl or mortar used for grinding and crushing spices, accompanied by a wooden pestle called a *pengulakan*. Alternately, it is a volcanic rock basin with a rock pestle. Simple *sambal sere tabia* combines shrimp paste, large and small ground chilies, lemongrass (*sere, sereh* or *serai*) and salt fried together and served with a modicum of coconut oil. *Sambal pelecing* has become so deeply ingrained in the Balinese kitchen that it has become a generic term for a way of cooking chicken and vegetables. The bases of *sambal pelecing* are tomato and *belacan*. Finely chopped and roasted rice field eel mixed with shallots, chilies and coconut oil is another extremely popular Balinese *sambal*. Increasingly avant-garde *sambal* concoctions include Bali's "naked" *sambal matah*, the most beloved *sambal* on Bali. An invaluable part of many Balinese meals, *sambal matah* is an uncooked dressing composed of chopped onion or shallots, garlic, diminutive hot chilies, *terasi*, kaffir lime, lemongrass, salt and coconut oil; the latter is the most important ingredient. It is a tongue-teasing seafood mainstay at the string of grilled fish *warung* guarding the island's culinary coastlines.

Extravagant "acquired taste" *sambal* include stir-fried chili with shrimp paste, onion, garlic, bitter melon and egg; complicated *sambal goreng hati ayam* or chicken liver *sambal* with sweet chili and potatoes; grilled anchovy *sambal; sambal tuwung* (*tuwung* is eggplant in Balinese), a tomato-based roasted eggplant *sambal;* and *sambal kukus bongkot*, steamed torch ginger *sambal. Sambal tomat*, a spicy tomato-based chili sauce, is the Latin salsa of Indonesia. This fiery red paste is a mix of fresh tomatoes, garlic, shallots, red chili, lime leaves and pungent *terasi* (shrimp paste) ground in a volcanic rock *cobek* or *tjobek*. The intensity depends on the piquancy of the chili used. *Saur* (in *Balinese* and *serunding* in Bahasa Indonesia) is grated coconut pulp mixed with palm sugar or spices like turmeric and beans and fried. It is used in simple *warung* cooking as well as for ceremonies as a condiment to sprinkle on top of the type of rice that is served.

Taucho sauce, yellow fermented soy bean paste, is descended from a group of Chinese foods or condiments known as *jiang* (pastes) or more specifically as *jiang* made from soybeans (*doujiang*), first referenced in AD 535. The Chinese word for soy sauce is *jiangyou*, meaning the liquid pressed from *jiang*. Soybean *jiang* is the earliest known ancestor of Japanese *miso*, a fermented soybean paste made with soybeans, rice or barley, salt and water. As *doujiang* moved south from China into South-east Asia, the word became corrupted into *taucho* in the Indonesian language. In 1935, Burkiel described Indonesian *taucho*: cooked soybeans were mixed with roasted rice flour, then arenga palm sugar, and a paste of glutinous rice. *Taucho* is produced and consumed mainly in West Java where production is centered in the town of Chianjur. *Jiang* is produced by inoculating cooked, mashed soybeans with mold spores, crushing them, mixing them with salt or rice wine and water and then fermenting them in a pickling crock or jar for thirty to a hundred days. There are four soy-based varieties of Indonesian *taucho*: soft sweet *taucho*, which contains 25 percent palm sugar by weight; salty liquid *taucho*, a black bean sauce; firm dried *taucho* (*taucho kering*; *kering* means dry), which is sold in sun-dried cakes; and smoked dried *taucho*. The most popular recipe is *sambal goreng taucho*. *Sayur taucho* is a flavorful vegetarian dish on Java combining a deep-fried, seared or simmered repertoire of tofu, *tempe*, onions, garlic cloves, ginger root, galangal, *salam* leaves, lemongrass, green chilies, coconut cream, green beans, *peteh* or *petai* beans (a smelly, edible bean, *Parkia speciosa*), tomatoes and canned *taucho* black bean sauce or salty black soybeans. Soybean *jiang* appears as a sauce ingredient, typically in peanut sauce, in neighboring Bali.

Bali's widely used natural dark brown, caramel-flavored palm sugar (*gula merah* or *gula* Bali) is produced in backyards throughout the island by boiling nectar extracted from the unopened flower bud of the majestic areca palm, sugar palm or lontar palm tree. To produce palm sugar, the sap from the flower bud at the summit of the tree is harvested and boiled until the water evaporates. The resulting dark brown sugar is allowed to solidify in round molds. Villagers also make palm sugar from the white inside of the coconut tree trunk. Boiled at medium heat, the thick golden syrup that emerges is set and incubated inside a round coconut shell or a tubular bamboo stalk for five days until it becomes a solid palm sugar block. Produced in Karangasem and Klungkung regencies, palm sugar is typically intubated in a cylinder and vended in round or cylindrical cakes in Bali's markets, reflecting the shapes of their molds. Palm sugar (*gula merah*) can be made into liquid palm sugar syrup by simmering it in water for fifteen minutes with a pandanus leaf dropped in to give it extra flavor.

The Balinese are known for the liberal use of mixed species of tongue-numbing chilies (*cabe* or *cabai* in Indonesian) in their cooking. Chili peppers, the fruit of capsicum genus plants, originated in South America and were brought to Southeast Asia by Portuguese and Arab spice traders in the sixteenth century. They are an essential year-round ingredient in Balinese cooking and are abundantly used to turn up the heat. Although not native to Indonesia, the introduced chili quickly insinuated itself into the resident array of the fresh Southeast Asian herbs and spices needed to cook and create local fare. Before the arrival of chilies, the Balinese used gingers and black pepper. Peppers grow here profusely and there are thousands of varieties, each with their own flavor. As chilies are sensitive to variations in soil and climate, the same species grown 150 miles apart can have a very different taste and pungency. The Balinese are gastronomically addicted to capsaicin, the chemical substance that gives chilies their heat, and will not suffer being parted from their beloved chilies. A dish is only considered appetizing and palatable when it is gunpowder hot or served with a hand-prepared chili-infused raw or cooked *sambal*. Chilies are eminently practical in a hot climate as a convenient, natural food preservative. They are always used in ceremonial *lawar merah* (red *lawar*), which traditionally contains raw pig's blood. The peppers are believed to kill the bacteria.

Chili bushes are grown in local front yards, enabling the Balinese to use this sun-ripened fire alarm force for free. Traditionally, each village only cooked with the chilies that it grew but now there is a large chili repertoire in the market, among them red hot, mild maroon, pungent white, orange, medium hot yellow and emerald green, sold in plump, thin, long and short packages. Traditional markets and modern supermarkets are filled with aptly named *cabe merah besar* (big, plump red chilies), *cabe merah keriting* (slim, curly red chilies), *cabe merah kecil* (tiny red chilies), *cabe hijau besar* (big green chilies) and *cabe hijau kecil* (petite green chilies). Tiny, devastatingly hot peppers are used in *acar*, a raw sweet-and-sour pickle salad, and as a typical accompaniment to fried tofu, which would otherwise be bland. Among the three most common pepper varieties in Bali is, first, *tabia kerinyi* (*cabai burung* in Malay) or bird's eye chilies, so-called because of their small size and bird-like shape. The hottest of the hot, the bird's eye chili is the tiniest and most popular blazing firebrand in Bali and is often eaten raw as a condiment with snacks. Secondly, *tabia* Bali, otherwise called *tabia biasa* (common) or *cabe*, is a one-inch-long medium-sized red-yellow chili that packs a moderate punch for its size. Thirdly, the VIP list of culinary mouth burners is completed by the finger-length red *tabia* Lombok, which is larger, sweeter and milder. This long red chili also packs a punch but is gentler than the small, mean green ones! Lombok is the island of the chili and is famous for its spicy dishes. Indeed, the word *lombok* means red chili, and thus the island was named after its notorious hot pepper. Long pepper, *tabiabun* (*tabia* is chili and *bun* means vine) is hot and aromatic. This tropical climbing plant (*Piper retrofractum*) is common in the villages and wends its way into many traditional dishes.

Local Balinese garlic cloves (*kesuna* in Balinese, *bawang putih* in Indonesian) are sweeter, smaller and milder than their Western counterparts. Their skins intact, they are deep-fried and added in a typically Balinese double-cooking process to deep-fried coconut for extra flavor. *Bawang merah* (Balinese shallots) are very small, mild, purple-red onions and are a vital ingredient in almost all Balinese recipes. The Balinese also use a lot of strong, small local onions, believed to protect young children from black magic. Miniature golden pieces of fried shallots or onion (*bawang goreng*) are sprinkled on dishes as a garnish, including plain steamed rice and thick, congee-like Indonesian rice soups (*bubur ayam*). *Bubur ayam* is usually served for breakfast with a wide choice of side condiments and add-ons: pickled ginger, fried onions, peanuts, croutons, shredded chicken, thick soy sauce and tiny green chilies.

Rare but popular leaves like *salam* (*daun salam*), a member of the myrtle family, rule many of Bali's culinary roosts. *Salam* are long grass-green, pointy-ended oval leaves that grow on trees. They are thrown into the daily steamed rice to add both freshness and fragrance. *Salam* is alternately known as Indonesian bay leaf, *daun salam* (Indonesian) or *jangar ulam* (Balinese). The scientific name for *salam* is *Syzygium polyanthum*. Aromatic *salam* leaves, either fresh or dried, are used as a spice in multiple Balinese dishes. The *salam* leaves are added intact early on and are left to cook with the dish, as their flavor develops only gradually. Distinctive, scent-laden, spear-like pandanus (screwpine) leaves (*daun pandan harum*) are used to add green color, a subtle scent and a sweet flavor to cakes, porridges and teas, and to enhance cauldrons of sticky steaming rice. There are many different species of and uses for pandanus in Bali. Minutely shredded worm-like pandanus leaf squiggles are a routine topping on offering baskets seen and placed everywhere in god-conscious Bali. The Balinese do not cook or eat the thorny pandanus species growing on dry Nusa Lembongan. Like the inventive cooks of cosmopolitan Singapore and Malaysia, the Balinese only use the correct pandanus varieties as valued rice or dessert flavorings and artful but functional food wrappings. *Ulam* refers to cold, raw, young leafy vegetables eaten as a side dish (*lalapan*).

An essential component in ceremonial cooking and in everyday village fare, the coconut (*kelapa*), inexpensively purchased for Rp.1,500–2,000 in the market, adds to the idiosyncrasies—and calories—of Balinese cuisine. The equatorial coconut palm is considered sacred (many special offerings are made to it) because young, smooth coconut leaves (*busung*) provide the critical raw material for fabricating and weaving hundreds of different types of Balinese *canang sari* offerings, plaited containers for offerings, *ketupat* baskets and elaborate decorations required at temple ceremonies and religious celebrations. The whole round coconuts themselves are used in a large number of ceremonies as containers or as offerings. The coconut tree also plays an important secular role in the culture and economy of Bali, providing the Balinese with food to eat (coconut cream, milk, water, meat, palm sugar and grated coconut), cooking oil, and hard, strong wood for house construction. If a tree is cut for lumber, the bud or "palm cabbage," called *empol*, is eagerly eaten. Grated coconut flesh enters into almost every Balinese recipe. Frying of ingredients for dishes is done exclusively in coconut oil, and much of the food in Bali is simmered in either rich coconut cream or light coconut milk.

The Balinese name for coconut is *nyuh*. Young coconuts (*kelapa muda* or *kuwud* in Balinese) have a green-colored husk and are moist and juice-heavy at ten months old. These young, mature coconuts are filled with a naturally sterile, sweet, clear watery liquid (variously termed coconut water, coconut milk or coconut juice) that is sold all along the main highways as an inexpensive, natural thirst quencher. Young coconuts also have a thin jelly-like, transparent white coating that lines the inner wall of the nut, and this is often scraped off with a spoon and eaten as a snack. Older, fully mature coconuts have thick, fibrous brown husks. They yield a hard, dried white flesh known as copra. Coconut oil is derived from copra. Mature coconuts are cultivated on the northern coastal plains as a major international export crop.

Coconut milk (called *santen* in both Indonesia and Malaysia) is a sweet, milky white cooking ingredient derived from the grated meat or flesh of a mature coconut. Coconut meat is not normally eaten by itself. Rather, the meat is scraped from the shell, grated, mixed with hot water, squeezed and then strained to produce a freshly pressed thick or light coconut milk called *santen*. The word *santen* itself refers to both thin coconut milk and rich coconut cream. Its characteristic color, rich taste and high calorific count are due to the high oil content. Fresh *santen* is produced at two essential dilutions or strengths: thick ("first squeeze"), thin ("second squeeze") and an optional thinner milk ("third squeeze"). *Santen* is produced by repeatedly squeezing, soaking and straining the meat of a fresh coconut. The thickness of the milk (or cream) is determined by how much coconut or water is used. Thick milk (first squeeze) is prepared by directly pressing grated coconut meat (pre-soaked in water) through a piece of cheesecloth or a thin towel into a receiving bowl. The squeezed coconut meat is then soaked again in warm water and squeezed a second or third time for progressively thinner coconut milks. The first squeeze (thick creamy milk) is used to make desserts and rich, dry sauces. Thin milk is used for soups and general cooking. A typical *santen* preparation method is to place a cup of grated coconut flesh in a bowl and add an equal amount of hot to boiling water. The flesh is kneaded with the fingers for several minutes to release its oils into the water. Handfuls of the coconut flesh are then squeezed over a strainer and a clean bowl to release the thick coconut liquid (first squeeze). The process is repeated with more water for a thinner batch of coconut milk (or the two batches can be combined). One cup of coconut meat generally yields one cup of thick and one cup of thin coconut milk.

The Balinese use coconut milk (and secondarily cream) as an ingredient for cooking vegetables, seafood, meat, curries and dessert bananas.

Deliciously pungent and piquant, *nasi gurih*, which is made with thick coconut milk plus pandanus and *salam* leaves, has a salty taste like fried fish. Chunks of fresh white coconut meat are often roasted semi-black in a charcoal fire or over an open flame before the outer burnt layer is scraped off and the flesh grated, mixed with water and strained to make a sweet, smoky Balinese specialty—roasted coconut milk. After making fresh coconut milk, the Balinese save the pressed coconut to feed to the pigs in order not to waste any part of the fruit. Fresh coconut oil (*minyak kelapa*) is extracted from this same dried coconut meat and is the preferred home cooking oil in Bali. It is also called *minyak goreng*, meaning fried oil. Cheap, widely available coconut fruits are hand-processed into coconut oil in Balinese compounds and then used to fry meat, fish and vegetables. Local people can also manufacture their own coconut oil at home by boiling down coconut milk and ladling off the oil that rises to the top. Even the hard shell of the coconut is used, often as a sacred vessel to hold cremation ceremony ashes or as a container for other small items. The outer husk fiber of the coconut makes an excellent charcoal for grilling satay as well as a smoky fuel for grilling the fresh fish catch of the day on Jimbaran Bay.

Balinese Spice Paste Mixture

(BASE GEDE)

People live here in the hot tropical air under the glittering sun in an intoxicating and passionate collage of fragrant aromas and delightful sought-after spices. The fabled Spice Islands were the hotly contested colonial jewels in the Indonesian crown. The stuff of European war, conquest and naval dominance, the legendary spices (cloves, mace, nutmeg, pepper and cardamom) from the islands are seldom used, however, in domestic Indonesian and Balinese cooking! Base genep translates as "complete spice" and every grandmother in Bali has her own secret, passed-down recipe to make base gede. The legendary spice paste is the mainstay of many Balinese dishes and is easy to make.

The cuisine of Bali is distinguished from cooking in other parts of Indonesia by a multitude of spices and flavorings not, or comparatively rarely found, on the other islands. A characteristic feature of Balinese cooking is the absolute passion for grinding fresh rhizomes—ginger, greater galangal, lesser galangal and turmeric—into a paste. There is also a heavy use of lemongrass, kaffir lime, pandanus leaves and Indonesian bay leaf (salam) compared with their use on Java. Another flavoring much liked by the Balinese is terasi, a pungent and strong-smelling paste of fermented shrimps.

Recipe courtesy of Ni Wayan Murni, Murni's Warung, Campuhan-Ubud.

7 oz (200 g) shallots
7 oz (200 g) garlic
3½ oz (100 g) lesser galangal
2 oz (50 g) fresh turmeric
2 oz (50 g) galangal
½ oz (10 g) fresh ginger
½ oz (10 g) candlenuts
½ tbs coriander seeds
½ tbs black peppercorns
½ tbs grated nutmeg
1 tsp shrimp paste
1 stalk lemongrass
salt to taste

Peel the bulb and root spices and place with the rest of the ingredients in a traditional Balinese mortar. Chop until they are very fine.

Pound and crush the chopped bulbs, roots and spices using a hand-held pestle until a smooth paste forms. Add a little water if too dry.

Fry the mixture in a little coconut oil for a few minutes. Do not scorch.

Serves 4–6.

CHAPTER SIX

Breakfast in the Morning of the World

———— ≠ ————

BREAKFAST ON BALI IS A FORM OF PRAYER. The Balinese ritually cleanse themselves first, traditionally requiring a dawn walk through the rice fields to a river for a chilly morning bath, and cleaning up the kitchen before receiving spiritual nourishment from the soul of the rice. The first meal of the day is a gift from the benevolent gods and is treated and eaten in respectful silence. Many Balinese women only have a drink of water when they wake up because they must head right out to the market and then cook the entire day's food supply before taking nourishment.

The Balinese breakfast (*makan pagi or* morning food) usually consists of freshly cooked fried golden bananas (*pisang goreng*) or local Balinese rice cakes (*jaja*) composed of rice flour dough, coconut and palm sugar, and a piping hot, very sweet glass of thick, strong locally grown black *kopi Bali* (coffee) with extra sugar but no milk because it is too expensive. Industrious village women wake up before sunrise to fry *banjar*-size quantities of golden bananas in batter and walk door to door in the early morning selling the warm *pisang goreng* fritters from a bamboo carrying basket. Traditionally, *jaja* is a breakfast food and a mid-morning snack, either fried, steamed or boiled. Freshly cooked in the wee hours, hot off the stove, various types of *jaja* are available in the local village market stalls by dawn. A wife might buy a tasty breakfast treat for herself and her family consisting of a few small, moist *jaja* sprinkled with fresh coconut and palm sugar syrup.

Spring roll-shaped coconut-filled pancakes (*dadar*) are another stand-ard Balinese breakfast food. *Dadar gulung* (*dadar* means crepe or pancake and *gulung* means roll or to roll) are sweet, rolled-up, crepe-like pancakes in blinding pink, aquamarine and lime green colors stuffed with a filling (*unti*). Made of rice flour, pandanus, *suji* leaves, sugar, salt, egg and coco-nut milk, *dadar gulung*, also called *dadar unti*, are renowned for their addictively sweet, chewy filling, the luscious *unti*, composed of fresh coarsely grated sweet young coconut, pandanus leaf and *gula Bali* (brown palm sugar). *Dadar gulung* are most often found in a luscious spongy green with a bubble-pocked texture. Aromatic pandanus leaves are used as the natural food coloring agent. *Urab jagung*, sweet corn kernels integrated into grated coconut, sugar, salt and coconut cream, and *jaja injin* made with steamed black and white glutinous rice, pandanus leaves, grated coconut, coconut cream and palm sugar syrup also fortify the Balinese in the early morning hours.

Godoh biu, fried bananas, are one of the most popular morning treas-ures, usually enjoyed with hot, super sweet Balinese coffee or tea. These crispy finger bananas, dipped in a batter of rice flour, plain flour, water and salt, are slow-fried in coconut oil over low heat until golden brown and served with palm sugar syrup or honey. The bananas are cut in half lengthwise and each piece then cut in half. Since the batter is made with-out eggs, it yields a light, crisp result. Many *warung* regulars break the overnight fast with a variation of fried bananas called *jaja pulung biu* (fried, mashed, overripe bananas) served with coffee. To make *jaja pulung* (small ball or pellet) *biu*, the Balinese first mash very ripe bananas, add plain flour, water, sugar and salt, and mix them into a soft elastic dough. Tablespoons of the mashed banana batter are deep-fried until crisp and served with palm sugar syrup. Some Balinese make fried rice in the morn-ing or purchase small portions of rice with vegetables as breakfast from a nearby *warung*. A local *warung* breakfast may consist of spicy free-range village chicken, coconut vegetables, salted egg and *sambal* combined into a mini-feast for Rp.10,000. *Nasi campur* and sweet or savory rice porridges (*bubur*) are also offered in the local markets as early morning take-out breakfast fare in waxy banana leaves or small plastic bags.

Breakfast in the sacred "morning of the world" can also begin with one of the most exquisite and satisfying breakfast sensations: *bubur mebasa* (*bubur* is porridge in Indonesian and *basa* spice in Balinese). The rice porridge is cooked with saffron, spice paste and tasty leaves found only on a rare tree (*bulan baon*) in select housing compound gardens and also, somewhat secretly, sold in the market. *Bulan baon*, a member of the Loganiaceae (cabbage tree) family, has a number of names in Indonesia: *kayu bulan* (Kalimantan), *bebira* (Sumatra), *bira bira*, *bubira*, *malabira* and *melabira*. Its thick, broadly rounded teardrop-shaped leaves have prominent veins. To make *bubur mebasa*, washed white rice is boiled in water or chicken stock and a fried spice paste mixture composed of ground garlic, ginger, lesser galangal, turmeric, galangal, red chili and shrimp paste is added. Near the end of the cooking process, the magical cabbage leaf is inserted. Crowned with fried shallots and served on a banana leaf if you are Balinese, or in a bowl for crockery-dependent Westerners, this dish is out of this world, especially for the flavor of the leaf delicacy. *Bubur mebasa saur* is a soupy Balinese breakfast rice porridge blessed with *saur* (fried grated coconut pulp mixed with palm sugar), traditionally served in a an environmentally friendly banana leaf receptacle. Flavored with *salam* leaves, it is often served with fried shallots, a hard-boiled egg, diced cooked chicken or any other easily digestible food.

Bali boasts a wide range of these velvety breakfast or snack porridges, among them *bubur sumsum*, a sweet, creamy, boiled rice flour porridge made with Balinese palm sugar, rice flour, pandanus and freshly squeezed coconut milk. The rice flour is flavored and colored with liquid produced from *pandan harum* leaves, creating a brilliant green color and fragrant taste. The soft, emerald *bubur sumsum* is served with extra coconut milk, nestled in a crater of melted brown sugar. Eaten primarily as a snack, it is widely available in the markets. *Bubur sumsum* is always served after cremation ceremonies without the melted palm sugar. *Bubur mengguh* is porridge mixed with meat, either chicken or shredded fish, vegetable (usually spinach) and spices, and is served on special occasions like family gatherings. Old-fashioned compound *bubur* consists of soft-boiled rice topped with steamed greens and soy bean sprouts mixed with shredded coconut, shrimp paste, chili seasoning and coconut sauce. *Bubur ketan* is sticky rice porridge; *bubur merah* is rice porridge with palm sugar, and *bubur nasi pulut* is rice porridge made from *beras pulut*, a sweet, glutinous rice. Another secular variety of porridge is made from ordinary rice served with mixed vegetables, coarsely grated half-grilled coconut, chicken broth and coconut milk. It is usually sold at markets and village food stalls. At home, the Balinese also make *bubur* for people who are ill.

As an extraordinarily religious community, the Balinese view food as something only partially intended for nutrition; it is more often intended for ritual use. To show veneration to God and his creations, villagers give offerings to plants and animals to represent the harmonious, interdependent relationship between humans, animals and plants The ritual to honor plants occurs every 210 days on Saniscara (Saturday in Balinese) Kliwon Wariga. The day is also known as Tumpek Wariga or Tumpek Bubuh because the offerings contain various *bubur*. To start the ceremony, *bubur* is smeared on the bark of a tree as a symbol of fertilizer, the proper food for vegetation. For this celebration, offerings are accompanied by flour porridge and palm sugar syrup. Special offerings are also made to coconut trees. *Bubur* is put inside offerings that are attached to the tree and each tree is commanded to produce a bountiful crop of coconuts in the year ahead. The Balinese also ask the gods for prosperity for their vegetation so that it can provide food for mankind. A blessing ceremony is given to it for good crops, held at every plantation and farm throughout the island.

Another mouth-watering, very rich morning dish is black rice pudding or *bubuh injin* (*bubuh* is Balinese for pudding and *injin* is black rice). Dense in texture, warm in flavor and full of home-cooked goodness, *bubuh injin* is made with a galaxy of the more expensive black glutinous rice, or combined with a small admixture of white glutinous rice, and cooked with palm sugar syrup, vanilla bean, pandanus leaf and salt. It is topped with white roasted coconut milk or thick coconut cream, fresh coconut shavings, palm sugar syrup and banana wedges or jackfruit pieces. Bali's luscious *bubuh* are customarily served with shaved coconut or coconut milk mixed with liquid brown sugar. A simpler traditional version of *bubuh injin* consists of black *injin* rice cooked and served with brown palm sugar and coconut milk. The Balinese normally buy *bubuh injin* from a *warung* since it takes time to prepare and they often eat it as a substantial afternoon snack.

Bubuh Injin

(BLACK RICE PUDDING)

Murni cooks bubuh injin (bubuh is Balinese for pudding) and other exquisite local dishes a bit differently at the Warung than the way she would cook them for herself at home or for Balinese friends. At the restaurant, the recipes are toned down out of consideration for Western clients. Murni's former American husband, Pat, lovingly remembers Murni in the kitchen: "Murni is a great cook. But she doesn't do it the same for herself as she does for tourists. I wish you could have seen her in action before we started selling food some thirty years ago. We would eat in Denpasar and she would say, 'They use some shallots and turmeric and garlic, but not much. They cook at a very high temperature. They do this. They do that. They keep their acar in vinegar for at least one day before serving it.' It was a remarkable display. She could deconstruct almost anything we ate anywhere. And then duplicate it. A genius!" 2007.

This is Murni's black rice pudding recipe as served in Murni's Warung; the amount of water used and the cooking time may need to be adjusted according to the quality of the black rice. It can be kept in the refrigerator for 3–4 days, but do not add the coconut milk until the pudding is served.

Recipe Courtesy of Ni Wayan Murni, Murni's Warung, Campuhan-Ubud.

1–1¼ cups black glutinous rice
5 cups water
¾ cup thick palm sugar syrup
¾ tsp salt
¾ tsp vanilla bean
1½ pandanus leaves
2¼ cups thick coconut milk
banana slices or jackfruit wedges

Soak the black glutinous rice for 5 minutes and then drain.

Put the water and rice into a heavy pan and turn on the heat.

When the water starts to simmer, add the palm sugar syrup and pandan leaf.

Simmer over medium heat for about 30–40 minutes until most of the liquid has evaporated.

Add salt and vanilla.

Remove from the heat and allow to cool.

Put in bowls and top with coconut milk, slices of banana or wedges of jack-fruit. Palm sugar syrup and fresh coconut shavings are optional.

Serve at room temperature.

Serves 4–6.

Bubur Mebasa

(SPICED PORRIDGE)

Murni's menu emphasizes flavor, local natural ingredients and closely guarded traditional village (and family) recipes. Using fresh abundant produce from the Ubud market and seductive leaves from the lush surrounding interior highlands of Bali, Murni still enjoys experimenting at home and in the Warung kitchen, merging new ideas with traditional ingredients and time-tested family compound methods. As a professional purveyor of beautiful food on beautiful Bali, Murni gives her guests at Murni's Villas in Payangan the rare opportunity to sample some of Bali's best and most characteristic native dishes. Bubur mebasa tops the breakfast page on the highly inventive, highly spiced Balinese culture menu. Bubur is Bahasa Indonesia for porridge. Murni used to add tasty leaves to it from a rare tree (called bulan baon) growing in her father's garden. The leaves give bubur mebasa a remarkable, exquisite, delicious taste found nowhere else in the world. She has now planted the same leaf-bearing tree in the easily accessible gardens of Murni's Villas. Other Balinese commonly substitute salam leaves for the elusive bulan baon tree leaves. The best salam leaves to use are the old dried ones which have turned black in color. Spinach leaves are also a fine choice. Serve on a banana leaf if you're Balinese. If not, bowls or plates will do.

Strong, earthy, full-bodied, heavenly smelling kopi Bali (Bali coffee) locally grown in Payangan is the perfect complement to this outstanding breaking of the overnight fast. Planted and nurtured in rich volcanic soil, Bali coffee is cultivated in the higher mountainous elevations and cooler climes in Tabanan, Kintamani and Singaraja and is renowned for its strong and distinctive aroma and taste. The aroma of coffee in Payangan at harvest time is the first sign of other good things to come. Grown by local villagers, you can smell the beans as you drive up the road to the Villas at Ponggang. The local product tastes different from other varieties of Balinese or Javanese coffee.

Recipe courtesy of Ni Wayan Murni, Murni's Warung, Campuhan-Ubud.

⅔ lb (300 g) plain white rice, washed and drained
5 cups water or chicken stock
fresh *bulan baon* leaves (or a handful of *salam* leaves, washed)
3 tbs coconut oil
2¼ tsp salt
2 *salam* leaves
6 tsp fried shallots

FOR THE SPICE PASTE (*BASE GEDE*)
6 cloves garlic
½ in (1½ cm) ginger
¼ in (¾ cm) turmeric
½ in (1½ cm) lesser galangal
¼ in (¾ cm) galangal
pinch of shrimp paste
red chili (optional)

Wash the rice in cold water, then soak for 5 minutes. Drain and set aside.

Grind the spice paste ingredients using a mortar and pestle.

Heat the coconut oil in a frying pan over a low heat. Add the paste and fry gently for about a minute. Turn the heat off when you can smell the flavors and set aside.

Put the water or chicken stock in a deep pan, add the rice and boil. Add the paste, salt and bay leaf during boiling. Cook for 3–5 minutes.

Add the *bulan baon* leaves and cook for another 3–5 minutes.

Put the *bubur mebasa* on a banana leaf, in a bowl or on a plate.

Sprinkle about 1 teaspoon of fried shallots on each banana leaf portion, bowl or plate and serve hot.

Serves 4–6.

Dadar Gulung

(PANCAKE ROLLS STUFFED WITH GRATED COCONUT)

Dadar gulung (also known as dadar unti) is a sweet, scandalously green, thin rolled pancake wrapped around a sweet, chewy, grated coconut and palm sugar filling (unti). Dadar are one of the most popular forms of jaja in both Malaysia and Indonesia. The pancake batter and fillings will vary from island to island. Dadar gulung can incorporate fillings of either palm sugar, beans, coconut, bananas or sweet potatoes, but they will still retain the delightful, archipelago-wide, rolled crepe shape and presentation. The household ibu will adapt her traditional dadar recipes to local conditions and use the indigenous ingredients available in her area. She might substitute flour made from mung beans, white rice, sticky rice, sago, taro or cassava to create the much-loved, familiar dadar pancake.

What turns food into art? The presentation, the chef, the cooking process? Dadar are always rolls of modern art museum integrity, longing and beauty, a reminder that even the Balinese can sometimes choose to eat solely for pleasure! Blinding green dadar gulung can be found everywhere, from the little glass case stand outside Bintang supermarket in Ubud to the local take-out cake counter in Matahari Department store in Kuta. They are always packed in fragile, leaking, thin plastic containers, full of sweet wonder and divine promise. Delicious soft dadar are irresistible—even the mass-produced versions are pure Heaven on earth—and they are one of my favorite foods in Bali.

PANCAKE ROLL WRAPPING (BATTER)
1¼ cups thick coconut milk
1½ oz (40 g) *suji* leaves
3 pandanus leaves
5 oz (150 g) rice flour
warm water
1 egg
4 tsp salt
¾ tbs sugar
coconut oil

FILLING (*UNTI KELAPA*)
7 oz (200 g) coarsely grated fresh young coconut
10½ oz (300 g) brown palm sugar
2 tbs water
1–2 bruised, knotted pandanus leaves
pinch of salt

To prepare the *unti* filling, boil the water, brown palm sugar and pandanus leaves until the sugar is completely dissolved. Press through a sieve.

Boil the sieved liquid again, add salt, lower the flame and boil until the liquid thickens and becomes syrupy.

Add the grated coconut, mix well and continue to cook over a low heat for

10 minutes or until a thick, dry consistency is reached. Set aside to cool. Dispose of the pandanus leaves.

To make the wrapping, grind the *suji* and pandanus leaves, squeeze the resulting liquid through a sieve and mix with 400 ml of thick coconut milk.

Add the liquid extract gradually into the rice flour to make a batter.

Add the beaten egg, water, sugar and salt. Mix well until the batter is smooth and evenly colored.

Heat the oil in a frying pan over medium heat and pour in 3 tablespoons of batter for each round pancake. Fry at a medium heat until the visible layer is almost dry and tiny holes appear. Fry one side of the pancake only. Do not turn the pancake over. Repeat the frying process until all the batter is finished.

When done, put a spoonful of the moist, brown sugar colored coconut filling (*unti*) in the center of each flat pancake (on the unfried side).

To form into a roll, fold both sides of the pancake towards the middle over the filling and roll the pancake up from the short end until the filling is completely encased.

The rolls should be 4–6 inches (10–15 cm) long and 1–2 inches (3–5 cm) wide.

Makes 24 rolls.

Serves 4–6.

CHAPTER SEVEN

Dewi Sri and the Cult of Rice

———— ≠ ————

R ICE (*ORYZA SATIVA*) IS WIDELY CULTIVATED throughout Indonesia on both wet and dry lands in Sumatra, Java, Sulawesi, Kalimantan, Maluku, Nusa Tenggara, Irian Jaya and Bali. Always a subject of great passion, rice is the principal source of life and wealth on Bali. Critical to the indigenous eating experience, the romance and worship of rice dates back at least 2,000 years on this fertile island of the gods. Bali has a varied, complex vocabulary for rice, reflecting its importance as both food, the staff of life, and a ceremonial ingredient. "*Padi* rice" is rice on the stalk growing in the field (the English word paddy comes from the Malay *padi* or rice plant). The Balinese cultivate and eat several different types of rice: traditional white Bali rice (*beras Bali*); sticky glutinous red rice (*beras barak* or *merah*); sticky glutinous black rice (*beras injin*), sticky glutinous white rice (*ketan*); "new" green revolution, modern white rice; and a type of dry rice called "dryland rice" (*padi gaga* or *gogo)*. Dry rice is particularly tasty but is a labor-intensive strain planted in dry, non-irrigated hilly ground instead of in wet rice paddies. It is a mountain crop, along with cabbage, coffee, maize, ginger and oranges. *Beras* (in high Balinese or *baas* in low Balinese) is milled, ready for the pot uncooked rice sold in bags in the market. *Gabah* (in Indonesian and *jijih* in Balinese) is unmilled rice that has been separated from the stalks. Cooked rice is called *nasi*.

Black glutinous rice, whose short round grains are black on the outside but white in the center, is used to make cakes and black rice pudding.

Beras merah (red rice) is a colored rice variety, which is actually reddish-brown in aspect. Not as popular as normal white rice but with a distinctive and unusual taste, *beras merah* is still a common and nutritious staple in rural areas of densely populated Java. Deemed to be less fragrant than white rice and therefore less commonly consumed in the big cities, red rice is mainly made into a porridge for infants and elderly people. In Bali, red rice is rarely eaten because it is hard to chew, but it is used to make a nutritious red rice baby porridge. Very little black rice, red rice and glutinous white rice is grown compared to ordinary white rice, and it is more expensive. They are always available in the local market, however, as they are needed for offerings. *Ketan* and *injin* are less commonly used in cooking than the common white rice, *baas*. Thick, glutinous sticky rice is sweeter than the staple *baas*, and is used in rice cakes and desserts.

Bali's ancient irrigation system is complex in design, engineering, distribution and symbolism. It is this system that allows a large percentage of Bali to be covered with breathtaking green rice fields teeming with a life of their own—crabs, eels, dragonflies and legions of busy insects. Cool, sacred mountain lakes (Batur, Beratan and Tamblingan) and high, flowing upland rivers water the precious downstream network of rice fields all the way to the sea. The local district *subak*, a traditional Balinese irrigation cooperative, functions as a collective farmer organization-cum-irrigation association. It coordinates the planting schedule and distributes, allots and channels the water supply through a highly effective hand-built canal, dam and aquaduct-driven irrigation network. The *subak*, a traditional committee with roots in Balinese culture stretching back for many centuries, organizes the production of rice and the complex irrigation system. Groups of neighboring rice farmers with adjacent fields band together and cooperate to deliver water to all of their fields collectively. Everyone who owns a *sawah* (paddy field) must join their local *subak* and meeting attendance is compulsory. The association then insures that every member gets his fair share of this irrigation water, including the very last rice farmer in line at the bottom of the steep, stepped rice terraces. These *subak*, averaging 200 members each, control irrigation, repair aqueducts and dikes and prevent theft of water. The head of the *subak* decides on an auspicious date for planting the rice seedlings and harvesting, the appropriate times for offerings and ceremonies, the repair of dams, weirs, and canals, fertilizing and insecticide regimens, and seed procurement for the next crop.

A schedule of holy ceremonies and sacrificial ritual activities accompanies the rice planting, growing and harvesting cycle. These religious processes and practices have been inherited through the generations and remain firmly in place today. The women busily prepare offerings at each growth stage of the developing rice crop in order that the plants flourish and are protected from disease, bird predation and climate fluctuations. Every *subak* cooperative also has its own small *subak* temple located in the upstream part of the rice field territory. The *subak* temple is where the principal rice ceremonies are performed and where the deities associated with rice reside when invited to descend to earth. The Bali-Hindu community continually pays tribute for the proceeds of what they have undertaken, holding spectacular, complex ritual activities to express their gratitude to the gods for the bounty of the earth. Farmers in Bedugul (Tabanan regency) always hold a daytime *mesaba* ritual at their *subak* temple to thank God, manifested as the rice goddess Dewi Sri, for each rice harvest, approximately every three months. The *subak* temple is adorned with rich woven fabric and other traditional accessories. Tall *penjor* poles are installed outside the entrance gate and furnished with colorful ornamental paraphernalia. Farmers also place small *penjor* in their own rice fields, equipped with *sanggah cucuk* or bamboo shrines to hold required offerings. In the morning, before carrying out the *mesaba* ritual, the *subak* members gather to prepare and cook roast suckling pig, *lawar* dishes and starfruit leaf salad as a farmer's tribute and act of thanksgiving to the Hindu gods of Bali. Each farmer need only bring a coconut, banana leaves and firewood as they enthusiastically work together in a familial, harmonious group atmosphere. The *mesaba* ritual begins at noon, and the roast pig and other offerings are presented at the *subak* temple, usually attended by a local *pemangku* (priest). The festivities are normally accompanied by a joyous, dynamic *gong kebyar* gamelan orchestra. At the conclusion of the festivity, small portions of any remaining meat are distributed equitably to each *subak* member to take home for a modest family celebration.

A paddy is a small, level, flooded piece of land used to cultivate semi-aquatic as opposed to deep-water grown rice. Paddy fields are the predominant feature of rice farming throughout Southeast Asia. Bali's renowned tufted carpet of rice fields begins life post-planting as young yellow-green shoots rising out of giant mirror-like, reflecting pools of water. Two months later, the new paddy growth is a rich green, which then turns golden yellow when the crop is ready to harvest. After harvesting, the straw is burned, leaving ashy stubble and dried-out cracked ground. Balinese *padi* rice was always grown naturally using the labor power of local ducks. Released into the flooded fields when the rice plants are two months old, they happily take over the weeding, pest control and fertilization tasks until the harvest. Following a traditional cycle, the post-harvest field is rested and is then sown with peanuts or legumes (cash crops) to enrich the soil before it is planted again with rice. Bali's fat chemical-free "duck farmers" usually last for four rice growing cycles (eighteen months), while continuously producing eggs for sale. They are then vended off at a profit for Rp.35,000 each.

Rice farmers in Kacang Dawa *subak* in Klungkung regency cultivate crop plants twice a year and paddy rice once a year. Prior to planting the rice seedlings—the paddy season is November to December—they plough the fields twice using pairs of oxen. An auspicious day is selected to plant the rice seedlings and another to scatter the rice seeds. By selecting a propitious day to plant, the farmers believe that the seeds will develop vigorously and stay protected from plant diseases and cereal eating birds. Offerings to the gods accompany each specific phase of the rice growing journey. Soon after planting, women make offerings to Dewi Sri, the goddess of fertility and rice, to pray that the plants will flourish. Other ritual offerings must be made when the *padi* plants reach thirty to fifty days. The head of the *subak* chooses the right day for this ceremony. The next ritual (*biyukukung*) is performed when the rice stems are in their second month. They are now said to be pregnant as the empty young paddies inside will soon fill up with white milky liquid. Offerings at this sensitive juncture include *biyu kukung* (cakes made from yellow, brown and white rice flour), and *rerujakan* (mixed fruit salads). The ceremonies are to ask that the paddy grains grow normally and not fall prey to diseases.

Another ceremony, *ngalapin*, is carried out when the paddy grain turns yellow near harvest time. Three standing clusters of rice are tied, knotted together and embellished with a young coconut leaf arrangement and assorted flowers—like goddesses—at harvest time. This gorgeous religious rice field art expresses Bali's deep gratitude to the Creator for this rich endowment. The final rice crop ceremony occurs when the paddy rice stalks are cut and carried home by the farmers. The three festooned clusters are cut and placed in a bamboo offering basket (*keben*), laid to rest with simple offerings and three handfuls of unhulled rice on top and then placed in the family's traditional rice granary (*lumbung*). Bali will continue to eat for another season as a benediction from the gods.

Bali's original short-grained white rice (*beras Bali* or *padi Bali*), grown since time immemorial, has now been largely replaced by a tidal wave of faster growing, high-yield and hybrid commercial rice varieties that are disease and insect-resistant. The government first introduced the "new" or "miracle" long-grained dwarf rice strains in the 1970s—accompanied by the use of chemicals—to feed Indonesia's exploding population and avert a food supply crisis. The new strains have a much shorter growing season than the old rice, around 120 days instead of the 150 days required for traditional *padi Bali* to mature. Stewards of the land, Balinese farmers have always been intimately connected to their island and had respect for Ibu Pertiwi (Mother Earth). As such, they would allow the land to either rest and regenerate for a few months between harvests before planting more rice, or plant a soil-friendly legume crop. After the Green Revolution, farmers were ordered to grow as much rice as possible and thus had to abandon the healthy practice of crop rotation, planting a legume like soybeans to enrich and rejuvenate the soil in between rice crops.

Fussy, opinionated connoisseurs of rice, the Balinese still universally dislike and reject the taste and quality of the new short-stemmed hybrid rice varieties which now account for 90 percent of all rice grown in Bali. They strongly prefer to eat their now much more scarce and expensive but better tasting old strain of flavor-rich traditional *padi Bali*. Restricted to a few areas and used as a ritual food, this old-style rice is now mainly grown in northern Bali. *Padi Bali* is a tall, beautiful, graceful, 55-inch-high plant. When cut and harvested, *padi Bali* rice stalks are always tied up into picturesque round 10–12 kilo bales to be carried home on the heads of the women field workers. They will be placed in the family's home rice storage barn (*lumbung*) and the rice grains will be separated out and threshed later as needed. To receive the fresh *padi Bali*, a storage ceremony is necessary. The rice barn is elaborately decorated with palm leaf plaques, *lamak* (decorations on bamboo poles) and cloths. *Dewa nini* (*nini* is a term of address to an old woman or grandmother) and small basket offerings are spread out on top of the newly cut rice bales inside, accompanied by prayers to thank the gods. In sharp contrast, newly harvested dwarf rice cannot be removed from the field because the grains fall off the heads. As the stems are short and the grains are easily dislodged, the "new rice" must be shaken loose and dislodged immediately after it is cut in the field, bypassing the traditional threshing methods.

Rice, religion and the gods are inexorably intertwined on Bali. After praying in the temple at important ceremonies and being blessed by the *pemangku*, the people place a few wet grains of white rice called *bija* on the center of the forehead, at the temples and at the throat as a blessing. Three grains are then swallowed and the rest of the rice is thrown over the head. Rice is also used in all offerings for all ceremonies. *Banten* (offering) *nasi* (rice) *wong-wongan* (people) is made every fifteen days for the ceremony called Kajeng Kliwon. A human-like figure is made out of steamed rice, intended to be positioned at significant places like village crossroads, outside large temples and even inside tourist hotels. To make one of these gingerbread man-like figures, the rice (but not the same rice that is cooked for eating) is first steamed. The rice is cooked only halfway through so that it is easy to fashion and shape the figure. *Banten nasi wong-wongan* are made and cooked at home but are never placed at home because this is not a house offering. The Balinese bring them to other symbolically significant locations for offerings. Very small triangular rice offerings, symbols of the mountain, are called *tumpeng*. The rice for these is steamed as usual and then pressed into a one-inch triangular pocket formed by a folded-over banana or coconut leaf strip. The rice is pushed down into this leaf mold for a moment to set the shape. The leaf is then opened and you have the special tree-shaped rice triangles. The *tumpeng* are used for the new year or for opening ceremonies for a business.

Bali's ever-pregnant rice fields produce reliable natural supplies of red (*merah*), black and white rice, representing three of the four sacred cardinal colors (yellow is missing). When the Balinese need rice offerings corresponding to each of the four holy colors and directions, they generate their own strain of yellow rice by dying white rice grains yellow (*kuning*) with turmeric (*kunyit*). *Nasi kuning* is in high demand in order to make ritually required offerings on Kuningan—during the important ceremonial holiday period of Galungan (Wednesday) to Kuningan (Saturday). Kuningan comes every 210 days on Saniscara (Saturday) Kliwon Wuku Kuningan. Served in a decorative peak-shaped cone crowned with a banana leaf cap as a symbol of Bali's most sacred mountain, Gunung Agung, the warm, freshly cooked rice is hand-shaped and prepared to both please and to represent the gods who reside at the summit of the mountain. On Kuningan Day, it is typically Balinese to eat a conical-shaped dome of yellow rice trimmed with fried chili, spices, green beans or peas cooked with coconut cream, chili, palm sugar and shrimp paste. *Nasi yasa* (*yasa* means decorated, ornamented or garnished) is *nasi kuning* combined with chicken, egg, raw vegetables and *saur*. It is usually served at religious ceremonies on Saraswati Day or Siwaratri Day, the night of Siwa when the Balinese stay up until dawn at the temple to pray, meditate and repent for past wrongdoings, and as a ritual offering for the ancestors. Mountains of pink and orange rice offerings will typically decorate the inner sanctum during temple anniversary (*odalan*) ceremonies.

In Bali, a hierarchy of multilayered government and village organizations supervises rice growing and irrigation. A large complementary body of religious observations, prayers, ceremonies, offerings, festivals and obligations also permeates every aspect of rice farming on the island of the gods. Rice and its rituals occupy a major portion of the time, energy and money of the people of Bali. Rice is treated with reverence and respect on Bali. The crucial role that rice plays can be gauged by the amount of religious importance and the diversity and number of periodic rituals, prayers, offerings and temple ceremonies accompanying each stage of the complex, labor-intensive planting, cultivation, irrigation and harvesting processes. These rituals range from tiny offerings placed in the corners of a field to keep animals away to huge, village-wide, multi-day temple ceremonies involving weeks of preparation, thousands of elaborate offerings and hundreds of people. The association between rice, water (as mentioned above, the *subak* irrigation society manages and allocates water resources) and religion reflects the dependence of rice cultivation on an adequate and constant supply of water, and of people upon rice for their survival. Rice thrives in the garden of the gods as the gift of the goddess of agriculture and rice, Dewi Sri, the most widely worshipped and beloved deity on the island. Dewi Sri, the female aspect of rice, is a potent symbol of goodness and fertility, protectress of the rice fields and guardian of rice barns. She is the favorite manifestation of God amongst the Balinese. The growth, preparation and consumption of rice in Bali gives rise to a lovingly crafted network of bamboo or stone rice field shrines and a lifestyle of thankful daily prayers and offerings to the life-giving rice goddess. Every face in Bali lights up with joy at the mention of her name. In every traditional family compound, there will be an elevated bow-roofed thatched granary near the kitchen called a *jineng* (Balinese) or *lumbung*, built far up off the ground on posts to deter rodents, with a storage area for rice and rice-related offerings. This rice barn is the house of Dewi Sri. The little rice access door can only be reached by a long bamboo ladder and the space below is often used as a sitting area.

Rice is "female" in the Javanese language, because, according to legend, the goddess of rice is Dewi Sri. In Central and East Java, there are also ceremonies honoring Dewi Sri. Dewi Sri is physically represented in Bali by an image called a Dewa Nini (grandmother) or *cili*, from the word *cantik*, meaning beautiful. At important times in the rice cultivation life cycle, these small, symbolic, doll-like rice stalk images of Dewi Sri are fashioned in the *sawah* as offerings. They also festoon every rice barn. At harvest time, farmers twine rice stalk bundles tightly together in the middle to resemble two triangles with a pinched waist and a wide conical skirt. These feminine-form *cili* are often attached to the growing rice itself. This double triangle, or hourglass figure, is enshrined in Balinese offerings and in endless art forms—paintings, statues, wood carvings—as the de facto symbol of Bali. In every elaborately sculpted and irrigated rice field, often straddling mountainous geography, deep gorges and steep rugged slopes, there is at least one shrine for Dewi Sri, and every six months there is a special rice day for the goddess.

No religious effort is spared to nurture and protect the developing rice crop, the central part of the village economy. Fluffy tufts of golden Balinese rice adorn handcrafted bamboo poles (*penjor*) erected in front of every house gate for the festival of Galungan and during temple *odalan* to symbolize and invite prosperity. Cooked rice, bounty of the earth, plays a huge role in *subak* rice ceremonies to thank Dewi Sri. The largest ritual, *ngusaba nini*, occurs just before or after the all-important harvest. Offerings of plaited coconut leaves, colored rice, flowers, brilliantly dyed rice cakes, fruits, roast ducks, suckling pigs, rice wine and palm brandy are placed on mats in the *subak*'s field temple and in large shrines hung outside the temple gate. After God has partaken of the essence or *sari* of the food, the people eat the offerings. One particularly spectacular offering consists of a three-foot-high cone of white rice. The men parade around the inside of the temple carrying the big rice cone, shouting loudly to thank the gods. The cone is then returned to the ground and it, and the suckling pig, are cut up and distributed to the members of the *subak*.

White rice is sacred, secular and social currency on Bali. The staple food of Bali, it forms the centerpiece and the basis and essential element of every meal on the island of the gods. In Bali, rice is virtually synonymous with food. Indeed, the word *nasi*, which means cooked rice, also means any kind of food or meal. *Nasi* is a synonym for food in general, naturally assuming that any meal will consist mostly of rice. All government employees and many factory workers in Java are given a segment of their salaries in rice in the form of coupons that can be exchanged for rice. Each civil servant receives an allowance of 10 kg of raw rice per month, 20 kg if married, and an extra 10 kg for each child up to a maximum of three, totalling 50 kg per family per month. The Indonesian government subsidizes the price of rice in order to keep it affordable and maintains huge rice stockpiles in warehouses near Denpasar.

The most common rice cooking methods are steaming, using a traditional *dangdang* pot and woven bamboo *kukusan* basket, and boiling. The Balinese strongly prefer steamed rice (*nasi kukus*) over boiled rice (*nasi jakan*). *Kukus* means cooked by steaming or vapor. The delicious end result is always presented in plump white mounds. To make boiled rice, the wife stirs washed rice into water already boiling in a clay or metal pot (*payok*), stirs it until the water returns to the boil, and then allows it to cook for another half hour. The wife cooks rice once a day in the morning, or sometimes twice in the morning and once in the evening. It is never reheated and is kept in a large container during the day. Family members help themselves to the cold contents at their leisure. Rice is never kept over until the next day as it deteriorates quickly without refrigeration.

As noted earlier, different types, qualities and flavors of rice appear in Bali. The Balinese also insist upon having their rice white. The brown parts are normally removed at home by placing the grains in a long wooden trough (*lesung*) and then pounding the rice with a six-foot-long wooden pole (*lu*) to strip off the husk and bran. The Balinese are reluctant to tolerate and eat inferior quality or incorrectly cooked rice. Fluffy, separate grains are mandatory, achieved only by steaming; the Balinese use boiled rice solely as a porridge. The ideal is to produce dry, separate rice grains not stuck together. Since people dry the rice kernels on the road on mats, passing vehicles flick stones among the grains. As the rice is not always winnowed or sieved well, there are occasionally tooth-threatening stones lurking in the beautiful pearl white *nasi putih*. In many small rural villages like Bongkasa, you can always see rice drying on the street by the side of the road, an old lady invariably in attendance nearby. Here, the ancient village and family-bound occupation of rice farming still anchors the community and the economy together.

Balinese meals consist of generous portions of humble, life-sustaining white rice (*nasi putih*) as the main course, accompanied by token amounts of two or three side dishes like fish, meat, poultry, vegetables or soybean products. Rice is the primary dietary food on Bali. It is eaten with every meal, every single day, and provides more calories than any other single food. The Balinese eat a lot of rice. The average rice consumption on Bali approaches a high 1.1 pounds of uncooked rice per person per day. Poor people, or those living in districts where water is not so abundant, live on corn and sweet potatoes, foods considered inferior to rice. In poorer or mountainous parts of Bali, where rice is not available, cassava or taro is substituted. Leftover rice can be made into snacks, puddings and cakes, but Balinese do not ordinarily carry food over from one day to the next. They prefer to prepare fresh rice from scratch for every dish. *Sambal orang miskin*, known as poor man's chili sauce, is a specialty of the Minangkabau region of Sumatra, renowned for its amazing culinary culture. The name comes from its three all-green half-ripe fruit and vegetable ingredients (green chili, *jengkol* and *leunca*), considered to be low-quality foods for the poor. *Jengkol* is a species of flowering tree in the pea family (*Archiden-dron pauciflorum*). Despite its overpowering smell and mild toxicity, which can cause kidney failure, its large brown beans are a popular food in Indonesia. Because of the odor, *jengkol* is considered a lower-class food. People who like it are often ashamed if others know about their clandestine eating habits. *Leunca* (*buah ranti*) is a small, green, round, bean-like vegetable resembling fresh shelled peas. Otherwise known as black nightshade or *Solanum nigrum*, and considered poisonous in North America, it is popular for making *lalap* or *lalapan*—fresh raw cold vegetables eaten with *sambal*.

The wide, gently sloping southern and central regions play host to Bali's famed, intensely cultivated, well-watered rice terraces, which are among some of the most spectacular in the world and certainly among the best in Southeast Asia. The gods blessed Bali with these majestic fertile stairways of bright green rice terraces. The legendary sweeping rice fields of Jatiluweh, the source of much of Bali's sustenance, are nature's own answer to the perfectly created splendor of the Taj Mahal. Staggeringly beautiful hills and dales of brilliant rice stalks stretch as far as the eye can see. These immaculate terraces step down far into the valleys below, celebrating the joy, sophistication and simplicity of rice born and bred in Bali's lush agricultural precincts. Whether bathed in coconut milk, stained yellow with turmeric or swathed in aromatics and exotic seasonings, rice and religion rule the Balinese diet. Early waves of Dutch colonial settlers also fell prey to the local lure and Balinese love) of rice, adding their own unique rice legacy to Indonesian cuisine in the process. Rice took on a new, European-derived personality in the form of a *rijistaafel* (literally meaning rice table in Dutch), originally served to hungry Dutch plantation colonists as a *makan besar* (big meal). The *rijistaafel*, now mainly reserved for tourists, consists of dozens of small, sequentially served, meat, vegetable and boiled egg courses plus condiments grouped around a lavish, always replenished central mound of rice.

Neighboring Singapore and Malaysia have their own love affair with the aromas, tastes and textures of rice. Distinctive and delicious *nasi lemak* (*lemak* means fat) is rice cooked in coconut milk and eaten with curry, chili paste, anchovies, peanuts, egg and cucumber, bundled together in a triangular green banana leaf packet. The gods have created a showcase of rice and rice cultivation in all of its beguiling, diverse glory throughout Southeast Asia—black, red, white, yellow, sticky and organic. The elaborate design and elegance of Bali's cascading rice terraces and ridges rivals that of the great gardens of the world but they were not created for aesthetics alone. If the rice bowl is full, the people do not starve. Carefully cut into the countryside, the glistening green rice paddies are the essential life blood of the grateful people of Bali.

Nasi Goreng

(FRIED RICE)

Versatile, beloved white rice is commonly reinvented as fried rice (nasi goreng), eaten throughout both Bali and Indonesia as a main course or as an accompaniment. The Balinese eat hot nasi goreng very often and with great joy at their local warung for as little as Rp.3,500 per serving. Although it is infrequently prepared at home, it is a very popular eating out treat for the Balinese. A true culinary journey, it includes such ingredients as pork, chopped chicken, beef or prawns, shallots, eggs, red chilies, garlic, ginger root, carrots, cabbage and mushrooms, often garnished with a fried egg on top, a chicken satay stick on the side, sliced cucumber, crisp-fried onions and crispy-fried shrimp or onion crackers (krupuk). Nasi goreng takes many delicious forms: nasi goreng ikan laut (fried rice with seafood), nasi goreng ikan bilis (anchovy) with all the trimmings, nasi goreng ayam (fried rice with chicken), vegetarian fried rice and nasi goreng mawut (fried rice with noodles). Nasi goreng sends chills of intensely familiar pleasure down the entire spine of the food-loving archipelago. At Ibu Dody's food court stall in Centro Discovery Mall (Tuban), it comes with fried egg, sayur, small chunks of ayam (chicken) and two pieces of sweet potato fritter for Rp.7,000–10,000. Nasi goreng is Indonesia's iconic food and its "national dish." Nearly every region and island in the country has its own special, creative version of fried rice. Nasi goreng Madura always contains small pieces of fried salted fish, while central Java boasts nasi goreng tempe with fried tempe sticks and nasi goreng kunyit with healthy, healing turmeric.

Recipe courtesy of the beautiful Pundi-Pundi Restaurant in the rice fields of Ubud. Recipe provided by their executive chef, Nyoman Suartajaya. Pundi-Pundi Restaurant, Jl. Pengosekan, Ubud. www.pundiubud.com, 2011.

1 lb (450 g) steamed white rice
1⅓ lb (600 g) chicken with bone, deep-fried
⅔ lb (300 g) chicken or beef for satay
6 eggs deep-fried (for the top of the *nasi goreng*)
2 tbs cooking oil
1 oz (30 g) white cabbage, chopped
1 oz (30 g) prawn crackers

SPICE MIXTURE (*BUMBU*)
2 oz (60 g) red chili
1¾ oz (50 g) shallot
1 oz (30 g) garlic
3 tsp oyster sauce
3 tsp sesame oil
salt and pepper to taste

For the spice mixture, crush the chili, shallot and garlic using a mortar and pestle until smooth.

Heat 1½ teaspoons of oil in a frying pan. Stir fry the spice mixture for 5 minutes.

Add the rice, cabbage, oyster sauce and 1½ teaspoons sesame oil to the frying pan, mix thoroughly and cook for 1–2 minutes.

Serve the fried rice with fried chicken, satay sticks, fried eggs on top, shrimp crackers as a garnish and a side condiment dish of acar.

Serves 4–6.

Nasi Kuning

(YELLOW RICE)

Nasi kuning is a very special sacred food. The Balinese will always endeavor to make it as spectacular and ingredient-rich as possible. It is prepared for many different ceremonies and is always fashioned in a beautiful, highly decorated conical shape to resemble Bali's most holy mountain, Gunung Agung. A critical Balinese ceremonial dish, nasi kuning is cooked in and embellished with lightly seasoned coconut milk or cream, butter and chicken stock with cloves, salam leaf, pandanus leaf, kaffir lime leaf, lemongrass, turmeric water, torch ginger, chili, peanuts, spiced coconut, laos (greater galangal) and fried shallots. Hoary basil (kemangi leaf) is added to the yellow rice for such special ceremonial occasions as the day after Saraswati Day. Carefully crafted and presented, nasi kuning is mandatory for the important high holiday of Kuningan (but not for Galungan or Saraswati Day). Nasi kuning will also be created for a son's birthday (one-year, two-year and five-year ceremonies), and also for the birthdays of men and women.

Recipe courtesy of I Wayan Sudirna, Balinese chef at the superb Tanis Villas resort, Nusa Lembongan. www.tanisvillas.com, December 2011.

2⅔ lb (1.2 kg) steamed white rice
2½ cups coconut milk (2 squeezes)
2½ cups chicken stock (obtained from boiling a chicken)
1 lemongrass stalk, whole
½ tsp sea salt
½ tsp pepper
½ tsp chicken powder
4 oz (120 g) turmeric
6½ oz (180 g) shallot
2 oz (60 g) garlic
2 oz (60 g) ginger

Peel and wash the turmeric, shallot, garlic and ginger, then cut into very small pieces and grind until smooth using a mortar and pestle.

Boil the coconut milk, chicken stock and whole lemongrass stalk for 5 minutes.

Add the steamed rice and ground spices to the same pot and simmer another 10 minutes. Season the rice with salt, pepper and chicken powder.

To form the *nasi kuning* into a mountain, take a banana leaf and fold it into a funnel shape. Fill the banana leaf funnel to the top with rice. Turn it upside down on a tray.

Garnish the rice mountain with sliced tomato, whole red chilies, sliced scrambled eggs and cucumber pieces. Place a wreath of cucumber around the base of the mountain. Use the scrambled egg pieces to decorate the circumference of the mountain one-third of the way up and near the top of the mountain.

Crown the *nasi kuning* mountain with a flower.

Serves 4–6.

CHAPTER EIGHT

The Hanging Ketupat Basket: Rice on the Run

———— ≠ ————

PICTURESQUE AND QUINTESSENTIALLY ASIAN, *ketupat* rice cakes in handwoven frond basket shells have widespread historical and cultural roots throughout all of Southeast Asia. Indeed, *ketupat* is one of the most significant foodstuffs fabricated and filled at home and eaten during the important Muslim festival of Hari Raya Idul Fitri. The archipelago's widespread tradition of leaf weaving even came to be called "making *ketupat*". In most of Indonesia, *ketupat* is made with glutinous rice, the pockets are triangle-shaped and they are wrapped in fan palm leaves. By contrast, in Bali plain white rice is used, the classic everyday basket is square in shape and coconut palm leaves, not fan palms, are used to weave the shell. The Balinese version of *ketupat* is called *ketipat* or, more commonly, *tipat*. Balinese villagers in northern Bali say that the word *ketupat* is for Muslim people as distinct from the common Balinese term *tipat*. *Tipat* benefits from legendary Balinese artisanry, local talent for food practicality and invention, peasant farmer culinary skills, tropical topographical raw materials, and an island-wide reverence for rice. In Bali, *ketipat* baskets are normally constructed out of young white or pale green coconut palm leaves. The central spine is removed first with a paring knife to split the leaves off into two ribbon-like halves. The long, thin coconut leaf strips are then braided together in an intricate yet simple tango of vertical and horizontal interlocking loops. These charming rustic rice accomplices are a deeply ingrained part of Balinese food culture and the Balinese food environment.

Tipat is a common presentation in Balinese ritual cooking as well as a favorite daily food. Ceremonial offerings on such auspicious days as Kajeng-Kliwon command exotic, highly crafted constructions, while everyday *tipat nasi*, also known as *tipat biasa (*common or ordinary) is confined in unprepossessing three-inch-square pockets or in onion-shaped domes called *tipat bawang*. Balinese *tipat* is always made with plain white rice and eaten with local Balinese foods like *satay* sticks, *ayam bakar* (grilled chicken), *bakso* (meatballs and noodles in soup) and goat or chicken soup, while their cousins in Java are traditionally eaten with chicken curry, satays, *gado-gado* mixed vegetables with peanut sauce, *serunding, sayur lodeh* (a Central Javanese coconut milk and vegetable soup or stew) and beef or chicken *rendang*. Beef *rendang* is a classic Javanese specialty, usually consisting of soft, slightly chewy, reddish-brown, well-cooked beef which goes very well with hot white rice.

Tipat plays a significant role in Bali-Hindu rituals as a mandatory ceremonial offering. It is served at virtually every ceremony, not only because it is an easy food to prepare but because the hanging palm leaf parcels make decorative offerings. Wrapped up like presents, the rice cake snacks are fashioned into an array of intricately woven masterpieces with names such as *tipat kukur, tipat dara, tipat sidapurna, tipat belekok, tipat pesor* and *tipat pasung. Tipat belayag,* made from young palm leaves rather than coconut leaves, has a long lozenge-like shape so the rice is softer and tastes better. The palm leaves are wrapped and tied all around the package of rice inside. *Tipat sidapurna, belayag, pesor, pasung, tipep-engabian, sirikan* and *perististe jaya* are all made in different shapes. A *tipat gong* is square and has a protruding surface bulge in the center that makes it look like a musical gong. A turtle-shaped *ketupat* is created for special ceremonial usages. It can symbolically take the place of a real sea turtle in a sacrificial rite, thus sparing the life of one of these endangered creatures. These *tipat* are not used for daily food. Rather, they are constructed with great care and dedication as offerings, to complete a ritual ceremony. They typically stay for up to three days in the temple, after which they are fit only for feeding the villagers' pigs.

Ketipat is essential for ceremonial occasions such as Tumpek Landep, the day to honor metal objects like motorcycles, and Tumpek Kandang, the day to honor animals and pray to God that domestic livestock are healthy, grow big and breed well. Worshippers present a display of highly stylized offerings, including several kinds of *tipat* depending on what they can afford. Requisitioned for a large number of ceremonies, the standard, square-shaped *ketipat bekal* honors and feeds Bali's constellation of gods in myriad temples throughout the island. *Tipat telur* or egg tipat is a simple little woven bag into which an egg can be placed. This is a common offering made for many types of rituals.

Mothers teach their daughters from young the secrets of how to braid the many different styles of *ketupat*. Even a small child can weave a basic coconut leaf *tipat* container in under a minute, albeit one that is woven very loosely but not so open that the rice grains fall out. *Tipat* dexterity comes with experience. A woman may produce only a few *ketipat* as a contribution or manufacture large quantities depending on the ceremony at hand. *Ketipat* wrapping—how to contain and measure out a handful of rice—is both a festive and domestic art using leaves found in the environment, most commonly coconut leaflets. In the villages, the rice cakes are carefully prepared by women gathered around a tub of raw soaked rice amidst piles of coconut fronds purchased in the local market. They wrap the *tipat* in ingenious configurations according to farmer's wife wisdom and Bali-Hindu religious needs: "If it is too tight, it will burst. If it is too loose, it will spread out." Urban Balinese buy the leaves in the market in Denpasar and then cut them into strips at home. Fashioned for weddings, cremations or baby ceremonies, the Balinese are allowed to eat the *tipat* after the ritual. In contrast to everyday, secular kitchen cuisine, with its solitary eating habits, festive food is distributed among temple worshippers and home ceremony guests and shared. There is spiritual satisfaction in eating together and much meaning in wrapping and making *tipat* together at home.

Ketupat tipepengabian, also called *ketupat sirikan*, is made in a special shape for the six-month baby ceremony. Distinguished by two raised peaks, the offering represents a pair of legs and *susu kecil* (small breasts) and entails more intricate braidwork. Two of these special *ketupat* must be made for this ceremony. *Tipat perististe jaya* (*perisa* means delicious and *jaya* successful or prosperous) has three *susu* and is another crucial offering constructed for the gods for purification ceremonies (*melukat*). A *ketupat burung* (bird) is fashioned for Kajeng Kliwon, held every fifteen days. It is placed with salt and peanuts in the family temple as an offering to the gods in the morning. In the afternoon it can be taken out and eaten after the gods have inhaled its essence.

In Bali, the fabrication of complete *tipat* entails a lengthy and tedious preparation process. It is a risky food and a cook needs knowledge and precision to do it. She has to be able to gauge measurement and quantity—how many grains to use—as well as timing, or it may be under- or overcooked. To prepare the *tipat*, Balinese cooks pry open a space between the plaited leaves or use an opening in the top end to inject the raw rice grains (*beras*). They fill the little basket from halfway to three-quarters full with rice, close the opening and place it in boiling water for anywhere from thirty minutes to three hours. Many packets can be cooked simultaneously in a large pot. As it cooks, the rice absorbs the water and the grains expand and swell to fill the container. Due to lack of space in the basket, the grains are pressed against each other, resulting in a block of pressed rice. The compact square block can then be sliced for serving. Perfect *ketipat* rice is supposed to be springy and spongy to the touch with all the pieces stuck together, not as separate, individual grains. These attractive Balinese rice wrappings are then hung aloft from the kitchen ceiling. Due to the prolonged hours of boiling and the "swinging gallows" method of preservation, *tipat* keeps well and can house and store rice without deterioration for over two days without refrigeration. The air flow around the hanging basket provides ventilation, dries it out and effectively removes spoilage-causing moisture. The optimistic, cheerful, spiritually pristine Balinese swear to the longevity, staying power and protective properties of these cherished compound-born *ketupat* "rice *barong*."

Everyday *tipat* is more than just a snack food or a small repast to fill the stomach. It is a food to warm the heart, spirit and digestive system. *Tipat* is popular because leaf-cooked rice is softer in texture than regular steamed or boiled rice, and rice prepared this way also absorbs the good flavor and aroma of the coconut palm leaves. *Tipat* can also be deliberately overcooked, for up to eight hours, rendering it therapeutically soft and easy for elderly people to process. It is then called *ketipat nyaling*, meaning slippery *ketipat*. The little handwoven rice packages are also eminently portable. Not only can children can take them to school, but rice-filled *tipat* have long served as practical, convenient, easy-to-carry sustenance for the road. Called *tipat bekal*, they may harbor provisions, money, equipment or food brought on a journey or trip. They sustain the Balinese as they walk or ride over extended distances to work or to visit other villages. Laboring Balinese farmers often wake up before dawn, bathe and head out to the rice fields without breakfast. Their wives still cart diamond-shaped *tipat* cargo purses, along with portions of the day's home-cooked food, out to them in the paddies for a morning meal or afternoon break. These specially compressed rice cake treats partner well with peanut sauce and tofu. Wheeled *kaki lima* street cart sellers who cannot cook fresh rice sell the popular, resuscitative *ketipat* baskets as part of their standard village inventory.

The local people in Bali's sister island, Nusa Lembongan, eat a complete lunch of *ketipat* rice, fish, cooked vegetables and boiled egg for Rp.2,000 at the very friendly Adi Mini-Mart near Tanjung Sanghiang (Mushroom) Bay. Behind the counter, an *ibu* (wife) sells brown-leafed old *ketipat* packages nestled in a cracked crockery bowl. Inexorable filth and hygiene violations abound, but the *ketupat* plate is set at a very good price and the generous smiles are always free. *Tipat cantok* (or *santok*) is a vegetarian creation sold in small village *warung* for Rp.5,000. The *tipat* is served with *sayur* (vegetables), *tahu* (tofu) and *kacang* (peanuts) all mixed together on the plate. (The word *cantok* is derived from the utensil used for crushing the peanuts and spices.) The contents of the *ketipat* rice basket can also be paired with other vegetarian ingredients such as green beans, fried tofu, *kripik* crackers (sliced, fried, unripe banana, cassava or sweet potato chips), and peanut *bumbu*, a form of *tipat cantok* reminiscent of classic *gado-gado*. *Tipat tahu* is simple *ketipat* rice, spicy vegetables and tofu. *Tipat cantok kacang* is commonly found at roadside food stalls. Compacted rice wrapped in young coconut leaves is cut up into easy-eating chunks and seasoned with a ground-up mixture of peanuts, chili, kaffir lime juice, fried onions, palm sugar, soy sauce and *petis* (a mix of sweet soy sauce and fermented prawn paste). The crowning touch is a halo of a few green beans, bean sprouts and a hard-boiled egg! Another meatless version of *tipat cantok* combines *ketipat* rice served with seaweed, peanut sauce, onion, garlic and salt mixed together. This can also be bought as a dish in the local market.

CHAPTER NINE

Babi Guling and the Balinese Pig: From Secular Sausages to Sacrificial Offerings

———— ≠ ————

B ALI IS AN ISOLATED HINDU OUTPOST in predominantly Muslim Indonesia. The national religious prohibition on pork consumption therefore holds no sway here. Rural village Balinese share their bountiful island paradise with barnyard and farm animals raised and husbanded for food (meat, eggs, milk), other by-products, labor and sacrificial culinary splendor. Pigs, in particular, provide meat for dietary variation and for special ritual offering dishes for traditional ceremonies.

The Balinese pig (*babi*) is a unique breed. According to Bali observer Miguel Covarrubias in the 1930s, "It belongs to a monstrous variety that surely exists nowhere else. An untamed descendant of the wild hog, it has an absurd sagging back and an enormous, fat, protruding stomach that drags along the ground like a drooping sack suspended loosely from its bony hips and shoulders." Compound-coddled and fed, these huge pot-bellied Balinese pigs are plentiful and well cared for in Hindu Bali. The women of the household fatten them up with the standard Balinese pig food diet of freshly prepared soups and sliced-up sections of fibrous banana plant trunks that are too tough to be eaten by humans. The starchy stem fattens the animals quickly. Bali's farmers also take their rice crop to factories to remove the brown husk and the germ. Light feathery bran and the attached germ are by-products of this rice milling process. The material, called *oot alus*, is widely used as pig fodder on Bali. The rice hulls are purchased at the market and then mixed with water. Coarser fragments of the bran and the finer fragments of the husk, called *oot pesak*, are also produced in the course of milling rice. They are used for feeding pigs by Balinese who cannot afford the better *oot alus*, but they are more often burned or simply discarded. Pigs in Bali are also fed with commercially grown sweet potatoes, taro (*keladi*) leaves and sweet potato leaves. Villagers cut leaves that grow in their domestic gardens or sprout wild in the lanes, chop them up and cook them for the pigs, mixed with discarded shredded coconut leavings and brown coconut skins set aside from the daily family cooking and leftover family food from the daily meals. Old men or women are often seen carrying huge baskets of such green leaves on their heads or on bicycles as they head home on the roads.

Pigs are cheap to raise and provision and can be profitably sold at the market when they reach full maturity and weight. Loosely tied to a leash when they are small or left to frisk around freely in the yard, the fat pigs rummage alertly through the undergrowth and grass, squealing to be brought their evening dinner pails. They are only penned when they grow larger in the household animal pen (*kandang*) located in the lower, seaward-facing *kelod* part of the family compound. The kitchen (*paon*), bathroom, rubbish pit and pigsty are always located near this least auspicious section of the property. "Farthest of all from the holy (mountainward) area is the family pigsty—where there is always at least one occupant being fattened up for the next important feast." If Balinese next-door neighbours are jealous of each other or quarreling over something, the jealous neighbor will seek revenge by positioning the family's pigsty right by their neighbor's property wall to ensure a continual supply of noxious piggery odors.

Many local Balinese keep a family piggery as a small home business to supplement their tourism industry-related salaries. Other pigs are raised and ripened in small family-run, commercial egg farm-piggeries clustered around the village of Utu near Jatiluweh's verdant rice terraces. Since chickens and pigs can eat the same food, it is convenient and economical to rear them together. Pigs live in proximity to chickens in adjacent concrete enclosures. Snouts full of grainy, milky, mashed yellow gruel, the pigs are destined for the market rather than family consumption. Piglets (a baby pig is *kucit* in Balinese) are considered prime,

edible suckling pigs (35–50 kg in weight) at four months of age. At this
point, they are loaded up and sold to the market for Rp.400,000–
500,000 each. Once purchased, they will be slaughtered at home by the
customer and turned into Bali's most famous specialty, *babi guling* (spit-
roasted suckling pig). Larger pigs are usually picked up by distributors
and trucked to market at nine months of age, weighing 220 pounds and
earning the family Rp.1,000,000. By age five, pigs will weigh as much
as 330–550 pounds. These adults are usually kept for breeding.

Free-range pigs can also be encountered in Bali. Baby piglets trot
right across the rural back roads of Candi Dasa in eastern Bali, vanish-
ing quickly into the dense side vegetation. Wild pigs still inhabit the
mountains and less populated areas, always in danger of being lethally
kidnapped for food or vended in the market as a destined ceremonial
sacrifice. Wild pigs eat *sayur* (vegetables), *ubi* (sweet potato) and grass.
Bearing less body fat than bulbous domestic pigs, their meat is tougher
with a different but still good taste.

Pigs can periodically, and suddenly, change status from object of
sacrifice to object of devotion, affection and offerings on Bali. The
Balinese celebrate Tumpek Kandang as a day to ritually honor and thank
domestic animals for their service to and cooperation with man. Animals
all over Bali are given special foods accompanied by prayers for their
continued well-being, ample growth and prolific breeding. To this
effect, they are sprinkled with rice and holy water. Cows and buffaloes
enjoy a rest from their rice paddy labor, and no animals are allowed to
be slaughtered on this day. Pigs are embellished with a white cloth wound
around their stomachs. Swine find physical protection, but not the same
spiritual favor in the fishing community. Before launching a newly built
boat in the fishing village of Padang Bai, a holy man blesses the boat,
prays to Baruna, the god of the sea, for safety and sacrifices chickens
and ducks, but never pigs! Local fishermen believe that if they do, "the
prahu will act like a pig; it will roll around in the water and capsize."

Food sustains all life. It takes on the garb of raw survival in the Third
World, upgrades itself into a source of sustenance in the Second World,
and is a personal path to health, well-being and pleasure in the developed First World. In sharp social and economic contrast, scarce food
resources in Bali are primarily diverted towards spirituality. Food is the

traditional way to contact, please and honor the deities. Divinely blessed, and always cognizant of God, duty and religion, the ritual-driven Balinese celebrate the cyclical thanksgiving feast of Galungan every 210 days. One of the most important holidays on the Balinese religious calendar, Galungan celebrates the universal victory of good over evil as well as the historical defeat of the bad King Mayadenawa, who had once forbidden the vanquished, original Bali Aga people from practicing their religion. Fluttering *penjor* (bamboo offering poles) laden with coconuts and palm leaf ornaments symbolizing fertility and prosperity are erected in front of every house gate and temple. The curving upper end represents both the tail of the auspicious Barong and the peak of the sacred mountain, Gunung Agung. On Galungan, the hungry gods and deified ancestors descend from heaven to the family temples where they are welcomed, entertained, fed and presented with offerings and prayers. Massive, ritually correct Galungan feasts must include a roast pig on the menu. Local Balinese communities make arrangements one month in advance to purchase a male pig. The entire *banjar* (village association) pays for the coveted animal, which may cost as much as Rp.5,000,000). The pigs are mercilessly stuffed into rudimentary barrel-shaped portable baskets or carried home from the market "in the arms of the women like babies." Local trucks can be seen transporting these doomed sacrificial swine down village streets during peak holiday periods. The portly pink pig is typically lying down on its side inside a woven bamboo body cage with a bloody nose since the pigs tear their noses trying to get out.

Food preparations for Galungan begin days in advance. Bananas are ripened, rice pudding is fermented, cakes are baked, satays are twisted onto sticks and the ceremonial food slaughter begins. The day before Galungan is called Penampahan Galungan (from *nampah*, "to slaughter an animal"). This is a catastrophic day for a chicken, turtle or, especially, a pig on Bali. Domestic pigs are slaughtered (*nampah celeng*; *celeng* means "pork" in Balinese, usually from a male adult pig) at home by either the men or women of the house in the back yards of family compounds all over Bali. The sacrificial meat will be used to make *sesaji*, small food offerings, such as chopped *lawar* and satay. In the evening, these pork-based *sesaji* are placed in courtyards and houses and beside weapons or daily work tools.

Pigs, both small suckling pigs and adults, are killed while still alive. The Balinese take a long bamboo pole, force it into the pig's mouth and shove it all the way through the living animal until the pole emerges out of its rectum. Then they put the bamboo pole with the still-living, suffering pig over a coconut fire to roast it alive. For religious reasons, the Balinese will not kill the pig quickly and less painfully, for example by slitting its throat with a bamboo knife, before putting a stake through it, because there must be no marks on an animal's skin when making an offering to God.

The Balinese live very close to the ground and are used to hand killing and disembowelling live animals without a moral compass or humanitarian considerations. A whole pig will be slaughtered whenever there is a ceremony and many mouths to feed, or to sell to a *nasi babi guling* restaurant or to stock the family's own small *warung* business. En route from Ubud to Pacung, four Balinese villagers were squatting on their haunches in a rice paddy over a roadside river washing long slabs of fatty white meat—the same river where the community bathes, washes clothes, goes to the toilet and secures their drinking water. A recently slaughtered pig was visible lying on its side in the sun on a nearby flatbed truck, being systematically stripped of its flesh. There will be a generous ceremonial feast in this simple agricultural village tonight. The finely minced fresh pork meat and skin will be turned into offerings and sacred ceremonial dishes like pork satay, highly flavored traditional *lawar* (minutely minced ground pork combined with dozens of spices) and *babi guling* (a whole roasted, sweet suckling pig). The whole village will share the special, sudden windfall of always sought-after meat, which will be consumed in its entirety. All highland rivers in Bali flow down towards the seas. The year-round, often bloody detritus of these offering-filled sacred village ceremonies washes downstream on the rapidly rushing rivers and is dispersed into the oceans. The fabled white beaches of Bali are the place of last resort, the final resting place for the inevitable accumulated organic debris and waste materials (and the odd sacrificial/suspicious animal corpse) generated by thousands of inland ceremonies.

Covarrubias discovered the startling pig-centric pinnacle of Balinese ceremonial cuisine ahead of the rest of the Western world, recounting the complex, ritualistic *babi guling* cooking process: "Balinese cooking attains its apotheosis in the preparation of the famous *be guling*, stuffed suckling pig roasted on a spit, the recipe for which was given to Rose [his wife] by the Belaluan [village] cooks. After the pig has been killed, pour boiling water over it and scrape the skin thoroughly with a sharp piece of coconut shell. Open the mouth and scrape the tongue also. Cut a four-inch incision to insert the hand and remove the viscera. Wash the inside of the pig carefully with cold water. Run a pointed stick through the mouth and tail and stuff the pig with a finely chopped mixture of red chili pepper (*lombok*), *bogaron tinke* (nuts resembling ginger or the red-yellow, nut-like seeds of the melinjo tree), garlic, *tjekoh* or *cekuh* (lesser galangal, an aromatic root of the ginger family), red onions, black pepper (*meritja*), turmeric (*kunyit*), *sra* (concentrated fish paste), ginger (*djahe*), aromatic leaves (*saladam* or *ulam*), salt, and *kerbah* (a variety of peppercorn) mixed with coconut oil. Place a piece of coconut bark inside, and then sew up the cut. To give the skin the proper rich brown color, bathe the pig—before roasting—in turmeric crushed in water, rinsing off the excess root. Make a big wood fire and place the pig not directly over it, but towards one side. Forked branches should support the ends of the stick that serves as a spit, one end of which is crooked to be used as a crank by a man who turns the pig constantly (*guling* means to turn). Two people are required to cook the pig: a second man simultaneously fans the fire with a long, paddle-like object to direct the flame and smoke away from the pig. The heat should be concentrated on the head and tail and not in the middle so as not to crack the skin of the stomach. After a few hours of slow roasting, the juiciest and most tender pork is obtained—flavored by the fragrant, interior, trap door spices—and complemented by deliciously brittle skin covered with a golden brown glaze. Few dishes in the world can be compared with a well-made *be guling*."

Covarrubias comments further on the food-related Balinese tax system: "The most hated of taxes is that paid every time a Balinese kills a pig, no matter how small, for which he needs a certificate. This has led to clandestine slaughter and with it the reduction of the pig supply; the reward promised to denouncers has introduced the element of discord into otherwise unified communities. The population would prefer an export tax on cattle to the troublesome slaughter tax."

According to today's Balinese, the ideal, normal-sized live piglet selected for *babi guling* is four months old, typically 77–110 pounds in weight and costs Rp.500,000. The pig is either caught in the wild, purchased from a piggery or procured at the market. All-purpose pigs are on sale at the larger village markets held every three days. The small, squealing pink-nosed pig is usually carried home alive by *sepeda motor* or rickety public *bemo* in a commodious bag or bamboo basket. A tolerant camaraderie is achieved between Balinese passengers crammed into the back benches of worn, market-bound *bemo*. They smile and socialize despite being tightly packed in among flapping chickens and noisy, squirming swine-filled sacks. After the homeward-bound pig is killed with a bamboo knife to the throat, its hair is shaved off the skin with a home-made Gillette razor device in which the blade is placed inside a bamboo stick cylinder with long, rolling pin-like handles on either end. A square, middle slot section secures the sharp edges. The shorn pig is subsequently boiled in hot water for complete hair removal and then fully disembowelled. All of the stomach innards and viscera are removed and the empty cavity is washed clean. The Balinese then insert a thick bamboo pole through the entire pig from its mouth to its rectum (same process with a goat) so that it can be carried to the cooking site. A male chef fills the cavity with Bali's renowned, magical *bumbu* spice paste mixture (*bumbu rajang* and *sere*) specially hand-chopped, crushed and selected for *babi guling*. *Sere* is lemongrass and *rajang* means to cut into small, thin slices or mince finely.

The lengthy list of herbs and spices for *babi guling* typically includes shallots, garlic cloves, ginger, fresh turmeric, galangal, pepper corns, coriander seeds, candlenuts, bird's eye chilies, sliced lemongrass stalks, whole cassava leaves, salt, dried shrimp paste, lime leaves, *salam* leaves and oil. The stomach is sewn (*jarit*) closed to seal the flavorful spice mixture and the symphony of flavors inside. The Balinese make a hole in the ground and build a coconut husk fire to "burn" the pig. The pig is suspended on the pole over the fire on two Y-shaped wooden stick supports at either end. A man continually turns the pig around and around by hand for two and a half to three hours. When fully cooked and ready to eat, the Balinese will serve and share the entire animal, or will first cut the roast pork into small square slices. Because of the high fat content of the pot-bellied Balinese pig, *babi guling* is also extremely fatty. The Balinese love their *guling* fatty, and the golden brown, crispy skin is considered to be the best part. A small, whole suckling pig typically feeds up to a hundred people.

Culinary revolutions and innovations do not occur in Bali. The Balinese people remain wedded to their inherited traditions, the Bali-Hindu religion and their unique food intimately linked to the gods. To eat and to cook is to also praise and thank the deities that bless Pulau Dewata. Bali's best-loved food, *babi guling*, owes its romantic, religious and high-status reputation not only to the long cooking process required but also to the family care of the resident livestock. Pork is routinely eaten as a traditional festive food on such important childhood ritual occasions as the foot-touching ceremony at three months of age, marking the first time that a baby is allowed to come in contact with the lowly ground, and the *otonan* ceremony, at eighteen months. The mandatory three-month ceremony is carried out to mark the baby's transition from holy angel status to mere fallible human. A small suckling pig is always ordered for this happy, well-attended celebration. Settled on a large silver tray, the pig is judiciously surrounded by piles of small offering baskets and coconut leaf decorations. A young coconut leaf sash is wrapped around its waist. Balinese culinary artistry stretches the potential of *babi guling* to the maximum. Its crisp, honey gold skin shines with promise and the carnal scent of rich roast pork seduces nearby nostrils. Blessed, ceremonial *babi guling* is also slowly becoming a more frequent everyday splurge, available at locally known, eagerly patronized *warung babi guling* and other small eateries. A young pig is stuffed with a spicy *bumbu* paste and leaves that will later be eaten as vegetables. Then the pig is spit-roasted over a fire of coconut shell and bamboo roots for several hours until the skin is crisp and the meat is done, but moist. The succulent treat is traditionally served with rice, the leaves that were cooked in the cavity and a spicy relish (*sambal*) of fried garlic, shallots, tomatoes and chilies.

Located across from the Ubud Royal Palace on Jl. Suweta, Ibu Oka's *warung* produces the best *babi guling* on the island of the gods. Crowded to the rafters whenever it is open, for lunch only from 11 a.m. to 3 p.m. or until they run out of suckling pig, patrons literally "pig out" on the leaf-lined pork smorgasbord basket: sliced roast pork nestled under a giant square piece of crackling hard, crispy pork skin, pork sausage, steamed white rice and *lawar* (a mixture of shredded vegetables, coconut, chilies, spices and congealed pig's blood to impart a red-brown ceremonial color). Ibu Oka closes on certain days, and often suddenly and at random, but local Ubud customers know to follow the secret scent to her private home compound a few minutes away, further up Jalan Suweta. Here, the cooking continues and the swine specialties pour out of her bustling rear kitchen. Ibu Oka is the high priestess of pork in an island of many high priests. Her *babi guling* stands as a reference point for the great pork dishes of the world. You can sit down at communal wooden tables to spoil yourself with *babi guling* or order thick, luscious portions to go in a styrofoam box. The *babi guling* here is famous for its particularly succulent, tender, flavorful lean meat derived from the live pigs that are brought down the hill every morning and slaughtered out back. They are then stuffed with a secret concoction of chili oil, *salam* leaf, herbs, spices and peppers. When full, the abdominal cavity is stitched and sewn closed. The rotating pigs are slowly turned on a spit and roasted over an open wood fire for six hours, continually basted by hand with coconut oil to produce an unparalleled caramelized, roasted sweetness.

Other Balinese residents insist that the best suckling pig recipe on the island is prepared by the chefs of Gianyar village. Here, the abdominal cavity is stuffed with an orgy of roots, herbs and spices: chopped, crushed, sliced and shredded shallots, garlic, ginger, turmeric, galangal, pepper, coriander, candlenuts, chilies, lemongrass and whole cassava leaves. The cassava leaves spread the spices evenly while the pig is being slowly roasted (the stuffing is later eaten as a vegetable). The outside of the pig's body is rubbed with turmeric juice to make the final skin color a shiny, golden yellow-brown. It is then impaled on a long wooden pole and hand-turned (*guling*) rotisserie-like over an open burning fire of dried coconut or corn husks and wood for two to three hours depending on the size of the pig. *Babi guling* is mostly served at feasts but it is increasingly being made in commercial kitchens for sale at certain street food eateries and night markets in the larger villages. A famous family-run *be guling* stall in Gianyar attracts a constant stream of Balinese customers to its heaping pork platters. Cut into small portions, the *babi guling* is paired with *sayur nangka* (jackfruit), pork *lawar*, cooked blood, Balinese *urap*, satay, legendary *urutan* sausages and steamed rice. A *babi guling* stall can always be found at the Gianyar night markets, a noisy, crowded and littered local showcase of the wonderful sights, sounds and aromas of Balinese foods and spices.

Highly seasoned fried or steamed Balinese pork sausages (*urutan celeng*, also known as *urutan babi* and *celeng oret*) are made of pork meat combined with spice paste (*bumbu*), conveniently encased in the roast pig's reserved tubular stomach intestines. This meaty mélange of pig flesh and pig stomach is diced into small bits and then mixed with *bumbu*. The Balinese then construct a hand-held funnel carved out of bamboo, insert a coconut leaf spine in the middle as the tube and squeeze the *daging* (meat) *babi* through it into the attached intestinal casing below. The stuffed *urutan* is then placed outside in the sun to dry for approximately two days: it is then fried (rare, or well done until red or brown). Once cooked and ready to serve, the thick, full-blooded Balinese pork sausages are sliced into small, easy to eat round sausage pieces. Aromatic *urutan*, usually served with Balinese rice wine, is always found at Balinese food stalls that sell whole roast pig. The deceased pig's head is usually on display as a trophy-talisman in a glass display cabinet with a black tongue and its mouth and teeth wide open. *Urutan* is served with *nasi putih* (white rice) and various kinds of raw *sambal matah*: *sambal lemu* with salt and green chili pepper or grilled *terasi* with coconut oil. *Be celeng menyatnyat* is a pork casserole combined with substantial Balinese *urutan*. *Oret,* a different, black-colored fresh blood sausage, is made of pig heart and blood, with no flour added. Fried blood sausage (similar to Scottish black pudding) is also made. Another special side dish sourced from the excess of *babi guling* production consists of pig intestines packed with sweet potato, coconut, a little red palm sugar and a *bumbu*, and then boiled.

Be celeng base manis (pork simmered in sweet soy sauce) is flavorful pork cubes smothered in sweet and salty soy sauces, ginger, chilies, shallots, garlic and chicken stock. It often appears on festive occasions when a whole pig is slaughtered and plenty of meat is available. "Balinese spice pork curry" is made with Bali's coconut-fed pork in a mild curry with root vegetables, steamed rice and *sambal ulek*. *Balung nangka*, another integral element in festival cuisine, is braised pork ribs (*balung* means bone) with young jackfruit or papaya cooked with the pork still on the bone. The creative play of flavors and ingredients is rooted in local lemongrass, *salam* leaves, ginger, red chilies and spice paste. *Babi gorengan* (fried pork) consists of solid, square white chunks of pork fat with skin and browned pork pieces on the bone. The meat is first boiled and then well fried. This cooked pork dish is specially made for the gods on the day before Galungan or Nyepi. It is also designated for the souls of the dead. *Babi gorengan* is usually prepared for a *megibung* feast, served on a big communal plate to be shared among the participants. The *megibung* ritual is mainly only still carried out in Karangasem regency, one of Bali's more traditional areas. In an economy of chronic scarcity, the Balinese are necessarily very thrifty and practical when it comes to food. To ensure that no part of the coveted pig goes to waste, they utilize the knuckles to create *kikil celeng mekuah* (pork knuckles in spicy sauce). Balinese food stands in busy night market streets like Teuku Umar in Denpasar specialize in *lawar, ayam betutu,* popular pork satay (*saté babi manis* is a Balinese favorite) and renowned *babi guling*.

Traveling food sellers arrive unexpectedly on Kuta Beach with a full kit of pork-based dishes, plastic bowls, banana leaf squares and food serving equipment. Four bowls are set up on the broad sands under the trees. The red bowl on the left contains the *bumbu*. Second from the left is the banana leaf-lined bowl of *urutan* pork sausages covered by a black and white striped plastic bag. The *urutan* is made by mixing all parts of the pig's stomach together with *krupuk* (crackers) and then frying them together (*gorengan*). The large plate in the center resting on a bamboo basket holds the *babi serapah*, eaten with rice. The *serapah* is sliced and then mixed by hand. The Balinese believe that the dirt of the hands makes the *serapah* delicious. It tastes both sweet and hot from the use of chilies. The round metal tub sitting on the sand to the right takes pride of place. This is the *lawar*, a combination of *babi* and *nangka* (jackfruit) mixed together. The *lawar babi* is mixed by hand with blood in the big center bowl and is served to customers on a traditional banana leaf plate (*tekor*). The old lady seller prepares *nasi campur* (mixed rice) in a banana leaf wrapper consisting of *serapah, lawar* and rice ready to eat. She also sells *urutan* sausage with rice in a banana leaf *bungkus* packet to go for Rp.10,000 to the local beach massage ladies.

The Balinese are naturally gifted artists. They sculpt their food as they carve their temples as a form of divine creation or prayer. For a temple anniversary celebration (*odalan*), a massive pagoda-shaped statue made from perishable fried pork and pork fat will stand near the central shrine. It takes pride of place alongside other opulently constructed food-based offering structures dedicated to the gods. A striking, spiky bouquet arrangement of all-pork satay sticks is commonly produced as a cremation ceremony offering (pork skin, pork liver, pork *saté lembat*, bacon and pork meat). Visually arresting *saté isi* (*isi* is Balinese for meat) is another local food masterpiece. Meaning "meat satay" and it can be made from the meat of chicken, duck or pork. It is created both for ceremonies and for commercial consumption. *Saté isi* can take the form of three alternating pieces of pork—pork meat alone, pork meat with skin in the center and pork meat solo configured as three alternating balls or chunks threaded along a satay stick. The Balinese make these for ceremonies, weddings and tooth filings for family, guests and neighbors and for personal eating. The Balinese also like to eat internal organs of pigs and chickens as part of their repertoire. Skin, kidney, liver, heart and brain meats are either grilled or fried and presented to the gods on diverse ceremonial occasions.

Babi Guling

(WHOLE SPIT-ROASTED STUFFED SUCKLING PIG)

Pork is a luxury commodity in Bali. It is usually eaten only as a ceremonial food as it is too expensive for everyday consumption. Pork-based babi guling is the most famous religious food creation on the island of the gods. A spectacular Balinese delicacy, babi guling (literally "turned meat") is a whole, spit-roasted suckling pig, although the pigs used are technically too old to be considered suckling (from three to six months in age). More than mere holy haute cuisine, babi guling (be guling celeng in Balinese) is an important window into Balinese history, religion, tradition and culture. Prepared more to honor the gods than for personal eating relishment, classic babi guling is the island's favorite, unofficial "national dish."

Composite recipe Courtesy of Made Aryawan, Tabanan, Bali, and Nyoman Wardana (Mr Black), Denpasar, Bali. Made (an expert tennis player and artist, who drew a lifelike picture of me and my dog Chessie in Bali) spent months talking with me about the foods and culture of Bali, including babi guling. Nyoman took me to his house to meet his family and see his swine-filled home piggery business in Kerobokan. He sells the suckling pigs that become legendary babi guling. My two great Balinese friends, Made and Nyoman, both worked as funny, friendly poolboys at the beachfront Inna Kuta Beach hotel in Bali (now renamed the Grand Inna Kuta). We enjoyed many scrumptious whole pizza pie and black Russian bottle parties on Friday nights at the hotel pool! 2008.

1 young suckling pig, about 35–50 kg in weight
10 shallots, peeled and sliced
6 garlic cloves, peeled and chopped
2 in (5 cm) ginger, peeled and chopped
15 candlenuts, chopped
4 in (10 cm) fresh turmeric, peeled and chopped
2 tbs coriander seeds, crushed
2 in (5 cm) *greater* galangal, finely chopped
lesser galangal
25–30 bird's eye chilies
red Lombok chili peppers
10 stalks lemongrass, sliced
1 tbs black peppercorns, crushed
bogaron tinke (ginger-like nuts)
1 tsp dried shrimp paste, roasted
5 kaffir lime leaves, finely shredded
2 *salam* leaves
chili oil
5 tbs fresh turmeric juice
whole cassava leaves
1½ tbs salt
2½ tbs coconut oil for basting

Obtain a four-month-old piglet in the market and slaughter it. Scrape or shave the hair off the skin, remove the internal viscera and wash the inside.

Impale the pig from the mouth through to the tail on a thick bamboo pole. Rub salt over the outside of the pig and inside the cavity. Then stuff the cavity with the *bumbu* collection of hand-chopped spices, herbs, chilies, roots, seeds, chili oil and whole leaves.

To seal the pig, either sew up the stomach or use sharp bamboo sticks.

Grate the fresh turmeric, mix with 1 tablespoon of water, then press to yeild 5 tablespoons of juice. Rub 2 tablespoonfuls of turmeric juice on the skin to make it turn yellow-brown and glossy.

Build a large wood or dried coconut husk fire. Suspend the pig on the spit above it, supported by forked branch supports at both ends. If dried coconut husks are used as the fire source, their aroma will penetrate the meat and give it extra flavor.

Turn the spit by hand continually and slow roast over the open, burning fire for anywhere from 2½ to six hours.

Baste regularly during the roasting process with the remaining turmeric water and with coconut oil to keep the meat moist.

Serve with steamed white rice and vegetables.

Serves 25–30.

Babi Kecap Bali Style

(PORK IN SWEET CHILI SAUCE)

Pork features prominently on the devout, devotional Balinese menu and a large proportion of ceremonial dishes are based on pork meat. Traditional babi guling is difficult to recreate in the Western kitchen. This recipe for babi kecap captures all of the exciting flare and flavor of Bali while being much easier to prepare. A popular pork creation cooked in a spicy Balinese sauce and sweet soy sauce, it is always eaten during the great Balinese festivals of Nyepi and Galungan. This luxurious pork stew can be prepared ahead and refrigerated; the flavor improves and can easily be reheated. We understand people at a very profound level through the food they eat. The Balinese anticipate and covet the almost sticky richness of this slow-braised pork dish bathed in an enlivening, spicy sauce.

Murni's recipes reflect and reveal magical local spice secrets from her native, nearby village of Penestanan and from her own family compound kitchen. Murni offers a spectacular fresh yogurt and honey taste sensation to her customers at the Warung. Murni's mother created the forty-year-old culture and passed the secret on to her daughter for the benefit of future generations. The honey is dark in color and piquant in taste. It is collected by hand from wild bee hives that thrive on the fragrant flowers that bloom almost all year round (frangipani, hibiscus and honeysuckle). A gracious living legend of Ubud, Murni actively promotes and preserves Bali's food heritage. When cooking at home, her personal preference is still for this authentic kampung cuisine (village fare) that she grew up on as a child.

Recipe Courtesy of Ni Wayan Murni, Murni's Warung, Campuhan-Ubud, Bali, 2006.

3 lb (1½ kg) pork fillet, cut into bite-sized pieces
10 oz (300 g) shallots
½ lb (250 g) garlic cloves
5 oz (150 g) lesser galangal
2½ oz (75 g) galangal
2½ oz (75 g) turmeric
1 tbs ginger root, peeled
½ oz (15 g) candlenuts
1½ tsp coriander seeds
1½ tsp cumin seeds
1½ tsp shrimp paste
3 red peppers (capsicums), roughly chopped
3 crumbled chicken stock cubes
¼ cup coconut oil
8 tbs sweet soya sauce
8 tbs tomato sauce
6½ cups chicken stock
salt and black pepper to taste

Place all the ingredients except the pork and chicken stock in a heavy stone mortar and grind with a pestle to a smooth paste.

Quickly brown the pork on all sides with a little oil, in small batches in a heavy pan. Take care not to burn and do not overcook.

Bring the chicken stock to a simmer and add the spice paste and salt and black pepper to taste.

Mix and add the browned pork and simmer until tender.

Serve with steamed white rice and a selection of *sambal* sauces.

Serves 4–6

CHAPTER TEN

Bebek Betutu:
The Balinese Duck

———— ‡ ————

BEBEK BETUTU BEGINS IN BALI'S IRRIGATED emerald green rice fields. Ducks traditionally are bred and live near the island's stepped rice terraces, their preferred early morning feeding grounds and source of food. Hungry ducks are banned from the newly planted rice fields but for one month after the harvest they are introduced to naturally perform ground weeding chores. They are released into the flooded fields when the rice plants are two months old and take over the weeding and fertilizing until the harvest. The field is rested and is sown with peanuts or other legumes to enrich the soil before it is planted again. After the harvest and the rice is cut, duck farmers drive their flocks daily to the flooded, newly shorn *sawah* and set them free to splurge on organic matter, discarded and leftover rice straw, rice grains, worms, snails, eels, baby frogs and small water animals. As the land needs to rest, there is usually a one-month "happy duck" feeding frenzy interval between the harvest and the planting of the next rice crop. Few people keep ducks in either mountainous or dry limestone areas like the Bukit and Jimbaran because there are no wet rice fields nearby. But ducks form an integral part of Bali's rice belt ecosystem, from the Tabanan countryside (Kerambitan, Pupuan, Antosari, Pejaten) to Sanggingan to Tegallalang and Jatiluweh through to the central highlands of Batukaru. Ducks judiciously protect the growing rice crop habitat from destructive insect pests like brown planthoppers and grasshoppers while simultaneously making compost and fertilizing the ripening fields.

Brown, white and black battalions of busy, quacking Balinese ducks swim, dive, duck, weave and take cover in the flooded rice paddy waters to escape the midday heat, obscured by the tall sea of green growing stalks. Balinese ducks have evolved into an essentially flightless species. Living in a year-round tropical climate, they have no need to migrate south for the winter. They emerge to waddle in long, orderly rows one behind the other through the green-brown irrigation ditches, duck herders wielding bamboo switches close behind. Paddling along the raised emerald green ridges between the rice paddies, the long straight line of trained ducks obediently follow a flag held by their owner, perhaps an old man dragging a machete, or a boy, to go home at sundown. This traditional hand-made guide is a long bamboo pole with a fluttering white cloth flag three-quarters of the way up and a duster of white feathers decorating the tip. As recently as the 1970s, the duck farmer would be bare-chested and dressed in an old Balinese-style cotton sarong hiked up between his legs like a loin cloth. Today, he is more likely to wear white shorts but will still shepherd his flock carrying the tool of his trade: a long, white feather-tipped bamboo pole with a white flag hanging halfway up. During the day, the ducks feast on cut, post-harvest, flooded *sawah* detritus. He uses verbal commands to round them up in a mad 5 p.m. dash towards a fenced-in, tarpaulin-covered enclosure at the side of the field for safekeeping overnight. The bamboo pole is planted upright in the ground at the secured gate of the enclosure.

The Balinese admire the strength of the duck because, like the turtle, it is the only creature able to survive on land as well as water. Ducks are deemed more intelligent, forthright and purposeful than chickens. "Royal palace ducks" rule the reception area, forecourt and off-limits floating lake pavilion in the great inner courtyard of the Puri Kanginan, an eighteenth-century palace of the Karangasem royal family in Amlapura. The Balinese prefer to eat duck over chicken but expensive duck meat is not everyday village compound food. The Balinese normally only treat themselves to a duck delicacy for a ceremonial feast. For quick simple cooking, they either remove the skin and boil the duck whole with *bumbu* spices, chop it and sliver it into more sophisticated *lawar*, or wrap it in banana leaves and roast it on the stove over an open fire. Farmers raise ducks mainly for their eggs—yellow, white, pale blue and black—rather than their meat. (Brown eggs are chicken eggs.) Duck eggs are available and sold in almost every market. The yellow eggs are called *sumba* eggs (*sumba* means dyeing or color in Balinese). To color the white eggs yellow, powder is mixed with a little water to make a yellow coloring liquid. Pale blue duck eggs are widely available and also appear in almost every village *pasar*. *Telur asin*, cooked and salted duck eggs, are a local favorite and appear in innumerable village *warung*. *Telur asin* are always made from black duck eggs laid by the *bebek selen* (a black duck in Balinese, also referred to as *bekasem*). To prepare *telur asin*, raw duck eggs are put in a basket, barrel or bucket full of mud made out of ashes taken from the traditional wood-fired kitchen stove, combined with salt and spicy *sambal*. A little water may be added to make the mixture more muddy. The eggs are left in the mud bath to absorb and mix with the spices for one to two weeks, after which they are steamed or boiled. The duck eggs emerge a dappled black-gray and white in color and have a spicy taste. Duck eggs are also needed, indeed preferred, as cremation ceremony offerings, although people can use either duck or chicken eggs to satisfy this religious requirement.

In the larger local markets, live flapping ducks are sold in pairs (Rp.30,000 for a small duck, Rp.45,000 for a large one). Tied together by the feet, they are bundled home on speeding, unsteady *sepeda motor* (motor scooters ridden by women are affectionately called *bebek* by local Balinese). There, they will be slaughtered by slitting the throat and turned into ceremonial *tum bebek* (highly seasoned, paste-like minced duck parcels steamed in banana leaf purses), *jukut ares bebek* (duck soup with banana stem) or duck *lawar* (minced duck prepared with stir-fried spice paste, chicken stock, thick coconut cream (*santen*), blanched green papaya, grated coconut, palm sugar, garlic, fried shallots, chilies and kaffir lime leaves). The duck used for this *lawar* is a different species to Bali's ordinary village *bebek*. For ceremonial *lawar*, Bali people use the rarer *entok* or *mentok* duck, also called Manila duck. It is a lot larger and is a mottled black and white color, with a short neck and a red face with short, bumpy, rooster-like wattles. Bali's ducks also leave their webbed footprints on succulently steamed crispy duck, a popular tourist specialty of the Ubud area and of the Bebek Bengil restaurant, in particular, which is renowned for its culinary duck culture, creative duck cuisine and local duck preparation practices. Here, the birds are marinated for thirty-six hours in a secret recipe of delicately calibrated Balinese spices before being steamed and then rapidly deep-fried at high temperature to yield the crispy duck exterior belying an interior wealth of soft, delectable duck meat. The dish is served with water spinach (*kangkung* or *urab*) and steamed white rice (*nasi putih*). Balinese *bebek* also wobble to the dinner table as *bebek mabuk* (drunken crispy duck) or as *bebek goreng* (a half duckling marinated with *bumbu* spices and deep-fried till crisp). Bali's pièce de résistance and the most famous traditional dish on the island, is succulent, well-seasoned *bebek betutu* (whole smoked Balinese duck). The outside of the duck is first rubbed with a carefully balanced mixture of roots, herbs, spices and vegetables, small bird's eye chilies, large red chilies, shallots, garlic cloves, ginger, turmeric, lesser galangal, greater galangal, ground pepper, black peppercorns, white peppercorns, cumin, coriander seeds, nutmeg, sesame seeds, candlenut, sea salt, lemongrass, lime leaves, dried shrimp paste, tamarind, sweet soy sauce, *salam* leaves, palm sugar and fresh coconut oil. The cavity, and even the throat, of the duck is then stuffed with the *bumbu* mixture. The duck is wrapped in banana leaves or, more traditionally, sheathed in sheets of sliced banana stem, bamboo, betel nut leaf, coconut tree bark or the husk of an areca palm branch. It is then buried in a smoldering pyre of rice husks or burning coconut fiber and smoked underground very slowly for anywhere from three to eight hours (some say overnight) until it is so tender that the spiced meat falls off the bone and melts in the mouth.

Indicative of its worth and importance, Balinese worshippers always present *bebek betutu* bought from a specialty *warung* to *pemangku* (lay priests) and *pedanda* (high priests) as a *banten* (offering) in conjunction with a major temple ceremony or ritual. The *pedanda* prays over the duck and blesses it as he chants and rings his sacred bell (*gente*) in a rhythmic, side-to-side motion. His song evokes the sound "AUM," meaning spiritual power, to speak to God. After the *pedanda* finishes praying over the duck, he gives it back to the people (some Balinese say the *pedanda* can eat the duck offering while others disagree). Once the ducks are blessed by the high priest, the *pemangku* and all the people will be served the sanctified ducks to eat in the *pura* (temple). True ritual Balinese foods such as *bebek betutu* are less often created in the compound kitchen nowadays. People lead busier lives, families are becoming smaller, young women are less interested in cooking and fast food snacks and fried rice are available everywhere. It is only the old people who will still spend ten hours to prepare and cook a smoked duck in this traditional way.

The Balinese only prepare time-consuming, traditional *bebek betutu* on special ceremonial occasions such as Hari Saraswati, the day dedicated to Dewi Saraswati (goddess of literature, fine arts, books, learning, wisdom, science, knowledge, music and education). Saraswati Day occurs every six months (on the last day of the 210-day Balinese calendar). Books, libraries and educational tools are cleaned and honored with offerings, the Balinese refrain from reading and writing and it is a school holiday (but children take offerings from home to the school and pray). Books in individual homes are collected and cleaned and offerings are made to them. The day after, Banyu Pinaruh, is marked by mass self-purification rituals and spiritual activities at the temple or on the beach, and a major feast beginning at 9.30 a.m. The Balinese begin Banyu Pinaruh by taking an early morning bath to clean themselves and receive blessings. There is a tremendous amount of cooking to do at home in the compound as this special Balinese banquet includes *bebek betutu*, yellow *nasi kuning* (ceremonial *nasi kuning* is decorated on top with dried omelette cut into small pieces and cucumber), vege-table *lawar*, raw eggplant, small red peanuts, salted fish and other foods to represent the diversified bounty of the earth. Although modern Balinese may bake the *bebek betutu* in an oven for only four hours, the rich gourmet festival food is still culinary and visual perfection, a veritable, edible form of installation art. Strong-flavored *bebek betutu* imbued with its trademark medley of fragrant leaves, roots, and spices is mandatory for the thanksgiving feast because the duck is the sister of the pure white swan that the beautiful goddess Saraswati traditionally rides as her mount. The swan symbolizes prudence so that Saraswati's devotees may use their knowledge to distinguish between good and evil. Next-door neighbors traditionally visit each other to share the food. The wife will bring samples of *nasi kuning* and *bebek betutu* for her neighbor to taste.

Bebek Betutu

(WHOLE SMOKED DUCK)

Bebek betutu (whole smoked duck) is Bali's most famous dish. Inundated with spices, this delicious duck can also be steamed, barbecued or roasted in the oven. An award-winning Balinese masterpiece, bebek betutu explodes in your mouth like a flavor firecracker. It is full of hot, hand-crushed peppers, spice-driven excitement and a deep, abiding love for the gods. Embrace the sheer luxury of this elaborate duck dish as you let the intensity and integrity of the flavors slowly unfold, moment by moment, piece by perfect piece. The traditional Balinese cooking method is to smoke the duck in a special pit in the ground for three days, the reason why it has to be ordered in advance in restaurants.

Recipe courtesy of Ni Luh Sudiani and Taman Rahasia Resort & Spa, Ubud, 2009. Ni Luh Sudiani was born in the mountain village of Kintamani. She grew up in the northern coastal town of Singaraja and has been cooking since the age of ten. She is the popular cooking school teacher at the gorgeous Taman Rahasia Resort. Ubud is known for its art museums, woodcarvings, paintings, yoga studios, natural healing centers, temples, powerful royal palace—and superlative cuisine. www.tamanrahasia.com

1 whole duck, 3¼–4½ lb (1.5–2 kg). Chicken can also be used.
10 oz (300 g) cassava leaves, boiled 30 minute and drained
   (*optional*)
5 stalks lemongrass, thinly sliced
5 kaffir lime leaves, thinly sliced
7 *salam* leaves (optional)
15 bird's eye chilies (optional)
⅓ cup vegetable oil
seasoning powder or chicken stock if needed
5 banana leaves (60 cm x 25 cm)

SPICE MIXTURE (*BUMBU*)
40 shallots, peeled
9 garlic cloves
1¼ in (3 cm) lesser galangal
1¼ in (3 cm) turmeric
2½ in (6 cm) greater galangal

3 tbs coriander seeds
1½ tbs black peppercorns
3 pieces candlenut
3 dried cloves
¾ tsp ground or grated nutmeg
1½ tbs salt
¾ tsp sesame seeds
¾ tsp dried shrimp paste
5 tbs water

Peel and chop or crush the spice ingredients and make a paste using a mortar and pestle (or a modern blender or food processor).

Fry the spice paste in 3½ tablespoons vegetable oil. Add the *salam* leaves and cook a further 3 minutes.

Put the spice paste in a big bowl. Add the kaffir lime leaves and sliced lemongrass and mix well.

Put the whole duck in the sauce, rubbing it thoroughly inside and out. Leave to stand for 5 minutes.

Stuff the cavity of the duck with the sauce and the cassava leaves.

Sew up the cavity with string or secure with bamboo slithers. Wrap in banana leaves and tie the bundle together with string.

Steam the duck for 1–2 hours on the stove top over moderate heat, adding more water to the pot if necessary.

Then grill or put in the oven for 30 minutes. (If grilling, leave the banana leaf wrapping. If using the oven, remove the wrapping. The oven temperature should be approximately 140º C. (Traditionally, leaf-wrapped *bebek betutu* was smoked for an extended period in an underground pit.)

Carve the duck and serve with steamed white rice and *sambal* sauces.

Serves 4–6.

Bebek Renyah

(CRISPY FRIED DUCK)

Bebek renyah (renyah means soft and crunchy—crisp but easy to eat) is served with delicious hot nasi putih (white rice), spicy Balinese vegetables (usually urap), krupuk and fragrant, field-fresh sambal matah. Crispy duck is not a traditional Balinese village food but it has become a characteristic culinary invention in the village of Ubud. (Ducks are abundant in the ever-pregnant and prolific wet rice fields surrounding Ubud.) The succulent, double-processed duck masterpiece is served in several Ubud restaurants and is highly sought after as a regional delicacy. Life doesn't get any better than this!

Recipe courtesy of the green, peaceful Pundi-Pundi restaurant in Ubud, situated among quietly growing rice terraces in the primeval heart of the Balinese countryside. It is a gift from the gods to enjoy an Ubud specialty—crispy duck—surrounded by the pageantry, piety and silence of what is still a very traditional village. Recipe provided by executive chef Nyoman Suartajaya, Pundi-Pundi Restaurant, Jl. Pengosekan, Ubud. www.pundiubud.com, 2011.

2–3 whole ducks (total weight 4 kg)
2 oz (60 g) shallots
1 oz (30 g) garlic
30 red chilies
½ oz (15 g) hot chilies
½ oz (15 g) ginger
½ oz (15 g) galangal
½ oz (15 g) turmeric
½ oz (15 g) coriander
½ oz (15 g) lemongrass stalk, cut into pieces
salt and pepper to taste
3¼ cups coconut oil

Peel and chop or crush the spice ingredients and make a paste using a mortar and pestle (or a modern blender or food processor).

Cut each of the ducks in half lengthwise.

Heat 1–2 tablespoons oil in a stock pot, stir fry all the spices, then add 3 quarts (3 liters) of water to the pot. Put the duck in the pot and simmer for about 3 hours until the flesh is tender.

Heat 8½ fl oz (250 ml) oil to a very high temperature and deep fry the duck for 1–3 minutes until crispy.

Serve the duck with steamed white rice and Balinese *urap* vegetables.

VEGETABLE MIXTURE (*URAP*)
5 oz (150 g) long beans
5 oz (150 g) round white cabbage
5 oz (150 g) spinach

2½ oz (75 g) bean sprouts
¼ cup grated coconut

Boil the vegetables for 3 minutes, then cut into small pieces according to preference.

Mix with a Balinese spice paste made from the same spices as for the duck and grated coconut.

Serves 4–6.

CHAPTER ELEVEN

The Village Chicken: Ayam Kampung

———— ≠ ————

EIGHTY PERCENT OF ALL HOUSEHOLDS in Indonesia keep live poultry. Indeed, the island abounds with chickens, roosters, hens and miniature trains of fluffy, cheeping chicks raised and husbanded as self-renewing sources of meat, eggs and sacrificial offerings. In a typical rural village like Sibetan in Karangasem regency, villagers work as farmers and fruit growers, raising livestock on the side. Sibetan has a typical animal population profile and animal species ratio. In 2007, it had 1,416 pigs, 468 cows, 312 ducks, 103 goats, 103,312 *kampung* chickens and 1,050 non-*kampung* chickens. The Balinese distinguish between two types of chicken (*ayam* in Indonesian, *be siap* in Balinese): *siap kampung* (homeyard chickens) and *iap Java* (meaning any place outside of Bali). The free-range *siap kampung* are left to roam the village compounds and eat whatever they can find while the *siap Java* are typically raised in enclosures with special feed. Bali's thin, sprightly village chickens run, cluck, scratch, groom themselves, drop feathers and peck incessantly at grass, ants and ground throughout every family compound and meticulously broom-swept Balinese yard. They pay a price for their relative freedom, however, making exhausting, sometimes futile attempts to fly up into the small compound trees at nightfall to sleep in safety above the aggressive reach of the free-range family dogs. Highly preferred natural "local chickens" are smaller, thinner, tougher, bonier, tastier, less fatty and healthier than Western battery-produced broiler chickens. The Balinese believe that this is the way chicken is supposed to taste. Demand dictates that the scrawny village *siap kampung* are much more expensive than their fat *siap Java* counterparts.

Tethered in open-backed vans or strapped across the rear of speeding *sepeda motor*, village chickens rattle their way towards bustling local markets to be bought and sold. While chickens cost Rp.25,000 at the market, fighting cocks cost a handsome Rp.300,000–400,000 each. Chicken farms regularly home-deliver poultry to steady restaurant and household customers. If a family wants live chickens, they just call up the local chicken farm and the delivery truck will be sent out to sell birds by the kilo or by the number of whole chickens required. Balinese families slaughter both domestically raised and externally purchased chickens at home by slitting their throats with a knife. Flatbed pick-up trucks also deliver chickens door to door, where they are sold by weight, in more remote mountain regions like Pacung. The chickens travel in stacked rows of metal wire cages fitted to the length and breadth of the vehicle. The desired number is taken out and placed in large round bamboo baskets to be weighed on a hanging scale and hook mechanism attached by a rod at the rear of the vehicle.

There are virtually no classical egg dishes in Balinese cuisine because eggs were seldom eaten in the past. Chicken and duck eggs were left to hatch to guarantee that there would be enough poultry available for use as offerings and sacrifices for Bali's temple ceremonies. But egg consumption in Bali has increased in recent years with the establishment of commercially run chicken farms, leading to a more plentiful and reliable supply of both birds and eggs. Egg-laying compound chickens still abound but the egg supply is now augmented by small family-run commercial egg farms, usually combined with piggeries, clustered around the village of Utu near Jatiluweh's rice terraces. Readily available and cheaper, eggs have begun to insert themselves deep into the Balinese food chain: *telur ayam kampung* (village chicken eggs), *telur bebek asin* (salted duck eggs) and *telur burung puyuh* (quail eggs). In the absence of refrigeration, eggs do not last long at this hot, humid latitude. Much kitchen effort has to be expended on treatments to preserve them. One method, which turns the edible unopened eggs jet black, involves coating the shells with kitchen ashes, salt, red cement, brick powder and vinegar! Creative Balinese egg recipes include *telor sambal kesuna* (eggs in coconut garlic sauce) and *tumis telor* (stir-fried or poached eggs in stock). *Telor base lalah* (chicken eggs in spicy coconut sauce) is flavorful Balinese creation. The eggs are hard-boiled, peeled and then deep-fried whole until golden brown. They are then drenched in a thick sauce of chicken spice paste, shrimp paste, red chilies, bird's eye chilies, chicken stock, coconut cream, *salam* leaf and kaffir lime juice.

Chickens eggs are commonly used as fertility offerings. A symbolic wedding basket containing a shaved coconut, a string of Chinese *kepeng* coins and an egg is secreted under a newlywed couple's bed and must remain there for six weeks to promote fertility, despite the pernicious smell of decomposing egg! A raw chicken egg is the central component in a complex offering basket called a *daksina*, coupled with rice, coconut, a small *canang* offering tray and money (usually a Chinese coin). The *daksina* is made for a new building so that the gods will take up residence and look after the people. The *daksina* must be placed inside the house and altar room (the *plangkiran* or offering box) along with other offerings. The raw egg is left there for one to six months before it is changed and replaced with a new one, or sooner if it breaks.

Chicken adapts easily to local cooking methods, dietary regimes, religious requirements and budgets. It plays a dependable role in satays, *lawar*, curries (*kare ayam*), coconut milk dishes (*ayam gecok* is a soupy dish of grilled chicken with roasted coconut milk), soups (*calon be siap*, Balinese-style chicken *bakso* soup, or *sop ayam*, Balinese chicken soup with vegetables and noodles), Indonesian *soto ayam* (chicken soup thickened with coconut milk) and chicken stock (*kuah siap*), widely used in a range of recipes. Chickens sacrificed as ritual offerings are later cooked as ceremonial dishes. One of Bali's best-known traditional ritual recipes is *ayam panggang mesanten* (roasted chicken with coconut sauce). Grilled chicken (*siap mepanggang*) and fried chicken (*siap megoreng* or *ayam goreng* in Indonesian) appear in elaborate temple offerings and play a role in many traditional ceremonies.

Some chickens that arrive on the Balinese table are defeated heroes from local cockfights, often given to friends and neighbors as food gifts. *Cran cam* (Balinese), a clear chicken soup with lemongrass stalks, *salam* leaves and fried shallots, and *siap gerangasam* (Balinese), a slowly simmered sour (*asam*) chicken soup-stew with *sambal* and burnt grated coconut are traditionally prepared after a local cockfight when the winner receives the losing bird as a reward. Well-seasoned thick *komoh* soup is also used for ceremonial purposes. The Balinese drizzle one cup of grated coconut and half a cup of fresh chicken blood into it.

Chicken also shines in a workaday stable group of classic village dishes. Its most famous incarnation on Bali is as *saté ayam*, sold along every roadside and at every temple festival and night market in Bali. Crunchy *siap megoreng* (fried chicken) is served throughout the Indonesian archipelago and varies from island to island. A simple dish, fried chicken in Sumatra is always made with domesticated chickens (*ayam kampung*) set on culinary fire with a hot sauce dip. Bali, of course, spices up its spring chickens with aromatic chicken spice paste, bird's eye chilies, shallots, lemongrass, tomatoes, palm sugar, garlic, black pepper, *salam* leaves, kaffir lime leaves, chicken stock, coconut milk, rice flour and vegetable oil. Ordinary charcoal-grilled poultry, *ayam bakar* (*siap mepanggang*) is cut in half—butterflied flat open—and dressed up with a gallery of Balinese spices: chicken spice paste, black peppercorns, lemongrass, *salam* leaves, bird's eyes chilies, kaffir lime leaves, chicken stock and coconut cream. Once cooked, *ayam bakar* is trussed up on the ceiling until eaten to keep it out of reach of hungry household dogs and cats. *Ayam bakar* with *ketupat* rice is the quintessential "people's food" on Bali. Ceremonial *lawar ayam* is a complex, highly spiced green bean with minced chicken village product, while *pesan ayam jamur* (mushroom) is grilled chicken with mushrooms in banana leaf.

Similar to Bali's famous *bebek betutu*, *ayam betutu* (smoked chicken in banana leaf) is marinated with a medley of salt, black peppercorns, shallots, garlic, turmeric, greater and lesser galangal, candlenuts, bird's-eye chilies, red chilies, lemongrass, palm sugar, oil, cassava leaves and *salam* leaves. Wrapped in several layers of banana stem and smoke-roasted in the ground, it is served at traditional Balinese *odalan*, *otonan* and wedding ceremonies. The Balinese of Nusa Lembongan traditionally cooked *ayam betutu* underground in a palm and banana leaf covering for an entire month. *Ayam betutu* (*betutu* means chicken fillet in Balinese) was a sacred food of Bali a long time ago. The people would make it and give it to the high priest to eat following the conclusion of a ceremony. *Ayam betutu* is for the highest caste; it is *pedanda* food and only the high priests have the right to eat it after a ceremony. *Bebek betutu*, however, is very different. It is made as an offering to the gods and the *pedanda* cannot eat *bebek betutu* brought to the temple.

Freshly roasted *be siap pelalah*, hand-shredded chicken with chilies and lime and a stuffing of black pepper, chicken spice paste, *salam* leaves, lemongrass and kaffir lime leaves, is a firm favorite. It is tossed with spiced tomato *sambal*, lime juice, fried shallots and the remaining spice paste stuffing. Fragrant *be siap base kalas*, chicken marinated in spices and coconut milk, is a home brew of simmered chicken parts (thighs and legs), chicken spice paste, lemongrass, *salam* leaf, kaffir lime leaf, coconut cream, chicken stock, black peppercorns and shallots. *Ayam kampung*, simple Bali-style village chicken, is simmered in a rich spice paste and chicken stock until tender. *Ayam kecap*, chicken in sweet soy sauce enlivened by green and red sweet mild peppers, is a surprising Balinese play of color, aroma and zest. *Ayam sambal matah*, shredded chicken with a raw shallot, chili, lemongrass and coconut oil sauce, and *jejeruk ayam*, coarsely grated or shredded chicken with jackfruit or vegetables, add to the fame of the humble Balinese rural chicken. Another recipe for *jejeruk* (milky shredded chicken) uses both coconut milk and coarsely grated coconut flesh. *Jejeruk* is usually presented as *jotan* (a food gift) to friends and relatives to maintain relationships when people organize a ceremony. Such gifts usually consist of white rice, *lawar*, twisted satay and *jejeruk* packed in a covered bamboo basket. *Jejeruk* is also a favorite Balinese food served at local *warung*. To make *jejeruk*, the ingredients consist of 250 g of chicken breast and half a coconut. The spice list includes 4 shallots, 2 garlic cloves, 1 small chili, 1 large chili, ½ tsp coriander, ½ tsp pepper, 1 slice lesser galangal, 1 slice turmeric, 1 stalk bruised lemongrass, 2 pieces *salam* leaf, 1 tb cooking oil and 200 ml coconut milk. The chicken is boiled until cooked, removed from the pot to cool and shredded. The finely ground spices and grated coconut are then fried with the shredded chicken, coconut milk, grated coconut, salt, lemongrass and *salam* leaf until thick, then served on a banana leaf mat. Curry-like Indonesian *opor ayam*, Javanese chicken coated with and boiled in a hot, spice paste-based broth topped with white coconut milk, extends the impact of the Balinese compound chicken throughout the length and breadth of the archipelago.

Ayam Kampung Bali
(BALI-STYLE VILLAGE CHICKEN)

Local village chickens (siap Bali) are totally free-range and taste very different from the commercially produced chickens in the West. While they may not be as fat and meaty as their Western cousins, the indigenous chickens (ayam kampung) make up for it in natural flavor. This recipe uses the typical "base genep" (literally, complete spice) and recreates the flavor of Bali.

Recipe courtesy of Ni Wayan Murni, Murni's Warung, Campuhan-Ubud, Bali.

30 chicken pieces (breast, thigh or leg), washed and dried
3½ oz (100 g) shallots
7 oz (200 g) garlic cloves
3½ oz (100 g) lesser galangal
1¾ oz (50 g) turmeric
2 tsp ginger root
1 tbs (10 g) candlenuts
1 tsp coriander seeds
4 tsp chicken powder or 4 crumbled chicken stock cubes
1 tsp shrimp paste
1 tsp salt
1 tsp black pepper
2 tbs coconut oil
4½ cups chicken stock

Place all the ingredients except the chicken pieces, coconut oil and chicken stock in a heavy stone mortar and crush with a pestle until reduced to a thick paste.

Fry the paste in the coconut oil for a few minutes, taking care not to scorch.

Stir in the chicken stock, mix well, and add the chicken pieces. Gently simmer until the chicken is tender.

Serve with steamed white rice and *sambal* of your choice.

Serves 4–6.

Tum Ayam

(WRAPPED CHICKEN PARCELS)

Tum is usually made from either chicken or boneless fish like tuna, marlin or mahi-mahi as these forms of protein are "easier to get" (expensive pork tum is only for ceremonies). A Balinese wife will prepare tum at home once every one or two weeks for her family for lunch or dinner, whenever she can afford to buy the chicken (a costly ingredient). Eel tum is a traditional village dish although the availability of eel is sporadic, seasonal and geographical as it is sourced from nearby rice fields. Tum requires considerable time to make, an almost obsessive sense of devotion, craftsmanship-like art work and manual dexterity, but this delicious, visually adorable dish is well worth it!

Recipe courtesy of Mr Dolphin (Gede Masda) and Mrs Dolphin (Kadek Astini), the very friendly owners of the delightful Warung Dolphin, a small, local, beachfront restaurant opened in 1999 in Lovina. Situated right across from Banyualit beach, it specializes in boat-fresh seafood (Mr Dolphin has his own prahu in the waters daily). Mr and Mrs Dolphin pamper and indulge all of their (mainly Western) customers and will pick up guests by motorbike anywhere in Lovina. They made it their business to learn exactly what their many Dutch and German clients want, and have implemented extremely stringent hygienic standards in the preparation of their food. Mr Dolphin personally leaps to attention to serve the guests and takes their orders with a huge, happy smile and a joyous welcome for returning guests from previous years. Everyone is welcome, taken good care of, protected and treated as family. The food is among the best in the world, ranging from Balinese specialties like gado-gado to luscious tuna, shrimp and squid. Mr Dolphin and the local boys also have an open guitar and music session every night after 9 p.m. in this relaxed, intimate, comfortable café. The ever-smiling beautiful Mrs Dolphin is the chef extraordinaire in the rear kitchen, and allowed me into her spotlessly clean, well-organized cooking stronghold (2008) to watch this magical preparation of traditional Balinese tum. Warung Dolphin, Jl. Laviana-Banyualit, Lovina, Singaraja, tel. 081353276985, www.dolphinlovina.com.

5 chicken pieces on the bone, cut up (or deboned chicken pieces
   or fillets)
10 shallots
4½ tsp sea salt
4½ garlic cloves

9 slices fresh ginger

9 slices fresh turmeric

9 whole candlenuts

1 packet spice ingredients (*base genep* or *wangenan*), including
candlenut, white pepper, cloves, peppercorns and *jebug arum*
(a spicy fruit), ground to a powder

9 small red chilies

4½ red Lombok chilies

1½ glasses coconut milk

12 *salam* leaves (one for each parcel)

3 kaffir limes

8-inch (20-cm)-square sheets of banana leaf

Put all the ingredients except the chicken, coconut milk, *salam* leaves and kaffir limes in a stone mortar and pestle and grind to a smooth *bumbu* spice paste.

Add the spice paste to the chicken pieces and the coconut milk and mix well.

Cut the kaffir limes in half, sprinkle the juice over the mixture and add the rind from half a lime for extra flavor. Then add the *salam* leaves.

Use a double layer of banana leaf squares to wrap each packet of *tum*. Place the uncooked chicken and spice mixture on the double-layer banana leaf, add a *salam* leaf and fold into a chunky triangular packet. Seal with fine inch-long bamboo sticks (*semat*) or toothpicks.

Trim any extra leaf on top of the parcels with scissors to tidy them.

Steam the parcels for 15–20 minutes.

Makes 4 parcels for 2 people.

Ayam Panggang Mesanten
(GRILLED CHICKEN WITH COCONUT MILK SAUCE)

This recipe is for a Balinese family to cook and eat at home, not for ceremonial offerings. Chef Ni Wayan Sulastini will cook it at home for her family, maybe 2–4 times per month.

Grilled chicken (ayam mepanggang) is a common, core, required ceremonial food. The Balinese construct massive, colorful, banten tegeh (pyramid-shaped offering towers) to honor the gods. Village women balance them on their heads as they march in single-file street processions to their local temples. These offerings contain a wide, veritable orchard of local tropical fruits (salak, apples, mangosteen) and such rice-based cakes as tulip-shaped kué mangkok. They place the ayam mepanggang (grilled chicken) on top, at the summit of the imposing, celestial food tower. Nothing that is fried can be used as an offering; grilling and roasting have a different theological meaning. The grilled food must be all freshly cooked; used food cannot be offered to the gods. The food, as well as the cooking pan, must be new and pure. The chicken will be grilled over a billowing, smoking fire fueled by burning coconut shells below the grill. After worship—after the conclusion of the ceremony—the Balinese always take the offerings back home. They will often use the grilled chicken as an ingredient to then make soupy ayam panggang mesanten ("me" means "with" in Balinese and santen is the coconut milk sauce). The ayam panggang mesanten will have a better taste because there is already a smoky tinge to the chicken from the grilling process. Visitors to the temples love eating the food offerings afterwards because of the extraordinary powers that the foods are believed to contain. The chicken will also taste exquisite because it has been doubly blessed: the priests have prayed over and blessed it, and the gods have inhaled its essence (sari). People in the villages cook a lot after a ceremony because they have smoke-grilled chickens or other meats at hand. The Balinese will not normally cook ayam panggang mesantan without a religious ceremony. It involves too much work because they have to grill the chicken first.

This delightful, flavorful recipe was prepared in the gleaming, high-tech restaurant kitchen of the very luxurious, beachfront Dolphin Beach Holiday Apartments resort in Lovina, northern Bali. Nestled in between a mountain range backdrop and the sea, the Dolphin Beach Holiday Apartments offers five newly built (2011), well-appointed apartment suites fronting a never-ending volcanic sand beach. Dolphins play in the waters off Lovina, and a snorkeling expedition over the coral reef completes the sensation of a Tahiti-like paradise. The intimate, ultra comfortable, upscale boutique property is owned by Australians David and Moira. Jl. Raya Singaraja, Seririt, Kaliasem, Lovina Beach. Phone: +6236242024. www.dolphinbeachbali.com

Recipe courtesy of cooks Ni Wayan Sulastini of Karangasem Regency and Ayu from Pemaran village, Singaraja, Bali, December 2011.

6 chicken breast cutlets
12 pieces lesser galangal, each 1 in (2.5 cm) long
6 pieces turmeric, each 1 in (2.5 cm) long
18 pieces garlic, each 1 in (2.5 cm) long
12 candlenuts

6 pieces shrimp paste, the size of marbles

1 packet spice ingredients (*base genep* or *wangenan*), including
chili, candlenut, nutmeg and white pepper, ground

6 big red peppers

6 small orange chilies

3 tsp sea salt

6 whole, old coconuts

1 packet Kara instant coconut milk

3 cubes Masoko chicken powder

shallots, sliced and fried for garnish

Fry the chicken in a little oil in a pan (or grill on a brazier over coconut husks).

Cut the fresh spices into small pieces, combine with the *wangenan* packet spices and peppers and crush with a mortar and pestle to form a paste. Add a little water if necessary.

Shred the chicken.

Put a little coconut oil in the pan and add the spice paste. Stir over a high heat for 1 minute.

Add a cup of water to the fry pan, then the shredded chicken. Cook at high heat over a gas flame. Season with ½ teaspoon sea salt and ½ cube of chicken stock.

Add another ½ cup of water to the boiling mixture in the pan. Add more if you want the dish to be more soupy or broth-like.

Pour in ¼ cup of freshly squeezed coconut milk (*santen*), stirring all the time to prevent it separating and becoming coconut oil.

Add the fried red shallot slivers to the boiling mixture for 10 seconds.

Serve with steamed white rice.

Serves 4–6.

CHAPTER TWELVE

Seduced by Saté:
The Balinese Twist

———— ǂ ————

SATAY STICKS ARE STANDARD FARE in many countries and cultures around the world who have invented their own versions of the popular dish. "Satay," from the Tamil word for flesh (*sathai*), comprises marinated pieces of meat (chicken, beef, fish, pork, goat and mutton) roasted on a wooden skewer and dipped in a special sauce before being eaten. South Indian Muslims brought satay to Southeast Asia, as the Tamil name suggests. Indonesia then developed its own satay tradition. The Indonesian archipelago has, in fact, a large range of satays in many different formats and meat combinations as well as regional satay specialties influenced by local cooking styles and ingredients. The countless meat satays reflect local food supply, availability, pricing and preference. Among them are *saté siap* or *ayam* (chicken), *saté babi* (pork), *saté kambing* (goat), *saté sampi* or *sapi* (beef), *saté anjing* (dog), *saté kelinci* (rabbit, more commonly eaten in Java), *saté kerang* (mussels picked from the shorelines), *saté siput* (in Indonesian or *kakul* in Balinese, garden, rice field or ocean snails), *saté udang* (shrimp, out of the economic reach of most people) and *saté languan* (sea fish impaled on lemongrass skewers). Served in Balinese ritual ceremonies, *saté languan* is made with green coconut, spices and brown sugar. Although it is a traditional specialty of Klungkung regency, it can be found all over Bali.

Regional satay specialities use the same popular meats (chicken, fish, goat, beef, mussels and lamb) but with a different construction or cooking style and ingredient list to standard Balinese satays. *Buntel* (or *pentul*) is a different style of winding the meat on the tip of the skewer into a round ball (*buntel* means wrapping, wrapped up, bundle, knapsack or packaging). *Saté buntel* most often refers to meat wrapped with another type of meat, for example, beef satay wrapped with pork. Variations of the most common and popular satays are available everywhere throughout the diverse island nation, including Bali: *saté banjar* (mackerel from Kalimantan), *saté betawi* (meaning Batavia, the former name of Jakarta), *saté Madura* (off Java) and *saté Padang* from West Sumatra (mostly water buffalo, beef or chicken). The Minangkabau people of Sumatra near Bukittinggi have created their own Padang-style culinary culture, including a Padang version of almost every dish in the country. In Padang Panjang, beef satay is grilled on a charcoal fire and the sauce is a unique thick brownish soup added hot right after the meat is cooked. The smoky satay is then served on banana leaves with *ketupat* rice packets. Diners soak up the excess peppery sauce with giant *krupuk rambak* (crackers made from fried cowhide). Other local satay styles include *saté ponorogo* (from one regency in East Java, mainly chicken or beef), *saté tegal* (a sea fish, finny scad, from Yogjakarta) and *saté khas ungaran* or sea perch (a specialty of Central Java).

Some satays are subject to consumption restrictions due to customary or religious beliefs. *Saté babi* (pork satay, not eaten by Muslims), *saté sapi* (beef satay, not usually eaten in Hindu Bali), *saté jamu* (dog satay, particularly available in the city of Solo on Java) and *saté penyu* (turtle satay), rarely eaten or available in Java but commonly used for ceremonial purposes in Bali.

Satays are the secular and religious workhorses of the Balinese and Indonesian diet. Pork, chicken, liver (*hati*), beef, lamb, goat, duck, dog, snail, minced seafood, fish or prawns are marinated in spice paste, chilies and brown sugar, sliced very thinly and threaded onto bamboo sticks (*tusuk*) to be grilled quickly at high temperature over burning coconut husks. (*Tusuk* means stick but not exactly a stick.) As with everything else in Indonesia, there is always the "seen" and the "unseen" and many mysterious layers of meaning in between. *Saté tusuk* means meat put on a stick but people do not always say *saté tusuk*, they simply say satay and everyone will know that it is any kind of satay on a stick. In Jakarta, *saté tusuk* is most often beef (tongue, skin and meat) or chicken (meat, liver, chicken organs and intestines). *Saté tusuk* on Java is usually accompanied by one of three kinds of sauce: sweet soy sauce with red onion and small green chilies, peanut sauce (peanuts blended with water and chilies, and not too spicy), or *saté Padang* sauce (a yellow-colored sauce for beef satay, originating in Sumatra).

Sizzling hot Balinese satays are an art form in themselves. Suspended on narrow, smoking skewers over hot portable braziers, they are lightly burned on the outside, imparting a particularly delicious, palm sugar-based caramel flavor. The Balinese generally eat freshly grilled satay as a snack at a *warung* or buy it from portable carts that specialize in chicken or goat satay on the side of the road. *Saté ayam* is the most popular and common market mainstay. Squatting streetside vendors string four to six tiny basted pieces of tightly packed chicken onto satay sticks, then turn and rotate them by hand over very hot, smoking dried coconut husks on a small ceramic or metal grille. To properly cook satay, the fire must be very low and the heat as high as possible. To achieve this, the satays are continually hand-fanned with a small bamboo mat or aerated with a small plastic rotating electric fan to blow air into the fire and energize the flames as they cook. Continual wet-basting further ignites the glowing coals below and imparts a delicious smoky finish to the juicy morsels. Customer-ready satays are then doused with a spicy-sweet peanut sauce, often referred to as *saus saté*, and wrapped in take-out banana leaves. Grilled satays are often served with a piquant or creamy peanut sauce, but in the villages the Balinese will normally dip the tip of the satay into a mixture of chopped chilies and salt or in a mixture of sweet soy sauce blended with chopped chilies. Artistically rendered skewers of succulent *saté ayam* are also teamed with a banana leaf-lined clay pot of steamed white rice, mixed vegetables and *sambal ulek*, a chili sauce made by grinding spices in a mortar and pestle.

Myth and mystery surround even the most ordinary of satays. The combination of goat satay and beer and dog satay and *arak* (liquor) are believed to enhance male virility ("strong") and guarantee hours of marital bliss in the family compound. The most popular styles of satay in Bali are plain satay (usually chicken, pork, or goat), *saté lilit* (minced seafood), *saté lembat* (minced pork, chicken or duck satay with spices and grated coconut), *saté babi manis* (pork with spice paste, sugar and *kecap manis*, a sweet, thick soy sauce), *saté serapah* (made of pork fat for temple ceremonies) and *saté asam* (meaning sour, marinated meat threaded through a skewer). *Saté asam* is renowned for its soft consistency. Boiled for only a few minutes, it escapes the flames and smoke of the traditional charcoal grill. *Saté asam celeng* incorporates pork loin or tenderloin with a basic spice paste, bird's eye chilies, palm sugar, and salt to produce a sharp, sour satay. *Saté asam sampi* is acidic-tasting beef satay. The three satay sisters—*saté ilit*, *saté lilit* and *saté lembat*—share sticks and spices but with significant differences. Pasty lookalikes, *saté ilit* and *saté lembat* are both wound around the end of a skewer but vary in shape, size and composition. The generous mix of spices is the same but *saté lilit* is blessed with coconut milk whereas *saté lembat* is always impregnated with grated coconut and is always made by men.

Saté lilit (*lilit* means to twist, wind, coil or wrap around in Indonesian) is a time-consuming indigenous Balinese specialty utilizing the choicest cuts of minced pork, chicken, seafood or duck. Prepared as an offering, it is usually only made for religious celebrations (Galungan-Kuningan, mass cremations, tooth filings or weddings) when lots of time and labor and large amounts of meat, spices and coconut are available. Seafood *saté lilit* starts out as a pasty, multiple fish mixture of fresh, finely chopped snapper, tuna, mackerel, swordfish or *mujair* (a kind of white water fish), prawns, coconut milk, seafood spice paste, sea salt, chilies, kaffir lime leaves, red or brown palm sugar (to give the slightly charred, caramelized glaze typical of Balinese satay) and complementary spices. The secret is to grind and blend the fish and spice batter to a chopped sausage consistency in order to twine it easily around one end of a flattened satay stick, a coconut leaf spin or a lemongrass stalk skewer. Thick bamboo sticks resembling ice cream paddles are Balinese-style skewers, while thin pointed sticks are Indonesian-style and are more appropriate for *saté ayam*. Drumstick-shaped *saté lilit* is particularly delicious when trimmed fresh lemongrass is used as skewers instead of bamboo sticks and it is grilled over a flavor-enhancing fire of coconut shell embers (the coconut keeps it deliciously moist) instead of charcoal. For duck *saté ilit*, villagers usually incorporate both ground duck meat and ground duck bones into the *lilit* batter in order to save money. It has a different taste and texture than the all-meat restaurant versions.

Saté lembat (pork, chicken, duck and, traditionally, turtle) is made with freshly grated coconut, crushed, ground raw meat, pulverized spices, palm sugar and coconut milk. A specialty satay exclusively hand-produced by males, it is always prepared for Balinese rituals and ceremonies. The number of sticks varies according to each occasion. The *tukang saté* (satay maker or worker) scoops up a small chunk of the thick, sticky, kneaded meat dough, then shapes the grainy mixture onto the flat end of a bamboo stick until it forms a thumb-sized, pear-shaped ball. The paste continues to be wound around until it reaches halfway down the stick, tapering to the diameter of the shaft below. Men cut a piece of banana plant stem, and several of the *lembat* sticks are thrust into it by their trimmed ends. The banana stem thus serves as a base holder as the *saté lembat* grills over the charcoal or lit coconut husks to a golden brown.

Superlative multi-stick satay presentations worthy of a royal palace *cokorda* are available in chicken, pork or fish ceremonial configurations. Ceremonies and satay sticks always go hand in hand as satays are one of the most important ritual foods on Bali. The larger the ceremony, the more satay sticks are needed. Priests consult the sacred lontar inscriptions to gauge the number of satay offerings required for specific ceremonies and how each offering should be made. Large-size satays are for common offerings while small satays are for *caru* offerings. An ordinary ceremony would require a ratio of thirty sticks (plus other food) to feed ten people. Miguel Covarrubias photographed a group of bare-chested saronged village men seated on the ground preparing ceremonial banquet quantities of "turtle meat en brochette" in the 1930s. The satays were affixed to a ten-foot-long two-strip bamboo pole border resembling steps on a fireman's ladder or a train track. The long straight row of a hundred or more satay sticks was being hand-fanned with square bamboo mats, twirled, turned and broiled to fruition over a bed of hot smoking coals. Very little has changed since then.

In ceremonial settings, the number of satay sticks offered in a particular bundle represents a family's caste or position in society. The more sticks (as many as eleven for a high priest), the higher the position. Practiced in the art of satay stick construction, communal groups of men eagerly hand-make the satay sticks for such rituals as a three-month baby ceremony. Sourced from felled bamboo poles, the satay sticks are painstakingly hacked and whittled into shape behind *warung*, in narrow alleys and in darkened family compounds on the evening before a ceremony. While most of the artistic palm leaf offerings are constructed by women, only men can prepare the elaborate offerings made of meat used on all major ritual occasions. The *gayah saté gede* offering represents the animal kingdom, a direct counterpoise to the plant life kingdom represented by women's offerings. *Gayah* means a lot of ornaments or beautifully decorated in Balinese, and *gede* means large, great, on a large scale or big in both Balinese and Indonesian. The beautifully adorned *gayah* or *saté gede* creation is meant to symbolize and include the "entire contents of the world" to maintain harmony and balance in the universe. A brown triangular offering, it resembles a dried-out floral arrangement or a Christmas pine tree with hundreds of protruding, needle-like meat satay sticks. A pig's head forms the carnivorous base. A different bouquet of tall, thin, all-pork satay stick offerings is required for cremation ceremonies on the beach. Many different types of pork satay appear in this white-clothed, bamboo-colored arrangement: pork liver satay, pork skin satay, tiny Q tip-shaped pork *saté lembat* and combined pork *saté embat* and pork skin bits strung along the same skewer. Five rectangular bacon or pork strips also crown five tiny, hairpin-like sticks.

Saté Lilit Ikan

(GRILLED GROUND FILLET OF FISH IN A BALINESE SPICY SAUCE WITH FRESH SHREDDED COCONUT)

Saté lilit differs from the usual Indonesian satay, which normally consists of chicken pieces threaded on a skewer. This satay is a combination of spices and minced seafood molded onto a skewer or, preferably, a thick stem of fresh lemongrass. Lilit (Bahasa Indonesia) means to wind, twist, turn, coil around, circle around or wrap around.

Saté lilit ikan (fish) is a main course and is usually made "when the Balinese have ceremony." This recipe gives "the exact taste of the Balinese ceremony food." The Balinese will make saté lilit ikan for a temple ceremony (dewa yadnya), a six-month baby ceremony (manusa yadnya) or a Mecaru ceremony (Bhuta yadnya). It is a favorite food for any religious event.

Recipe courtesy of the charming, natural Puri Lumbung Cottages in Munduk, North Bali, 2011. Their wooden rice barns are surrounded by gigantic red pagoda flowers, bunga lilin (yellow candle flowers) and lively (loudly croaking) frog-filled lotus ponds.

1⅓ lb (600 g) finely minced fresh tuna (or mackerel and white snapper)
¼ lb (120 g) palm sugar
30 bamboo satay skewers, each 8 in (20 cm) long and ¾ in (2 cm) wide or skewers made out of lemongrass stalks
½ large whole coconut, grated

SPICE PASTE (*BUMBU*)
3¼ oz (90 g) red chilies, seeds removed
5 oz (150 g) shallots
3¼ oz (90 g) garlic cloves
½ piece turmeric
½ piece nutmeg, pounded
2 oz (60 g) ginger root, chopped finely
5 oz (150 g) galangal, chopped finely
1 tbs shrimp paste
salt and pepper to taste

Chop then pound the chilies, shallots, garlic, turmeric, ginger and galangal in a mortar and pestle. Add the shrimp paste and a little salt and pepper.

Add the palm sugar and continue to grind for 5 minutes it until the mixture becomes a soft paste.

Put the tuna into the paste and mix thoroughly by hand into a fine dough.

Add the grated coconut to the dough and mix further. Taste and add more salt and pepper if necessary.

Divide the mixture into small balls using your hands and mold the seafood mixture onto the end of each lemongrass stick, tapering the mixture slightly so that the end is slightly thicker. It should look like a drumstick.

Grill for 10 minutes until golden brown on a modern gas grill or over glowing charcoals or a low fire. Rotate the sticks to make them evenly brown. The surface should not be too hard.

Serves 4–6.

Saté Lilit Ayam

(GRILLED GROUND CHICKEN IN A BALINESE SPICY SAUCE WITH FRESH SHREDDED COCONUT)

We integrate ourselves into, bind ourselves to and root our culture in the foods that we eat. Our shared food defines us as a group. These are the very primal ties that bind. All living things must eat and satay is crucial to the Balinese cultural and psychological landscape. Satay is also a cornerstone of Balinese religious offerings and is the most typical food on the island.

Recipe courtesy of Made Janur and Iloh, Janur Dive Inn, Jl. Laviana-Banyualit, Lovina, October 18, 2008. My good friend Made Janur invited me into the Balinese-style kitchen behind his sunny, relaxing, open-air restaurant. Janur and his assistant,"my sister" Iloh, demonstrated four authentic Balinese dishes for me. I took notes, photographed beautiful and mysterious spice pastes, smelled the scents of Heaven and ate some of the most delicious foods I have ever tasted in Bali. Janur (heavily inked with tattoos, wearing powerful, large Balinese rings with potent, protective stones) can always be found lounging with his friends in his small, streetside Dive Inn restaurant. Janur will go out back and cook you the best fresh mackerel, fried Balinese chicken or nasi goreng that you have ever experienced in your entire life! You can sit there for hours in the warm, safe, quiet cocoon of local Lovina life, sipping a sweet glass of iced tea among your new friendly family—the local Balinese.

½ **chicken cutlet**
11 **shallots, cut in half**
5 **garlic cloves**
5 **bright orange chilies, each 1½ in (4 cm) long**
2 **pieces lesser galangal, each 1¼ in (3 cm)**
3 **slices fresh turmeric**
1 **piece fresh ginger, ¾ in (2 cm)**
¾ **of a freshly grated coconut**
1½ **tsp sea salt**
coconut oil

Chop, then pound the chilies, shallots, garlic, turmeric, ginger and lesser galangal in a mortar and pestle.

Grate the coconut half, cut into two quarters for easier processing using a traditional *parutan* grater.

Cut the chicken cutlet into small pieces, add to the mortar and grind with the spices to a paste-like consistency.

Add the grated coconut to the chicken and spice mixture and continue pounding to yield a sticky yellow paste.

Heat the coconut oil in a pan in preparation for cooking the satay.

Wind and mold the paste mixture by hand around the top of bamboo satay sticks.

Fry the sticks in the hot coconut oil for 5 minutes, turning them over until both sides are a golden brown.

Serve with steamed white rice.

Makes 12 sticks for 4–6 people.

CHAPTER THIRTEEN

Seafood in Bali: Bounty of the Ocean

——— ≠ ———

IN HIS CLASSIC 1937 WORK, *ISLAND OF BALI*, Miguel Covarrubias had much to say about the Balinese relationship with the sea: "The mountains with their lakes and rivers are the home of the gods and the sources of the land's fertility; they stand for everything that is holy and healthy. To the Balinese, everything that is high is good and powerful. It is therefore natural that the sea, lower than the lowest point of land—with sharks and barracuda infesting the waters, and deadly sea snakes and poisonous fish living among the treacherous coral reefs—should be considered as *tenget*, or magically dangerous, the home of the evil spirits and negative powers. Few Balinese know how to swim and they rarely venture into the sea except to bathe near the shallow beaches, and then they go only a few feet from the shore. There are small settlements of fishermen who brave the malarial coasts of Kuta, Sanur, Benua, and Ketewel, but in general, fishing is done on a small scale—either with casting-nets, or in beautiful prows shaped like fantastic elephant-fish (*gadja-mina*) with elegant, stylized trunks and eyes to see at night. With their triangular sails apex downward, they go far out to sea at sunset to procure the giant sea-turtles required at the frequent banquets of this feast-loving people. Most Balinese seldom eat fish and remain essentially a rice-eating race. Their repugnance for the sea may be due to the same religious fear of the supernatural that prevents them from climbing to the summit of the great mountains. They dread the unholy loneliness of the beaches haunted by demons, and they believe that the coastline is under the influence of Djero Gede Metjaling, the Fanged Giant, who lives on the barren island of Nusa Penida. They are one of the rare island peoples in the world who turn their eyes not outward to the waters, but upward to the mountain tops."

Covarrubias described a well-delineated Bali-Hindu theological universe consisting of three distinct levels: the revered mountain peaks above, the abode of the gods; the middle world of earth, the province of humans; and the shunned, mysterious sea below, home of the spirits of the underworld. Yet, the sea is also a tool and place of purification as it receives the cremated ashes of the dead and purifies their spirits before they go to heaven. Singular among island peoples, the Balinese are reluctant fishermen. The island has no seafaring tradition, no history of exploratory or migratory oceanic voyages and minimal participation in national and international maritime trade. Some local night fishermen wade out onto the coral reefs at sunset, at low tide, to troll for fish (*ikan*) using kerosene lamps and rustic bamboo poles in Pemuteran, Lovina, Perancak and Sanur, but most of Bali's fishermen are migrants from Java or Lombok. These Indonesian men bravely navigate Bali's hazardous, inhospitable coastline. Bali has few natural, sheltered harbors or deep-water anchorages and is buttressed by a moat of dangerous breakers, coral reefs and wave-cut cliffs punctuating its craggy shoreline.

The men go out every day in colorfully painted, traditional, small *jukung* (double outrigger canoes) built in ramshackle fishing villages dotting the coasts and in larger ports like Amed, Padang Bai, Lovina, Kusamba, Singaraja, Jimbaran Bay, Pengambengan Bay, Kedonganan, Benoa Bay and Candi Dasa. In good weather, they normally set sail at night, sometimes late, and return early in the morning. Many Balinese farmers, employees and civil servants who live in coastal villages have side jobs as fishermen. They also join migrant fishermen from outside Bali based in scattered landing places across the island (Pengambengan, Medewi, Suan Galuh, Soka, Jimbaran, Sanur, Serangan, Kusamba, Tejakula). At some fishing nodes there is still a tradition called *ngajur*, assisting fishermen to drag their boats to and from the sea and to take their catch to auction houses or deposit them beachside. The Balinese helpers (*pengujur*) are paid for their services in the form of fish, often small, bony *cotek* fish.

The traditional Balinese *jukung*, a non-motorized boat made from a hollowed-out log, is crafted from a local wood called *kayu* (wood) *ganggangan* (put over a fire to dry or smoke) grown in the Karangasem regency villages of Manggis and Selumbung. Stabilized by bamboo struts, these local fishing vessels follow a trusted seaworthy, functional 7,000-year-old design. Mythological, crocodile-like visages are carved into the sweeping prow in the belief that these frightening open-jawed monster faces (*sudang*) will scare away the harmful forces. Their large, bulging, forward-looking eyes help the vessel to navigate at night and in bad weather, to avoid dangerous coral reefs and to spot fish. Wooden *jukung* in sister island Nusa Lembongan, part of Klungkung regency, have always been carved out of huge, whole *pohon mangga* (mango tree) or *pohon waru* (beach hibiscus tree) logs. These old forest wood resources have become scarce and new outrigger *jukung* are now built out of multilayered coated fiberglass. Only moderate size *jukung* requiring smaller, younger tree logs are still made out of local timber.

The warm tropical seas surrounding Bali shelter a god-given array of equatorial sea life: octopus and lobster off Uluwatu Beach, sea urchins in Sanur and shrimp and colossal-sized fiddler crabs with rose red/white claws in Benoa Bay. Saltwater fishing ponds at Benoa Harbor yield *kakap putih* (sea bass), *kerapu* (grouper), *bandeng* (milkfish) and crab. Kedonganan locals dig in the sand near the water's edge for *imis* (small cockles) to be used for a tasty soup. In Tanjung Benoa, as the tide recedes, locals harvest crabs and tiny fish trapped in rock pools by the ebbing waters. Inedible puffer fish and pipefish (a long, narrow, bony fish with a tube-like snout) populate the creeks meandering through Benoa Bay's mangrove forests. A mangrove forest in Suwung, Denpasar, is home to native crabs, shrimps and molluscs. It was briefly used for shrimp and milkfish embankment, but in 1992 Bali's government returned the mangrove to its status as a non-commercial forest preserve. Fish-burdened boats slide up Lipah Beach every day in Amed. Hotel managers roll up their sarongs to wade into the water and inspect the boat's catch, including red snapper, barracuda, tuna and mahi-mahi.

Underwater wildlife blooms along the offshore coral reefs. Amed Bay's spectacular coral wall teases distant divers and snorkelers with surgeon, cardinal, parrot and damsel fish and dogtooth tuna. The reefs around Bunutan (near Amed) teem with marine life: eels, white tip sharks, stingrays, barracudas, honeycomb moray eels, pygmy seahorses and rare whale sharks. Wild, undisturbed dolphin pods jump through the flat, tranquil waters around Lovina on Bali's northern coast, frequently visible offshore in the early morning hours.

Bali's inland rivers are alive with common river crabs, creek eels, goby fish (native to Bali and fond of stony rivers), gourami (a Southeast Asian freshwater fish) and several species of prawns in lowland rivers. Balinese men go fishing in local lakes and rivers, even in overpopulated Kuta, to snare freshwater mujair (cichlid fish), species *Tilapia mossambica*, delicious grilled and served whole. Guppies (native to Trinidad) are ubiquitous in every lake, river, canal and rice field, while edible tilapia fish (introduced from Africa) are found in lakes and rivers.

Aquatic life has been artificially injected into Bali's ecosystem since the mid-1990s. A commercial fish farm company established ponds in Tabanan regency to breed milkfish (*bandeng*) and grouper for the export market. Large milkfish are commercially grown in saltwater ponds along the coast in southern Bali for sale to Java. *Nener* are young, freshly caught milkfish, commonly traveling in thousand-strong schools. Bali cultivates freshwater fish like gourami, catfish, carp and nile in *minapadi* (separate "rice-fish" stations) in ponds, lakes or cages. Bangli regency produces fish bred in Lake Batur, spawning a popular regional fish delicacy known as "twisted" gourami *saté lilit*. Made from the fillet of the fish, the ground meat is blended with Balinese condiments into a malleable batter, twisted around a lemongrass stalk and then grilled until well done.

Benevolent sunlight, crystal clear waters and coral reefs surround Bali's three nearby sister islands, Nusa Lembongan, Nusa Ceningan and Nusa Penida. These conditions create a spectacular natural marine and sealife aquarium bursting with tropical life forms. Sea cucumbers (*trepang*), giant clams, reef sharks, thresher sharks, hammerhead sharks, sea turtles, manta rays, eagle rays, mola mola (ocean sunfish), starfish, anemone fish, sponges and blue marlin are all spotted or netted in these warm Badung Straits waters bracketing Bali.

Fishing is a new occupation in Nusa Lembongan, financially feasible only since the mid-1990s when the introduction of the seaweed farming industry infused money into the previously very poor local economy.

Seaweed dollars enabled local fishermen to purchase boats capable of traveling far enough offshore to net viable numbers of fish and make seafood an integral part of the island's diet for the first time. Nusa Lembongan fishermen sail out in their *jukung* at 5.30 every morning, flying the primary colors of the gods: yellow and white cloth is wrapped around each mast, crowned with palm leaf offerings, to pray for safety and success. Some boats go along the coast up the island heading towards Nusa Dua and Balinese waters while others go down the coast and round the island to the waters south of Dream Beach off Nusa Lembongan. Each *jukung*, owned by one man with four or five helpers, carries three or four green one-kilometer-long blue-bordered nets lined with a series of elongated weights. The nets are unravelled in the ocean, marked by colored sticks at either end weighed down with white styrofoam sinkers to anchor the boats in one area. Each fisherman has his own stick color denoting his specific fishing area, which can vary daily. If the current is strong, the net will float in a rounded arc or remain in a taut line if the current is weak. The boats return to shore an hour and a half later at 7 a.m. (if lucky) with a cache of very plentiful small tuna (*tongkol*).

Female cooks and hotel staff come to one end of Tanjung Sanghyang (Mushroom) Beach from 7 to 8 a.m. every day to buy fistfulls of tuna and carry them back to their commercial kitchens. The boatmen unceremoniously toss tuna to the hotel girls waiting on the sand or set them down on the shore in front of them. The girls shyly walk back up to the boat and hand the men folded rupiah notes (tens and fifties pass back and forth in a silent, ancient selling duet). The girls try not to wet their hotel sarong uniforms as they carry their fish trophies back to the Mushroom, Waka, Tanis Villas, Bali Hai and Nusa Lembongan resorts. The girls also buy fish for their own families and carry them home at the end of the day. Once the boats pull up on shore, easy-to-access tuna are thrown into round tubs for wives to transport inland and for instant sale to other local women. Tuna right off the boat costs Rp.4,000 per piece but prices rapidly escalate to Rp.7,000 once off the sands due to cartage costs. Unsold tuna are laboriously carried to the villages in heavy, plastic, head-borne tubs. By 8 a.m. all beachside vending is done and the catch of the day has disappeared. The fishermen and their crews spend another hour carefully and deftly removing and disentangling

individual tuna stuck by the tail or mouth in the precious, tear suscep-
tible nets. They fold the nets up and store them in special large green
plastic bags in small concrete sheds near the landed boats, blessed with
and protected by small offering trays to the gods.

Only small tuna are caught close offshore to Mushroom Beach but
Nusa Lembongan fishermen also provide a large variety of other freshly
caught fish. These are quickly sold and eaten (grilled) in the local
villages or vended to beachfront hotels. Straight from the fleet, blood
dripping out of the mouth, and on to the plate, most fish are consumed
the same day. Some hotels buy fish when the catch is plentiful and freeze
them until needed to guarantee a steady supply. Species include two
types of tuna (one the big *cakalang* or skipjack tuna), mackerel, expensive red snapper (*kakap merah* and *jangki*) and *tribang* (snapper with
tail). Snapper (red and yellow, black and brown) are found on the coral
reef near Nusa Lembongan but only in the evening and usually under
a full moon. Fishermen calculate correct fishing hours according to the
Balinese calendar. Lobsters are only caught in the afternoon. The
Balinese on Nusa Lembongan eat decorative anemone (clownfish) but
bemoan their small size. They dislike the taste of plentiful sea urchin
(*landak laut*) and omit it from their diet. Other locally consumed fish
include crabs, octopus, shrimp, catfish (*ikan kucing*), long-nosed jack-
fish (a large family of fish), *ikan kacang-kacang* (garfish) and moray eel.
Villagers go out and catch *ketepo* (*trepang* or sea cucumber) on the
shoreline at low tide. They dig it up out of the sand with a small pen-
size stick. The foot-long jellyfish-like *ketepo* is small and either red or
white in color. The yellow interior, filled with sand and water, must be
cleaned before it is cut up and either fried or grilled.

Covarrubias painted a cultural portrait of an isolated island landmass
haunted and tortured by impure fish and profane seas. Subsequent
historians echoed Covarrubias's thesis that the omen-vigilant Balinese
eschew fish in their diet. Although the sea is universally regarded with
deep suspicion, the Balinese take full advantage of the rich protein bounty
of their surrounding oceanic resources. Thousands of tons of edible fish
are netted each year in Bali. Ninety percent of the catch consists of ocean
fish. Seventy percent of this consists of one single species, the eight-
inch-long Indonesian oil sardine or *lemuru* (*Sardinella longicaps*).

Pengambengan Bay, on the southwest coast six miles from Negara, is Bali's largest fishing and fish processing port, reeling in 25 percent of Bali's entire annual fish harvest. Pengambengan and Kedonganan village fishermen plumb the rich sardine treasure trove in the Indian Ocean (Bali Sea) in between Bali and Java. At the height of the August sardine season, a hundred tons of sardines per day are carried ashore at Kedonganan in large baskets from early morning, water-bobbing *prahu* (*prah* means freight or cargo in Dutch) anchored close offshore. Purchased on the spot by buyers as whole or cleaned fillets, most sardines are packed in salt and ice, trucked directly to local canneries and processed for export. Kedonganan's beachside fish meal production facility also refines sardine heads, guts and off-cuts in huge vats into coarse fish meal used as chicken feed, fish oil and *petis*, a popular salty fish sauce. *Petis* is also a black fermented shrimp paste related to *terasi* or congealed fish, shrimp or meat paste.

The fishermen of Kedonganan village present simple offerings at their beachside guardian shrine every day before they set sail, rain or shine, to invoke and insure safety for the voyage. The same offerings are also placed on their pink, green, yellow and blue *jukung* outrigger boats and on the nets used to snare the fish. Further safety-oriented offering rituals are performed out at sea before commencing any fishing to ask for permission and blessings from the god of the waters or marine inhabitants. The fishing cooperative also carries out larger temple ceremonies entailing complex offerings presided over by a priest on the full moon of the fifth month in the Balinese calendar in November, a tradition inherited from their ancestors. The customary village of Kedonganan also stages an elaborate annual ceremony on the new moon of the seventh month in the Balinese calendar. Spectacular food offerings are cooperatively fabricated at the village temple to accompany prayers for the continued well-being of the entire fishing fleet and local community.

Twenty percent of Bali's ocean largesse consists of substantial (three to five kilogram, half to one meter-long) tuna (eastern little tuna, skipjack tuna, yellowfin tuna), striped mackerel and frigate mackerel caught by Jimbaran Bay's beachfront fishing fleet, a consortium of men from Jimbaran, Tuban, Kelan and Kedonganan villages. Fishermen in Bali enjoyed bumper years of tuna exports in 2008 and 2009 as global market demand continued to rise. In 2007, 6,898 tons of fresh tuna were exported internationally from Bali, mostly southern blue fin tuna, with a total value of US$59 million. Jimbaran Bay is home to Bali's largest fishing fleet. Its small *jukung* have a fishing range extending ten miles northwest to Soka near Tanah Lot and Yeh Gangga in Tabanan, and as far as the Uluwatu cliffs eight miles to the south. Shortly after sunrise, an incoming fleet of brightly painted wooden fishing vessels appears on the horizon. The larger, main *prahu* anchor offshore and are serviced by small boats that row out to offload and transfer their catch in relays to the shore. Strings of one- or two-man *jukung* and small fish shuttle boats land at Kedonganan-Jimbaran, the epicenter of southern Bali's main fresh fish market. Waiting co-workers rush the boats and hoist bursting fish-laden plaited bamboo baskets two by two to shore, suspended on ropes along traditional bamboo shoulder poles. This (mainly Javanese) fishing workforce heaves gill nets full of red snapper, squid, mahi-mahi, octopus, clams, crabs, tuna, and the odd gigantic marine specimen (an individual shark, swordfish, billfish, sailfish, large shrimp or lobster) sandwards to their wives who are squatting down with round black buckets between their legs at the water's edge.

Fishing families work together. The wives carry the blood-fresh morning catch on their heads in battered metal tubs straight to the Jimbaran market, with its makeshift corrugated tin roofs and plastic tarpaulin walls, one kilometer away. A bustling auction system and groaning weighing scales regulate buyers, bidders and sellers. Prices are negotiated, calculators click and Styrofoam coolers of fish are iced, salted and quickly trucked away. The auction house has its own secret language. An incredibly complex system of hand gestures and a rhythmic rolling commentary accompanies each sale, incomprehensible to the casual observer. Other women, wearing conical, woven bamboo Asian coolie hats for shade, bypass the official flea market-style auction and carry their own fresh sea fish to market or display and sell them to savvy Balinese buyers already positioned on the beach in search of the freshest fish possible. Renowned hotel and restaurant chefs and owners are also on the sand before dawn waiting to meet the colorful rag-tag fishing flotilla as it comes in with the night's catch after fifteen hours at sea. The sorting, weighing, bargaining and selection process for ocean-fresh fish begins right here at the low tide mark before the fish can cross over to the nearby established market stalls. The chefs come to gauge both the price and quality of the ocean catch they will serve that night in their restaurants. The waterside seafood pandemonium and excitement is over by 8 a.m. The returning fleet's pirate's capture has been fully secured and sold. Jimbaran's *jukung* boat operators and *prahu* will set sail again in the late afternoon, at 3 to 4 p.m., remaining afloat all night if the fishing is good.

In smaller ports like Padang Bai, the fishing community goes out twice a day, from two to eight in the morning and again from noon to six in the evening. In Jembrana regency in western Bali, fishermen in traditional Balinese *prahu* boats or *sampan* canoes leave their families behind to fish at night, returning home early the next morning. When they are not working, their *prahu* are parked high up on the beach to be repaired and repainted in contrasting colors, always adorned with the image of the beautiful goddess-queen of the South Sea, locally known as Nyi Roro Kidul. Moving quickly from the fishing armada to the plate, their lucky swag of fish, crab, shrimp and lobster is sold at early morning fish markets and the public market in town, and to restaurants and the fish canning industry. A fleet of government-owned deep-sea fishing boats and large trawlers ranges further out over the waters from Benoa Bay, scouring the bottom, middle and top of the Indian Ocean for yellowfin tuna, big eye tuna, albacore, barracuda and giant black marlin destined for the Japanese and Italian markets. Each year the boats press further and further afield to come home with a profitable catch as Balinese waters become increasingly depleted and market demand (more hotels, restaurants and people) expands exponentially. Additional massive diesel ships from Taiwan and China are permitted to operate in the Benoa Harbor area, catching large, nearby offshore tuna species for extradition to their countries. The remaining 10 percent of Bali's ocean catch is comprised of Balfour and hammerhead sharks and shallow coastal water coral reef fish (red snapper, grouper, hairtail shrimp, large shrimp, prawns and spiny edible lobsters). Sharks are soaked in salt, sun-dried and spirited away to covetous customers in Java. Baby sharks caught up in boatloads of tuna and mackerel are dumped on the beach and grabbed by restaurant owners. Overharvested top-quality reef resources like red and white snapper are becoming scarce and maintaining a continuous supply is difficult. Much fresh fish is now caught in the waters off Java and shipped over to Bali.

Embedded deep within the heart of maritime Indonesia, an equatorial archipelago of over 17,000 islands, the people of Bali depend on fish and seafood as a major part of their diet and a critical source of food, especially those living on or near the coasts. Seasonal fresh fish (bonito, small tuna, sardine and mackerel) are readily available and relatively cheap compared to meat, providing simple, delicious meals for Balinese families. The Balinese grill (*bakar*) and eat the freshly killed fish immediately. Available in the coastal markets and in Denpasar at the huge Pasar Badung, fish is iced, salted, sold and cooked within hours of being caught. On the north and east coasts of Bali, women from fishing villages line the sides of the roads sitting on the floor or behind makeshift wooden tables offering the day's catch (big snapper, tuna and mackerel) to a continual noisy, vehicular customer stream on trucks and motorbikes. Wet season rains and luscious red snapper run strong in Bali. In Banyualit village in Lovina, local fishermen return with exquisitely fresh tuna, mackerel, snapper and mahi-mahi ready for the grill. Owing to the limited availability of refrigeration and refrigerated trucks, inland markets sell these fish preserved in brine, dried, boiled in salted water or salted for longer storage, like *ikan teri* (anchovy). *Teri* are various kinds of small fish such as Japanese anchovy or whitebait (*teri asin*, dried salted anchovy). Small whole sardines (*pindang*) boiled and packed in brine, and canned catfish (*pindang ikan kucing*) can keep for months although the Balinese strongly prefer fresh rather than canned fish. *Pindang* also refers to a process for preparing eggs, meat or fish using salt, tamarind juice and other ingredients. When cooking fresh local *pindang*, the Balinese first boil the sardine in water until it no longer has any smell. Bali's renowned double-cooking process then comes into play, a technique typical of much Balinese food preparation. They fry or grill it again before eating.

The Balinese usually purchase fresh, small, silvery four-inch-long fish (petite anchovies are popular) and eat them whole in preference to fillet pieces cut from a large fish. Fish is favored because it can come in small portions, enabling the Balinese to consume it without wastage and without having to slaughter and use up an entire pig or cow, normally reserved

for ceremonies anyway. Because fish can be cheaply processed and preserved for extended storage, dried or salted fish is available at almost all
village markets. A popular Denpasar supermarket-department store, Tiara
Dewata, stocks an astonishing variety of both fresh and dried fish for
urban Balinese consumers: *cotek* (a small bony fish), *cumi-cumi bersih*
(squid that is clean), *cumi-cumi merah besar* (large red squid), *rajungan*
(small black crabs, sentinel crabs, marine crabs), *kodok batu* (a species of
frog used for frog's legs), *belanak* (gray mullet), *bandeng* (milkfish), *belut*
(rice field or swamp eels), *teri putih* (white anchovy), *mujair* (cichlid fish),
tongkol kecil (small tuna), *kakap merah* (red snapper), *cakalang* (skipjack
tuna), *tribang, kresi, baronang, lemujung, ikan layur* (hairtail or scabbard
ribbon fish), *ikan bawal hitam* (black pomfret), *jangki merah* (red snapper), *kerapu* (grouper), *kerang kukur* (grated clams, cockles, oysters,
mussels), *kul nener* (young milkfish) and *kepiting* (crabs). Expensive sea
and king prawns sold in the coastal markets and in Denpasar are a very
rare treat for the Balinese.

Local village fish dishes are very different from the sophisticated
seafood recipes, haute cuisine presentations, complex cooking methods
and types of fish presented in cookbooks and tourist restaurants.
Authentic Balinese seafood cuisine is rooted in the home. The Balinese
eat non-premier seafood species, relying mainly on mackerel, sardine,
eel and anchovy. Small portions of sardines are tossed in sauces while
crisp, deep-fried baby eels give rise to additional pleasure in the compound. *Sager*, dried anchovies with coconut, is a traditional Balinese
village food cooked and eaten at home, mainly in Singaraja. It is made
with dry seafood like cooked fried *teri*, whitebait (tiny juveniles of such
species as herring, sprat, sardine, mackerel, bass, anchovies, Japanese
anchovies) or dry chicken breast (cooked and shredded). Prise open a
coconut, remove the coconut flesh in large pieces from the shell, grill
them over hot charcoals, remove the dark brown skin, and coarsely grate
the flesh. Fry a *bumbu* assortment of spices and enjoy the instant good
smell! Add the crushed, grated roasted coconut, stir and add a little
water to make it wet (but not like soup-like). Cook some more, add the
teri or chicken and stir. Eat with *sambal*, hot steamed rice and *sayur* for
a full meal. *Sager gerang* (spicy dried fish and roasted coconut sambal)
is yet another sweet flavor feast of dried anchovy ingenuity (*gerang* are

ikan teri, small dried fish). The primary components are salted dry anchovies, Bali's famous *sambal goreng*, roasted grated coconut, kaffir lime leaves, shallots, garlic cloves, bird's eye chilies, lesser galangal, shrimp paste, *salam* leaf, palm sugar and tomato. The spices and sugar are pounded into a paste. The anchovies are then grilled, broiled, deep-fried or dry-fried and then chopped very finely into dust-like oblivion. The spicy crumbled anchovies are then combined with the *sambal,* coconut, *salam* leaf, tomato and spice paste to produce one of Bali's very best village dishes. *Sager goreng* (fried) is a different, less complicated home-cooked staple. Simple but perfect, it only consists of fried *teri* (anchovies) fried together with lemon, coconut oil and salt.

Ikan bilis, also called anchovies (*Anchoviella indica*) are popular throughout the island nation, including Sumatra. A small fish, it typically comes from Singkarak Lake near Kinari. Here, the fish is simply deep-fried to give a crunchy, tasty sensation. It is widely available in home-cooked, multi-plate Padang-style local restaurants. Seafood items on sale at the local market determine what will be cooked in the Balinese village compound kitchen that day, whether gleaming red tuna (*tongkol*), salted dried fish, *ikan asin* (salted, salty or briny fish), *ikan kembung* (a small local salmon found in Lovina) or smoked canned sardines (*pindang*). *Cotek* is a small, thin, very bony species of fish with an oblong body and large eyes, and is very cheap to buy. It is crunchy (you can eat the small bones) but it must be fried well. It is very often deep-fried and eaten with a hot-sweet sauce. *Cotek* are available in both the traditional markets and the supermarkets. Small young conger or sea eels are a perennial Ubud market commodity as they thrive in the muddy, life-filled rice fields. They writhe around in large wet marketplace buckets oblivious to their culinary fate, and are sold by the plastic bag as a deep-fried meal ingredient. The calm, practiced household *ibu* will either steam the eels, tuna, mackerel or whitebait in banana leaves, grill the spice-soaked treasures, or deep fry them till crisp, and then serve them with hot steamed rice.

East Bali's cuisine rests on an abundance of daily fresh seafood sourced from the Badung Strait, ever-reliant on the prowess of the local fishing villages. Rustic seaside *warung* are set up along Karangasem regency's east coast beaches serving a tidal feast of *jukung*-fresh seafood dishes with spicy home-made *sambal* and rice to local Balinese customers. The fishing village of Kusamba is known for such local specialties as fish *saté lilit*. The twirling sticks of fish are grilled to perfection over glowing coconut coals by squatting young staff tending braziers in the sands. A spicy fish soup, *ikan mekuah*, native to the Kusamba region and made with tuna, mackerel or swordfish, and *pepes ikan*, a spicy fish concoction wrapped and steamed in banana leaves, are hallmarks. Geared towards Balinese taste buds, these crowded *warung* range from decaying, utilitarian concrete blocks to temporary bamboo lean-tos, to quaint, thatched *alang-alang* beach burés. Selections are displayed at the front counter or in murky 1950s-era glass cases: grilled fish in banana leaves, fish curries and *sop kelapa ikan* (fish-head soup with tamarind and tomatoes). In the late afternoons, the last batch of fresh dayboat scallops arrives from the sea, headed straight across the black volcanic sands for these waiting, simmering *warung* pots and grills. Seafood stalls also abound in the port of Gilimanuk, while Pebuahan Beach has many seafood kiosks and *warung* rivalling the charm and quality of Jimbaran Bay's renowned restaurant row.

· Life is plentiful at the shore's edge, reflected in myriad, authentic Balinese seafood dishes such as *udang mepanggang* (grilled prawns) and *be* (fish in Balinese) *pasih* (sea in Balinese) *mepanggang* (grilled)— whole, marinated, charcoal-grilled snapper (or other fish) steeped in a *bumbu* seafood spice paste mixture. They are served with *sambal tomato* or *sambal matah*, *kangkung* and *nasi putih*. Tuna *sambal matah* is one of Bali's most characteristic native seafood specialties, but the Balinese normally substitute *pindang* (sardines) for the tuna. *Pindang* is always readily available, flies abuzzing, in the local markets. Sourced from Lovina or Jimbaran, the two main Balinese fish supply depots, the Balinese boil the *pindang* at home in water with sea salt as they prefer a salty taste. The fish is then boiled, fried or grilled, but it is always topped with a trademark raw, spicy *sambal matah* made of shallots, hot red chilies, lime, coconut oil and lemongrass. The Balinese also create a pineapple milkfish soup. The ingredients consist of milkfish, shallots, garlic cloves, small chilies, sliced turmeric, sliced ginger, candlenut, coriander and large, sliced red chilies. To make, the spices are ground very finely and then stir-fried in a pan until the fragrance emerges. Water is added to the spices in the pan, followed by pieces of milkfish to create a fish broth. When the water reaches the boil, the rest of the ingredients are added: ripe, peeled pineapple, galangal, lemongrass stalk, *salam* leaf, cooking oil and salt, and are mixed well. The pineapple eliminates the odor of the fish and gives the broth a sweet or slightly sweet-sour taste.

Pepes be pasih, grilled fish in banana leaves, is Bali's signature seafood dish (called *pepes ikan* in Indonesian). *Pepes be pasih* is made from fresh tuna (*tongkol*), snapper, *languan* (sea fish), *tenggiri* (Spanish mackerel) or any other saltwater ocean fish (*ikan laut*). The fish is ground using the traditional mortar and pestle for thirty minutes, and then gently spiced with coconut, chilies, *sambal* sauce, fragrant gingers, salt, black pepper and *bumbu* seafood spice paste. Left to marinate briefly in this fragrant mixture, the fish parcel is then individually wrapped in a young banana leaf sheet or other locally available frond and either baked, broiled, boiled, steamed, smoked or, most often, grilled to perfection. The small rolled-up little packages are grilled directly over dried hot coconut husks or embers to make dainty, sushi-sized morsels of pleasure. Porous banana leaves are perfect for grilling or steaming as they retain natural flavors while imparting their own special aroma. The wrapping is an art in itself that has to be mastered, distinguishing a great *pepes* from an ordinary one. The taste depends on the obtainable fish and spice ingredients peculiar to a particular fishing area, heightened by the distinct fragrance of the leaves. Served in its unfolded, organic banana leaf wrapper, *pepes be pasih* is often eaten at Balinese wedding ceremonies. Steamed prawns and rice paddy or river crabs are also wrapped and cooked in a banana leaf roll.

Local fish-based specialties such as *sambal udang* (plump prawns braised in a red, spicy, soupy sauce of chilies, onion, kaffir lime and coconut cream), *cumi-cumi panggang* (marinated grilled squid), fried seafood cakes, squid with green papayas and *ikan bakar* (whole fish or fish fillets marinated and grilled; mahi-mahi is very popular in Lovina) are cooking miracles emanating from Balinese waters. Another Balinese mainstay, *tambusan be pasih* (*tambusan* means grilled) is moist, slowly roasted, sliced whole mackerel or catfish fillets grilled and served. Locals in Kalibukbuk, Lovina, construct makeshift grills right on the beach powered by burning coconut husks inside a clay basin. A well-worn iron grill tray is placed directly over the embers and the fresh catch (snapper, mahi-mahi, tuna) is grilled in minutes under the shade of a beachside *waringan* tree.

Jimbaran beach transforms itself into a sunset-viewing strip of al fresco *warung* every evening where fresh seafood is grilled on open coconut husk fires under the stars. The numerous competing cafes begin to set up rows of tables and chairs along the beach in the late afternoon to greet the nightly influx of diners. Fire-ready whole red and white snapper, grouper, catfish, tuna, barracuda, king fish, barramundi, prawns, king bamboo prawns, squid, mussels, crabs, mud crabs, clams, giant clams, lobster and scallops are sold by 100-gram weights at the grilled seafood *warung* strung along the bay. Exquisite salty, mineral flavors are typically found in fresh shellfish such as oysters and to a lesser extent in grilled seafood. The marine splendors are served with very generous portions of steamed white rice, garlicky *kangkung* water spinach, peanuts, roast potatoes, a delicious *sambal* sauce and watermelon slices for dessert.

Grilled Tuna

(TONGKOL WITH SAMBAL MATAH)

Indonesia is a wide, curving archipelago with more sea than land. It follows that fresh ocean fish play an important role in the local Balinese diet. Tuna is plentiful in all coastal areas and the waters around Bali contain different species of tuna, weighing from three to five kilograms. This recipe for tuna sambal (sauce) matah (raw) can be made with tuna (Eastern little tuna or wavy-backed skipjack tuna are common), or any other meaty fish. Tongkol is available in Balinese markets, usually already cut into thick red steaks. Here, the bright, simple flavor of fork-soft, locally caught tuna is combined with a typical raw Balinese sauce.

Guided and motivated by Ni Wayan Murni and local Balinese chef and Dive Inn owner Made Janur, readers can embark on a private, armchair, at-home Balinese seafood eating escapade! This tuna with sambal matah recipe empowers and enlightens enthusiastic restaurant chefs, gourmet travelers,

*cooking aficionados and everyday, down-home family cooks in the heartland
who want to explore and experiment with new and unusual aquatic specialties.*

*Grilled Tuna Steak recipe courtesy of Ni Wayan Murni, Murni's Warung,
Campuhan-Ubud, 2006.*

6 fresh tuna steaks

Before grilling the tuna steaks, prepare the *sambal matah* (recipe below).

Then sprinkle the tuna steaks with lime juice, salt and freshly ground black
pepper and grill to taste. (The tuna steaks can be fried quickly on both sides
instead.)

Serve hot with steamed white rice, *kangkung pelecing* and *sambal matah* on
the side.

Sambal Matah

*Sambal matah is one of Bali's most frequently eaten, sparkling clean, delight-
fully fragrant sambal accompaniments, proudly served to add extra pleasure
and taste to almost any meal. Easy to prepare and healthy, it is always eaten
raw, and is always made and enjoyed completely fresh, right before consumption. It is my personal favorite, and I always request sambal matah with every
meal I eat on the island of the gods, from gado-gado to grilled mackerel.*

*Sambal matah recipe courtesy of Made Janur and Iloh, Janur Dive Inn,
Jl. Laviana-Banyualit, Lovina, October 18, 2008.*

24 shallots, cut into thin slices
6 red chilies
pinch of Masoko chicken stock powder
pinch of sea salt
3 tbs coconut oil
6 kaffir limes, juice and grated rind

Mix all the ingredients in a bowl except for the limes.

Cut the limes in half and drizzle the juice over the mixture. Add some grated
rind as well. Combine everything by hand and serve on a small plate.

Serves 4–6.

Pepes Ikan

(FISH WRAPPED IN BANANA LEAF ROLL)

Pepes ikan, wrapped in an elongated, loaf-shaped banana leaf bundle, is a common food item throughout the Indonesian archipelago. It is one of the most popular fish preparations in Bali, universally cooked and eaten at home and in local warung. Pepes ikan (pepes be pasih in Balinese) consists of highly spiced boiled mackerel, coral trout, tuna, snapper, mahi-mahi, sea fish (languan) or any other available meaty fish wrapped in a banana leaf and placed on the grill for cooking (traditionally grilled over dried coconut husks). It can be served with ceremonial nasi kuning and urab vegetables.

Recipe courtesy of Made Janur and Chef Iloh, Janur Dive Inn, Jl. Laviana-Banyualit, Lovina, October 18, 2008.

6 mackerel fillets
18 garlic cloves, cut into pieces
6 pieces of ginger, each 1 in (2.5 cm)
6 pieces orange turmeric
6 orange chilies, 1½ inch (4 cm) long
6 tsp sea salt
⅓ cup coconut oil
3 tomatoes, cut into wedges
6 candlenuts
Masoko chicken powder

Boil the mackerel fillets in a pan of water.

Pound the other ingredients into a wet paste in a mortar and pestle. Add a small amount of Masoko chicken powder for additional flavor.

Remove the mackerel from the water when tender, debone it and place large chunks of the fish (do not mash it) in the mortar with the spices. Use a spatula to turn the fish over and over so that it is covered with the spice paste.

Place the fish on a rectangular piece of banana leaf and fold the leaf around it to form a rolled packet. Secure both ends of the roll with bamboo stick toothpicks.

Place the banana leaf parcel directly on a grill (either indoors on a gas stove or outdoors on a dried coconut husk-fired brazier) for 5 minutes.

Serves 4–6.

TOP In this colorful Balinese ceremonial procession, women carry *banten tegeh*, tall, layered fruit offering towers.

ABOVE Luscious, shiny *babi guling* or spit-roasted suckling pig is a special sacred ritual offering.

RIGHT Temple priests dispense Bali's favorite drink, Holy Water (*tirta*), at the Cokorda Rai ceremony, Ubud.

1

LEFT This woman uses a traditional stone mortar and pestle to prepare spicy vegetarian *urab* in the Warung Dolphin kitchen.

BELOW A bamboo basket of uncooked rice (*beras*) for sale in the local morning market.

BOTTOM Mr and Mrs Dolphin create food magic in the kitchen of Warung Dolphin, Jl. Laviana Banyualit, Lovina.

LEFT Nyoman from Pemuteran and Budi from Lovina in traditional Balinese headdresses (*udeng*) illustrate the charm of Bali's people.

Top *Gado-gado*, lightly steamed fresh mixed vegetables with peanut sauce, soybean *tempe*, tofu, egg and *krupuk* crackers.

Above Succulent *saté ayam* (chicken satay) grilling on a brazier, served with a conical mound of white rice.

Right *Bubur mebasa*, a delicious Balinese breakfast porridge containing a secret scented leaf.

ABOVE Driver Wayan Sarma at a typical local *warung*, Taro village, Tegallalang.

RIGHT Silo and Santo eat lunch and smoke *kretek* clove cigarettes at a small side alley *warung* in Lovina.

BELOW Driver Made eats popular roast pork (*babi guling*) and rice for lunch, Singaraja.

RIGHT Wayan Sarma enjoys a glass of coffee at a simple village *warung*.

4

TOP Grilling and fanning *saté kambing* (goat satay) at a roadside stall in Lovina.

ABOVE The Bakso Malang mobile street cart sells *bakso* (meatballs in soup) to local customers.

RIGHT This RW "Kong" stall on the main road near Singaraja sells *saté anjing* (dog satay).

LEFT Flavorful chicken satay (*saté ayam*) partnered with rice and a light salad.

BELOW A couple grill *saté ayam* at a makeshift enterprise along the main road, Penestenan, Ubud.

BELOW *Nasi bungkus*, rice and *sambal* sauce wrapped in banana leaves, is a popular early morning breakfast in Lovina.

ABOVE A *jagung bakar* (roasted corn) seller fanning ripe ears of corn on the grill, Singaraja.

6

Left *Jaja uli*, steamed pink dessert cakes, drying in the sun in a huge barrel, Tegallalang.

Below A roasted peanut vendor with raw, unshelled peanuts (*kacang*) in V-shaped slings on a shoulder pole (*kander*).

Left *Urutan* (pork sausage) sellers at Kuta Beach entice local beach women with home-made sausages and banana leaf packets of rice.

TOP Women thresh rice grains in dry, post-harvest rice fields, Karang Dalem village.

ABOVE A farmer with a large bamboo basket in a lush emerald green rice field, Pacung, northern Bali.

RIGHT This man weaves a palm leaf basket to be used as a bird cage.

RIGHT A smiling *ibu* sells handmade leaf hats against a backdrop of Bali's legendary rice terraces.

BELOW A traditional thatched roof rice storage granary (*lumbung*) in Junjungan village.

BOTTOM A local farmer uses a machete to harvest wild leaves (*kangkung*) in the field.

Top Women examine the early morning tuna catch from a traditional outrigger fishing boat (*jukung*), Mushroom Bay, Nusa Lembongan.

Above Buying and selling fresh tuna on the beach.

Top left *Sayur pakis*, fresh green fiddlehead ferns for making fern tips in garlic sauce, Candi Kuning market.

Top right A basic home-based tofu factory with a goat pen to one side, Seririt.

Left Soft vegetarian fritters fried on the sidewalk, with chilies on the side, Pedawa village, Buleleng.

Below A traveling sunset seller cuts up fried spring rolls (*lumpia*) to be served with tiny green chilies, Tuban Beach.

RIGHT An itinerant *jamu* seller bearing a basket of colorful liquid health tonics. Lovina.

BELOW Raw *daluman* vine leaves (*daun cincau*), when mixed with water produce a gelatinous mass.

BOTTOM LEFT A tripod of sweetness: jade green *daluman* chunks, brown palm sugar syrup and white roasted coconut milk.

BOTTOM RIGHT Waitress Jero prepares the deliciously sweet, rural village drink *daluman*.

ABOVE Mr Sideman holding a bunch of ripe *pisang raja* (king bananas), Lovina.

TOP LEFT Workers with freshly picked local black table grapes en route to a winery, Seririt.

ABOVE Exotic equatorial fruits: mangosteen, rambutan, salak, mango, pineapple and banana.

RIGHT A sidewalk fruit seller hawks baskets of odiferous spiky durian—the king of fruits—Tegal-lalang.

13

TOP Pak Made Paten rotates coffee beans in a drum as he roasts them at his home compound business, Lungsiakan.

ABOVE Roasting coffee beans in a clay frying pan over a traditional wood-fired stove.

RIGHT Ibu Paten proudly holds a bamboo tray of freshly home-roasted coffee beans.

LEFT A woman pounding raw coffee beans using a traditional *lu* (pole) and *lesung* (mortar).

BELOW LEFT Wayan Sarma sipping élite *kopi luak* (civet cat coffee), Amertha Yoga Agricultural Farm.

BELOW Pure farm-fresh Kopi Bali in a nubby burlap bag gift sack.

BOTTOM A rare—and expensive—cup of *kopi luak* with classic coffee grinds around the rim.

15

ABOVE Sada, an ever-smiling beach massage lady, weaves *ketupat* rice casings while waiting for customers, Kuta Beach.

TOP RIGHT The casings are intricately woven from fresh young coconut leaves.

TOP MIDDLE The completed *ketupat tipepengabian* or *sirikan* (breasts and legs) offering for an upcoming ceremony.

RIGHT *Ketupat* rice cakes and boiled eggs in a food offering basket for the Cokorda Rai ceremony, Ubud.

16

CHAPTER FOURTEEN

The Perils of Penyu: Ritual and Dietary Turtle Meat

---≠---

Bali's underwater wonderland provides a perilous sanctuary for five of the world's seven remaining species of marine turtle: *penyu lekang* (olive ridley), *penyu hijau* (green), *penyu sisik* (hawksbill), penyu *tempayan* (loggerhead), *penyu belimbing* (leatherback) and *penyu pipih* (flatback). These sea turtles, hundred million-year-old remnants from the age of dinosaurs, are poised on the precipice of permanent species extinction. Despite a 1979 CITES ban on international trade in endangered green sea turtles and their products, Bali's turtles are still exploited for food, tortoise shell jewelry (tortoise shell is often cruelly removed from live turtles), handicrafts, turtle oil for cosmetics and mounted taxidermy displays. Flouting urgent worldwide conservation efforts, there is still open slaughter. Local shops continue to sell turtle shell artefacts and whole polished turtle shells near Bali's turtle tourist venues. The sale, possession and consumption of turtle meat was further prohibited by local legislation in 1990 and 1999 (Indonesian Government Act No. 7 on the Preservation of Wild Flora and Fauna), but the laws are randomly and inconsistently enforced. Bold illegal traders kill 30,000 wild (indigenous and imported) juvenile sea turtles every year in Bali, 6,000 of them ritually sacrificed in religious ceremonies as symbols of fertility, productivity, steadfastness and immortality). Majestic hundred-year-old adult turtles are also slaughtered while still alive and their meat vended covertly at local markets and in village *warung*.

Although turtles are considered sacred on the island of the gods—the second incarnation of the Hindu deity Lord Wisnu was as a turtle—turtle meat has a long, ingrained history of secular and religious usage as food. Bali-Hindu religious and cultural practices present unique and daunting obstacles to turtle conservation. Bali's most sacred ceremonial cuisine is created for important religious holidays such as Galungan and for life cycle or ritual occasions like weddings, tooth filings, cremations and temple anniversaries. Many of these occasions have traditionally called for mandatory turtle meat as an ingredient. There are numerous ways of cooking and presenting turtle.

Southern Bali has its own special spice and coconut-driven turtle blood and turtle meat ritual meal called *ngebat* or *ebat* (meaning chopped up). Its five requisite dishes are displayed on a woven coconut or banana leaf mat. At the heart is *lawar penyu* (turtle *lawar*), a tartare or raw meat dish made from slivers of turtle meat cut from boiled turtle cartilage mixed with fresh blood, chopped fresh spices and hand-grated coconut. *Urab* (ground coconut, turtle meat and *kekalas*, heated, thickened coconut milk with turmeric spice), *geguden* (pounded turtle meat, *kekalas* and boiled starfruit leaves), *jejeruk* (coarsely grated coconut mixed with *kekalas*) and *serandu* (leftover coconut milk pulp, blood, meat and spices) complete the sacrificial turtle quintet. Another dish, *serapah*, is made from turtle viscera (liver, intestines, stomach, lungs, heart and cartilage) boiled in a huge cauldron and then combined with turtle meat and turtle skin and cooked with herbs, spices and chilies. It is then grilled and cut into slices for serving. Thick *komoh* soup is also sourced from the remains of the turtle, including its blood, and spices.

The slaughter of sea turtles to make ritual food is largely confined to southern coastal Bali. Here, where turtles are readily available, their meat is the preferred choice for *ebat* whereas pigs are usually utilized inland. Turtles are generally killed at home for use in a ceremony, particularly on the day before Galungan. An offering is first made to the turtle begging its forgiveness for what is about to ensue. The helpless turtle is placed in a concave, crescent-shaped cement hole excavated in the ground in the backyard, specifically designed for this purpose. The turtle is flipped over onto its back and a knife is used to cut all the way around the perimeter of the turtle in order to pull it out of its shell in one entire piece. Traditionally slaughtered whole while still alive, the suffering turtles scream, make other noises and cry watery tears from tear ducts during this horrific, inhumane process. The Balinese insist that if you kill the turtle first by slitting its throat, as is done with pigs, the meat will not taste as good. Turtle meat does not keep long and must be consumed soon after it is cooked.

Miguel Covarrubias provided the first sobering Western description of traditional Balinese turtle cuisine in the 1930s: "On the road coming from the seaport of Benua we often met men from Belaluan staggering under the weight of a giant turtle flapping its paddles helplessly in space, and then we knew they were preparing for a feast. For days before the banquet, four or five stupefied turtles crawled under the platforms of the *bale banjar* awaiting the fateful moment when, in the middle of the night, the *kulkul* would sound to call the men to the gruesome task of sacrificing them. A sea-turtle possesses a strange reluctance to die. For many hours after the shell is removed and the flaps and head are severed from the body, the viscera continue to pulsate hysterically, the bloody members twitch weirdly on the ground, and the head snaps furiously. The blood of the turtle is carefully collected and thinned with lime juice to prevent coagulation. By dawn, the many cooks and assistants are chopping the skin and meat with heavy chopping axes (*blakas*) on sections of tree-trunks (*talanan*), grating coconuts, fanning fires, boiling or steaming great quantities of rice, and mashing spices in clay dishes (*tjobek*) with wooden pestles (*pengulakan*)."

Covarrubias recorded five customary methods of preparing ceremonial, turtle meat specialties: *lawar* (skin and flesh finely chopped and mixed with spices and raw blood), *getjok* (chopped meat with grated coconut and spices), *urab gadang,* meaning green in Balinese (chopped meat with grated coconut and spices cooked in tamarind leaves), *kiman* (chopped meat and grated coconut cooked in coconut cream) and special *saté lembat. Saté lembat* or *leklat,* essential to ritual banquets, is a difficult to make skewered delicacy of turtle meat and spices kneaded with coconut cream. It begins as raw turtle meat, which must first be chopped and then pounded in a large rice mortar to reduce it to a thick, paste-like consistency. Mixed with grated coconut, thick *santen* (rich coconut cream) and spices, it is wound around the end of a thick bamboo stick and roasted over charcoal. *Saté lembat* is presented with an equal number of ordinary *saté* (little dice-size pieces of meat strung through bamboo sticks) and either eaten dry or with a sauce.

Friendly Belaluan village cooks offered Miguel and Rose Covarrubias their closely guarded, prized *saté lembat* recipe: "Take a piece of hard, brown, ripe coconut skin (found in between the shell and the meat), roast it over the coals, peel it off, and grind it in a mortar. To prepare the sauce, brown some red pepper, garlic, and red onions in a frying-pan, and then mix with black pepper, ginger, turmeric, nutmeg, cloves, *sra* (pungent fermented fish paste), aromatic, ginger-like roots *isen* (greater galangal) and *tjekoh or cekuh* (lesser galangal or resurrection lily), *ketumbah* (a variety of peppercorn), *ginten*, and salt. [*Ginten* is an herb used in cooking and grows from the fruit of the tree. It looks like a small grain of rice with the skin still on and has an authentic smell like oregano.] Mash the sauce with the toasted coconut skin and fry the mixture until half done. Combine finely chopped red turtle meat (without fat) and the sauce in a bowl, using two and a half times as much meat as sauce. Add one whole grated coconut and mix well with enough *santen* (thick coconut cream) to obtain a consistency that will adhere to bamboo brochette sticks (not too dry or too wet). Knead for an hour and a half as if making bread. (Bamboo sticks ten inches long by a half-inch thick should be made ready, rounded at one end.) Take a ball of the paste in the fingers and cover the end of the stick with it, beginning at the top and working down gradually, turning it all the time to give it the proper shape, then roast over coals until done. Pork, duck, or chicken *lembat* are commonly cooked for modest feasts, but turtle remains the favorite of the Balinese of Denpasar. Live turtles are expensive, about twenty dollars for a good-sized one." Covarrubias passed on more 1930s Balinese cooking and social lore: "'He has to eat banana leaves,' is used to emphasize an individual's extreme poverty, but a delicious dish and a great delicacy is *kekalan*, made of tender banana leaf shoots cooked in turtle blood and lime juice!"

Contemporary consumption of turtle meat on Bali conjures up frightening, ancient forces of animism, hunger, anarchy and superstition. After the October 12, 2002 bombing of the Sari Club and Paddy's Bar in Kuta, the Balinese turned, as always, to their priests, for a karma-based theological explanation rather than a political rationale for these horrific events. Many people in Bali believed that it was divine punishment for their sins and for not making the correct offerings to the gods. The gods were angry. All over Bali, villagers constructed elaborate offerings to ask for forgiveness and to repent their mistakes. Other Balinese believed that the Kuta conflagration was related to a turtle incident in Klungkung regency, where a gigantic turtle was found by the seashore a few months earlier. When the Balinese see something strange, they normally consult their priests before taking action. This time they precipitously killed it. It is believed that the peaceful, primeval reptile was the mythical south Javanese princess Ratu Pantai Selatan who wields white magical powers. She was searching for 200 *panjak*, lower caste devotees or retainers who traditionally showed respect to and helped the kings in old Bali, and was killed before she could find the followers. Many people believed that she would take revenge.

Wanton turtle genocide displeases the gods and provokes the authorities. It is now illegal to kill turtles for any reason and individuals must seek special permission from their *banjar* to obtain a turtle for a religious rite. Legal safeguards and convoluted bureaucratic roadblocks restrict the acquisition and consumption of ritual turtle meat for village or household ceremonies. If an individual family or a village needs a turtle as a ceremonial food component, they must first get a written, signed recommendation from their traditional village chief. A village representative then has to present the certificate to a village head in Serangan Island, known as turtle island, or Nusa Dua, who then approaches the Bali government on their behalf to issue a special permit. The villager then brings the permit to official turtle sellers, fishermen concentrated on Serangan Island, who are allowed to vend a certain number of turtles to the Balinese for ceremonies and cyclical festivals. Skilled Bugis traders from Sulawesi, resident on Pulau Serangan, supply the green turtles needed by the Balinese on festive days. It is considered good luck for the vendor to sell a turtle even though the Bugis community itself does not eat turtle since Islam prohibits its followers from eating animals living in two worlds, water and land. The turtles are purchased from big fishing ships. As a conservation measure, only older turtles are used. Young turtles remain free to reproduce and repopulate Bali's decimated wild turtle population. Because of the scarcity, expense (a 30 kilogram turtle can cost Rp.3,000,000), difficulty and complex legal strictures involved, turtles are less frequently eaten in the villages now as either secular or religious food. Turtle satay is still utilized in Balinese religious rites, but for small ceremonies the Balinese will ordinarily substitute pork, chicken or duck. A holy man (priest) will advise them if a turtle is absolutely required, usually for larger ceremonies or an island-wide celebration at the mother temple, Pura Besakih, when many different animal species are assembled for sacrifice.

Although customary rituals dictate the use of turtle meat from both the turtle body and the head, in 2003 a leading Balinese high priest, Ida Pedanda Gede Ngurah Kaleran, stated that he could find no stipulation in ancient Bali-Hindu literature mandating the use of turtle meat in ritual practices. A venerated high priest from Sanur also spoke out against the turtle trade, stating that "It is not necessary to sacrifice turtles for ceremonies, but that it is a good excuse to slaughter turtles as their meat is delicious and only here to make the belly happy." He also claimed that by making simple *ketupat* (compressed rice cakes) in the shape of turtles, a common practice in Jimbaran, one would achieve exactly the same religious result as when butchering live turtles. Another respected Balinese priest offered a similar holy solution to this culinary conundrum. Instead of using a live turtle, one can draw an equally effective symbol of the turtle instead, especially as power-laden protective drawings are commonly made in Bali for the practice of both white and black magic. Badung regency religious authorities estimated that only seventy turtles are needed for customary and religious purposes in the regency each month, leading to hopes that Balinese ceremonial needs can be accommodated without sacrificing the future of the species.

Although turtle slaughter, consumption and cuisine are banned and turtles are under, albeit haphazard, government protection, people can still find *penyu* if they want it. Turtles are still being sold for daily, non-ceremonial purposes in response to a brisk, covert demand among the local population for turtle meat, turtle steak, turtle soup and turtle eggs. Since turtles can only be obtained for ceremonies, turtle hungry villagers will lie to officials about needing a *penyu* for an upcoming ritual. A supermarket in Bali's capital city of Denpasar continued to sell turtle eggs on its shelves until 1999 in clear violation of government regulations protecting an endangered species. The management agreed to stop selling the eggs after a visit by the local office of the World Wildlife Fund. A particular restaurant near the Dewa Ruci statue in Kuta continues to openly offer turtle as well as snake meat on its menu. Some of this still active turtle supply hails from Balinese waters while the rest comes in illegally on overloaded ships from other Indonesian islands, such as southern Sulawesi, Lombok, Java, Madura, Sumbawa, Flores and faraway Irian Jaya. The Balinese insist that the taste of Bali turtle is much better and that they can tell the difference. To them, Sulawesi turtle has a watery taste.

Market forces increasingly militate against clandestine turtle meat and egg consumption in Bali. It has become so expensive now that people are turning away from turtle meat. Pork frequently replaces or supplements turtle in local street food presentations. Enterprising sellers in Kuta, Jimbaran and Sanur fan sizzling satay sticks squatting down by the side of the road in the late afternoon. In the past, their satays were predominantly turtle meat. Uluwatu car park sellers found a ready market for *satay penyu* (barbecued turtle meat) among Balinese drivers and visitors from Asia. Today, they mostly hawk pork satays, still claiming that they are turtle meat to unwitting customers. They mix one-third turtle with two-thirds pork and sell it as pure turtle. Genuine turtle satays can be discerned by the particular smell of the smoke and the color of the meat. Local police periodically join the campaign to enforce national regulations protecting endangered green turtles. They sweep through local markets and arrest satay vendors who offer undercover police officers fresh turtle meat kebabs. Subsequent interrogation, however, often reveals that the sellers are defrauding customers into paying high "forbidden turtle delicacy" retail prices for what were, in fact, very ordinary skewers of Balinese raised beef!

Turtle conservation on Bali involves a long-term, two-pronged attack against deeply ingrained, centuries-old dietary turtle meat consumption and the continuing illegal Indonesian trade in a highly endangered species. Bali's steadily declining wild turtles have a small, intrepid band of non-governmental agencies (Profauna) and guardian angel expatriates fighting against all odds for their survival. One such person is Chris Brown, founder of Reef Seen Aquatics Dive Centre and its onsite Turtle Hatchery Project, who launched a rescue plan in the peaceful, off the beaten tourist track village of Pemuteran in northern Bali. It served as a much copied model for coastal wildlife preservation work in Bali. Chris designed a successful cash-for-eggs program to reduce turtle egg consumption (many newly laid eggs were prematurely lost to human and dog predation) and simultaneously opened up an important new income stream for local Balinese. Rather than digging up and dining on turtle eggs, the Balinese could sell them to his hatchery for the above market price of Rp.1,750 per piece. Formerly a threat to green, olive ridley and hawksbill turtles, area fisherman now scour the beach for freshly deposited eggs every day in the nesting season to trade them in at Proyek Penyu for eventual ocean release.

By compensating local people for changing their harvesting and eating habits and abstaining from part of their traditional maritime diet, Brown gave them an alternate eco-friendly way of earning money as well as an incentive not to kill the "fragile food species" that lays these precious eggs. Another savior, Heinz Von Holzen, celebrity master chef and proprietor of the beautiful Bumbu Bali Restaurant in Tanjung Benoa, is also at the dangerous, sometimes violent, forefront of turtle preservation efforts on Bali. Heinz initiated his own program, Peduli Penyu ("Take Care of Turtles"), to rescue and rehabilitate live green turtles and turtle eggs sold by Javanese fishermen at seaside fish and produce markets in Jimbaran and Tanjung Benoa, the epicenter of Bali's illegal, archipelago-wide, imported sea turtle trade. His staff continuously purchase any turtle eggs or adult individuals discovered for sale. These are transferred to Heinz's egg hatchery composed of restaurant holding pools for eventual release back to the ocean. Balinese community involvement is the way to save this severely endangered species from their traditional local fate as food and from the brink of extinction.

The author and the publisher do not advocate or condone the slaughter or eating of any species of live turtle. Chicken can be easily substituted for turtle in the recipe that follows without sacrificing either flavor or more sea turtles. The recipe is merely included to illustrate its authentic cultural and historical content and its role in the traditional Balinese secular and religious diet.

Serapah Penyu

(TURTLE)

The Balinese inhabitants of Nusa Lembongan used to go out in slow boats to fish for turtles but there are very few turtles left in their native waters. To obtain turtles now, men from Lembongan must travel approximately two hours by boat to Bali to buy a whole, living turtle and bring it back to Lembongan. They usually purchase a medium sized turtle weighing 10 kilograms, which costs Rp.500,000 (US$50 in 2012). Lembongan villagers incur additional costs to obtain a turtle from Bali. They must pay for the round trip interisland boat, plus transportation while in Bali to Benoa Harbor or Serangan Island where turtles can still be purchased with a permit, or bargained for without one. Once home, they kill the live turtle with a knife. They flip the turtle over on its back, cut all around the shell and take the meat out while the poor suffering creature is still alive and is crying out in pain. The turtle will be cooked that same day. Turtles are only procured and eaten for important ritual occasions such as Galungan, Kuningan, wedding ceremonies, a cremation or a toothfiling ceremony.

Recipe courtesy of I Wayan Sudirna, chef for two years at the Tanis Villas, Nusa Lembongan. Bali-Hindu religion, culture and cooking reign supreme on small, quiet Nusa Lembongan, Bali's sister island. Wayan's grandfather, the village cooking specialist, had originally taught him how to cook. The grandfather used to make the traditional food for all the village ceremonies. When Wayan was fifteen years old, he spent one year learning ceremonial cooking from his grandfather by watching what he did during ritual festivals.

The Tanis Villas is a very friendly, beautifully landscaped boutique hotel on the powdery white sands of peaceful, unspoiled Nusa Lembongan. It also enjoys a spectacular cross-island view of Bali's most sacred mountain, Gunung Agung, framed in a holy ring of impenetrable clouds. Tanis Villas, Mushroom Bay, Nusa Lembongan. www.tanisvillas.com, December 2011.

4½ lb (2 kg) turtle
1 whole young coconut
5¼ quarts (5 liters) coconut milk, two squeezes, medium dilution
3½ oz (100 g) small hot red chilies
7 oz (200 g) shallots
3½ oz (100 g) garlic

3½ oz (100 g) turmeric
3½ oz (100 g) ginger
7 oz (200 g) galangal
3 kaffir lime leaves
1¾ oz (50 g) lemongrass
1 tsp sea salt
1 tsp chicken powder
1 tsp black pepper

Boil the turtle in water for about one hour until tender.

Cut the turtle into half inch (1.5 cm) cubes.

Grill the young coconut for 5 minutes and then chop it into small, cube-shaped pieces.

To make the spice sauce, peel and chop the fresh spices into small pieces and then fry in coconut oil.

Simmer the coconut milk, lemongrass stalks, spice sauce and kaffir lime leaves for 5 minutes.

Stir fry the turtle and chopped coconut in coconut oil for two minutes and then season with salt, pepper and chicken powder.

Add the turtle mixture to the coconut milk ingredients and simmer a further 5 minutes.

Serves 4–6.

CHAPTER FIFTEEN

Bali: Emerald Vegetarian Garden of Eden

———— ≠ ————

FERTILE SOIL AND HIGH ANNUAL RAINFALL have long supported intensive agriculture in Bali, which remains the foundation of the island's economy. The thick ground coating of ash from Bali's active or dormant volcanoes is packed with an abundance of plant-friendly chemicals and trace elements. Past and present flows of volcanic mud (*lahar*) leave foot-deep layers of rich topsoil in their wake. Because of the enhanced soil quality, the Balinese can grow things at practically every elevation. Every inch of arable land is farmed. Vegetables are squeezed in among fruit trees, banana trees and coconut palms. Fruits and vegetables thrive in almost all backyard gardens. Family farms are inserted everywhere, from the lower slopes of sacred mountains to lush pockets of cascading rice field terraces. The small, individual, household nature of food production on Bali means that fruits and vegetables are picked at random whenever they are needed, or whenever they are ripe, and distributed locally. It is only two days from vine to busy compound kitchen.

In Bali, vegetables are simply called *sayur*, and all green vegetables are colloquially called *sayur hijau*, meaning green vegetable. Individual names and species are unimportant and are often not known. The vegetable dishes themselves are generically referred to as *jukut* (meaning grass or herb), including Bali's characteristically rich, thick soupy stews. Vegetables form a major part of the Balinese diet and are served with every meal. The Balinese normally steam or boil their vegetables, fruits, leaves and beans, mix them with grated coconut, spices or spicy sauces, garnish them with fried shallots and serve them with rice, meat and other dishes. Vegetables are never eaten on their own except as a side dish alongside rice. The Balinese prefer to eat them warm but they often cannot do so because there are no fixed household meal times. Vegetables are always well cooked, indeed limp or soft, and are never eaten raw, except for cucumber. Tomatoes represent a foreign flavor and were first introduced to Indonesia by the Dutch. They are grown in the cool mountainous highlands of Java and Bali. Tomatoes are condiments in Bali and are not commonly eaten alone as a vegetable or fruit, and are primarily used to make a hot chili and tomato *sambal* sauce. Small reddish, yellowish or green tomatoes are for sale daily in the traditional markets, ready to be added to *sambal terasi*. *Acar* (a colorful, piquant, red, orange and green pickled vegetable side dish with a sharp vinegar flavor) is a raw salad facsimile. Cucumber cut into thin matchsticks, carrot sticks, pineapple, round shallot slivers and whole hot chilies luxuriate in a slippery shield of sugar, rice vinegar, ginger, knotted lemongrass and sea salt. *Sayur kalas* are vegetables in coconut milk and spices, while *sayur mesanten* are vegetables braised in coconut milk. Chinese origin *cap cay* (pronounced chap chay), a descendant of mixed stir fried Chinese vegetables, appears on every Indonesian menu in Bali. *Timun mesanten* (cucumber in coconut milk) is refreshing. Scented spices, *sambal goreng* (fried chili seasoning), kaffir lime leaves, *suna-cekuh* or garlic-ginger paste (*suna* is garlic in Balinese, *cekuh* is lesser galangal), sea salt and roasted coconut milk turn these humble cucumber slices into a delectable Balinese vegetable dish.

Village markets (*pasar sayur*) are packed with garden fresh mounds of small red, hot orange and green chilies (milder, large red chili peppers are imported from neighboring Lombok), red shallots, tiny marble-like green, purple or white eggplant (turned into *terung tumis*, or stir-fried eggplant), frilly winged beans, mint green bitter melon, Chinese cabbages, local yellow Balinese carrots (*wortel*) from Bedugul, soybean and mung bean sprouts (*kacang hijau*), seaweed (farmed in Nusa Penida), and dependable local produce like morning glory (a twining vine with broad, heart-shaped leaves that bears large pale blue, pink, purple or white trumpet-shaped flowers that open in the morning.

Balinese cuisine is extraordinarily leaf (*daun*) heavy. Traditional markets and urban supermarkets have an overwhelming choice of leafy eccentricities, most notably frilly-leafed *bayam hijau* (green *bayam* or amaranth, with medicinal roots) that grows everywhere, *bayam daun singkong* (pointed cassava leaves) and *bayam potong* (large many-edged leaf pieces or slices). There are two main varieties of *bayam* in Indonesia, one with small leaves and the other with large. The leaves can be pointed or rounded and are light green, green or dark maroon red (*bayam merah*). Though often considered too ordinary, the nutritious vegetable can be cooked in soups, stir-fried, incorporated into wondrous wafer-thin tempura-like fried snack fritters or added to white rice. It is also a good source of vitamins A, B and C, calcium and iron.

Kacang panjang are thin, yard-long green or snake beans (*Vigna unguiculata*). *Jukut kacang panjang goreng* (stir-fried long beans) are a Balinese compound mainstay. Small red shallots, garlic cloves, red chilies, tomatoes, ginger, shrimp paste, *salam* leaves and sweet soy sauce turn these simple local beans (cut diagonally into shorter stubs) into an aromatic vegetarian banquet. The Balinese also cook and eat the leaves of the long beans (*daun kacang panjang*). Long, frilly, four-sided winged beans (*Psophocarpus tetragonolobus*; *klongkang* in Balinese, *kacang botor* and *kecipir* in Indonesian) are picked wild in or near the rice fields (*sawah*) and only occasionally appear in the market. Named for their angled, wing-like sides, they have a very clean, crisp taste and are best eaten when young, tender and light green in color. The beans are cut vertically, boiled, sliced and mixed with grated coconut and spices. They can also be braised in soy sauce, stir-fried with red and green chilies or cooked in a curry. The Balinese believe that their indigenous *klongkang* makes *sayur urab* particularly delicious. Winged beans also take full flight into a long bean salad with a coconut cream, vegetable spice paste, fried garlic and fried bird's eye chili-enlivened sauce crowned with crisp-fried fragrant shallots.

Serombotan, assorted mixed vegetables with grated coconut and hot sauce, is a delicacy of Klungkung regency in eastern Bali. The ingredients, typical of those grown in the area, include *kangkung*, spinach, cabbage, bean sprouts, long beans, winged beans, small round white eggplants and fried peanuts. The Balinese ordinarily do not make *serombotan* at home because it is too complicated and contains too many ingredients. Instead, they buy it in the traditional night market (*pasar malam*) in Denpasar where it is sold by Klungkung people. Although it is a common dish for Klungkung people, it is only available wherever they live in Bali. To make *serombotan*, the vegetables are cut into pieces, the eggplant is sliced and everything is lightly boiled. The sauce consists of freshly grated coconut combined with many spices (garlic cloves, fresh galangal, lesser galangal, big red Lombok chilies, small bird's eye chilies, shrimp paste, sugar and salt) ground into a paste with grated coconut added. For serving, the cooked vegetables are placed on a banana leaf and the spicy coconut sauce mixed in prior to eating. Fried peanuts can be sprinkled on top as a garnish. *Serombotan* can be eaten alone or with *ketupat* rice parcels or steamed white rice.

Bali's vegetarian palate pleasers reflect the full equatorial possibilities of Bali: green vegetable curry with sweet potato and eggplant, *tipat cantok* (boiled, sliced *ketupat* rice in a coconut leaf packet served with warm vegetables and peanut sauce) and *jukut rambanan* (made with mixed vegetables, shrimp paste and spices cooked with thick coconut sauce). *Jukut rambanan* usually consists of bamboo shoots, long green beans, cucumber, corn, spinach and sometimes young jackfruit. It is whipped into line with hot Balinese spices: chilies, garlic cloves, roasted shallots, greater galangal, *kemangi* leaf (hoary basil) and salt—and the twin trademarks of this particular dish—thick coconut milk (*santen*) and pungent *sambal terasi* (shrimp paste). Hoary basil, sometimes called lemon-scented basil, has slightly hairy pale green leaves and a peppery taste when chewed. It can be eaten either raw or cooked or used as a flavoring. Tasty round vegetable fritters are fabricated much more simply on ordinary *banjar* street corners by female vendors in small villages like Pedawa in Buleleng regency in northern Bali. Breaded with batter, fried in oil and dried in a clean white basket, the fritters (carrots, bean sprouts and flour) are eaten with tiny hot green chilies as a condiment. *Sambal goreng jepang* (choko in spicy coconut sauce) utilizes the pale green, pear-shaped, rib-skinned choko (or chayote), a tasteless watery member of the gourd family, native to Central America. The choko is peeled, cubed and then boiled and simmered with *salam* leaves, lemongrass stalk, white pepper, black pepper, hot spice paste and thick *santen* to create a soupy, viscous vegetable stew. A cheap, readily available vegetable in Bali, the choko (called *labu Jepang* or Japanese gourd or squash) propagates itself to the point of overabundance on rampant climbing vines in house gardens; the excess is fed raw to their cows and pigs. The Balinese also simply boil, steam or fry the smooth white-green-grayish flesh with pepper, chili, salt and garlic.

Gado-gado (*jukut mesantok* in Balinese) consists of an assortment of two or more very lightly steamed or parboiled fresh mixed vegetables, typically long green beans, cabbage, *kangkung*, carrots, cauliflower and bean sprouts, served with a tangy peanut sauce accompanied by hot steamed white rice. The visually appealing presentation includes other elements: crispy fried *tempe*, *tahu* (tofu), slices of *ketupat* rice cake, a boiled potato, a boiled egg, sliced cucumber, fried shallots and shrimp crackers. The Balinese rarely eat *gado-gado* at home but it is ladled out very inexpensively at most small *warung* in Bali or by street vendors, with aromatic peanut sauce, wrapped in a banana leaf to go. The Balinese have their own version of this classic Indonesian *gado-gado* specialty called *pecelan* (assorted vegetables with peanut sauce). In Bali, the vegetables are blanched in water instead of coconut milk and the peanut sauce (*base kacang*), ground by hand in a mortar and pestle, is served raw instead of cooked. Long beans, bean sprouts, spinach and cabbage, eaten lukewarm or cool, are dressed with a sauce of fried peanuts, garlic, bird's eye chilies, palm sugar, sweet soy sauce and lesser galangal. The vegetarian superstar is crowned with a finishing garnish of fried shallots and crushed, fried or roasted peanuts, with deep-fried *tempe* cakes on the side.

A feast for the palate as well as the eyes, *urab*, a mixture of cooked vegetables with grated coconut, is the star of vegetarian Bali. *Sayur urab* (or *jukut urab*) is a rich, pungent, spicy warm salad served at room temperature usually made with either one or two blanched, finely chopped seasonal green vegetables (long green beans, wild spinach leaves, Chinese cabbage, fern leaves or bean sprouts) combined with grated roasted coconut, chilies, kaffir lime, shallots, spices and Balinese fruit *sambal*. *Urab buncis* is a bean and coconut salad composed of five elements: red kidney beans (*kacang merah*), fragrant local leaves, freshly ground and fried spices, freshly roasted sweet chewy shredded coconut and fried *sambal*. The beans are first soaked in water for one hour and then fried to make them soft. They can also be kept in water overnight until they sprout, and are then fried or used as a vegetable in *nasi campur*.

To prepare this dish, the proper processing and handling of the coconut is paramount. The Balinese first roast a whole fresh coconut over a flame until it is charred, then clean the outer burnt skin by scraping it with a knife before shredding the sweet coconut flesh.

The Balinese gather many semi-wild local vegetables and glossy, leafy greens that grow at random or just below the surface in Bali's rich, lava-fertilized volcanic soil. Edible young shoots and leaves grace family compound trees and shrubs, while other greens border the lanes and edges of the rice fields. Local wild vegetables include shiny, dark green resurrection lily (lesser galangal) leaves, cassava plant bulbs and leaves, and acacia leaves (*pennata* and *farnesiana*), used in soups, curries, omelettes and stir fries. Abundant peanuts (groundnuts), maize and *kangkung* (water spinach, river spinach or water convolvulus (also known as water morning glory) keep Bali fed. *Kangkung* (*Ipomoea aquatica*) is an extremely popular semi-aquatic creeping tropical plant that grows in water and is used as a leaf vegetable. Since *kangkung* is cultivated across the island all year round, it is available at an affordable price. The Balinese love to eat their water or wet-soil grown *kangkung* with *sambal pelecing*, a very spicy Balinese sauce. Bali's trademark vegetable dish, *kangkung pelecing*, is made by hand mixing cooked spinach leaves and stems with a tomato chili sauce (white garlic, onion, tiny chilies, large red peppers, tomatoes, shrimp paste, shredded kaffir lime leaves and local sugar). *Kangkung pelecing* is commonly served with other dishes like grilled seafood. It is also served independently with white rice as a complete vegetarian meal.

Brightly colored young fern leaves and tips, blanched, boiled or steamed as *jukut paku*, are harvested wild by villagers or bought inexpensively in the market. They have a wonderful spinach-like flavor and an appealing texture. The Balinese use an edible, non-decorative species of marsh fern called *paku* (fern or bracken) *tanjung* (cape or promontory) (*Diplazium esculentum*) for cooking. Fern has an irresistible, fragrant earthiness. The Balinese choose to eat the young, tightly coiled fiddlehead frond (petal head), cooked as a vegetable or in a salad. *Urab pakis* (fern leaf coconut salad) is made with blanched fern leaves or tips, corn kernels, red chilies, grated coconut and fried shallots in a fried chili sauce (*sambal sereh tabia*) buttressed by kaffir lime leaf, lemongrass, salt, black peppercorns, palm sugar and lesser galangal. This delightful vegetable fern can also be blanched with chilies, shrimp paste, coconut oil, salt, black peppercorns, lesser galangal and fresh garlic in a crunchy Balinese specialty, *sayur pakis* (fern tips in garlic dressing). *Gulai paku* (curried fiddlehead ferns) is yet another fabulous use of the fern.

The *pete* or *petai* tree (*Parkia speciosa*) produces edible beans with a pungent odor called *pete kulit* (*kulit* means skin) in long, flat, wavy, bright green hanging seed pods. The beans are commonly called twisted cluster beans and stink beans. The seeds are the size and shape of plump almonds, with a rather distasteful smell, which permeates the entire body after they are eaten! An acquired taste, *petai* beans are best when combined with other strong-flavored foods such as garlic, chilies or dried shrimp. Widely eaten both raw and cooked, *petai* leaves are also harvested as animal fodder and as manure. (Scarce vegetarian resources must continually be diverted from the human consumption chain in Bali to feed domestic livestock. Men use machetes to cut grass daily to feed their cows, carrying the long green grasses home on their heads in huge round bamboo baskets. Beachside locals in Nusa Lembongan cut the leaves off the *pohon waru* (beach hibiscus) tree to feed their cows.)

An ubiquitous Balinese recipe staple, *daun salam* is sold fresh or as large dried-out leaves in a plastic bag for Rp.660. Bali's leafy pleasures also feature *daun kacang* (peanut leaves), papaya leaves, *daun jeruk* (orange leaves), long pointy-leaved *kangkung*, *kangkung akar* (leaves plus roots), *kangkung Lombok*, *gandola* (*Ceylon spinach*, similar to *kangkung* with softer leaves), *sawi ijo* or *hijau* (dark-colored mustard greens) and *ubi* leaves (an edible tuber or sweet potato). *Ubi*, a member of the nutritious underground tubers and roots family, includes purple-skinned sweet potatoes, red sweet potatoes, cassava, taro (*keladi*), wild taro, manioc, yam, buck yam and potato. *Labu* (bottle gourds, calabash, pumpkins and squashes) complement the natural vegetable bounty on Bali. *Labu* are available as *labu Jepang* (choko squash), *labu-air* (zucchini, squash, gourd for carrying water), *labu manis* (gourd), *labu merah* (red pumpkin), *labu kuning* (yellow pumpkin, also known as summer squash or marrow) and *labu ambon* (musk melon or winter squash). *Labu* grow in the villages on the ground to be eaten as either *sayur* (young *labu*) or as *jaja* (desserts), which utilize mature *labu*.

Cassava (*ketala pohon*) is a two- to four-meter-tall shrub (*Manihot esculenta*), also called manioc, that grows wild in Bali. A drought resistant crop, it is especially critical in places where the soil is relatively poor. In times of famine or food shortage, cassava, also called *singkong*, is used as a replacement for rice. Cassava leaves, cassava root and its derivative tapioca, are famous vegetables in Bali. However, the starchy, tuberous root, which has snowy white flesh inside, contains a toxic substance that, when eaten, can trigger the production of cyanide. It is edible only after being boiled or burned. It is then eaten plain (cubed or sliced) without spices. Young, tender cassava leaves are usually picked wild in the rice fields and thus appear infrequently in the market. To make them into *jukut urab*, the leaves are boiled then mixed with spices and grated coconut. The leaves, boiled and mixed with shredded coconut, also find their way into the Balinese kitchen as a delicious vegetable dish called *jukut daun ubi*. *Begala*, another typical, very popular and economical Balinese invention, also uses cassava plant leaves. They are boiled alone and then quickly stir-fried with fresh spices, roots, stalks and chilies.

Glatek is dry cassava, eaten as a carbohydrate in areas like the Bukit where rice cannot grow. The roots, which are crushed or chopped into small pieces and dried in the sun, can be kept for a long time and are carefully stored for times of need. *Glatek* is steamed like rice. Tapioca is a by-product of cassava flour production. The roots are cleaned, peeled, grated and ground to a pulp. The pulp is drained and squeezed dry and the remaining water allowed to evaporate, leaving behind fine-grained tapioca powder, which is processed into powder, flakes or pearls. The cassava tuber can also be sliced, dried in the sun until it is hard and then crushed into a powder for making sweet tapioca pudding. The Balinese make tapioca cake from the root by adding grated coconut. Pearl tapioca is made by pressing the moist starch through a sieve under pressure. Pearl tapioca is widely used in Asia to make tapioca pudding (with milk or cream added) and sweet drinks like bubble tea. Bubble tea consists of tea, milk, sugar and giant black tapioca balls that are gummy, soft and chewy. It is similar to Bali's beloved *es cendol*.

Several fruits are regularly cooked and prepared as vegetables. Papaya (*gedang*), jackfruit and mango in their unripe state are eaten as vegetables. *Gedang mekuah* (young papaya in spicy sauce) is an inexpensive village dish as papayas grow everywhere and are cheap in the markets. Unripe papaya has white flesh, whereas ripe papaya has orange-red flesh. The banana tree produces two vegetarian delights. At the tip of the inflorescence is a very large, maroon-colored bud called *pusuh biu* (banana navel) by the Balinese. After the bunched banana fruit forms along its stalk, the *pusuh biu* is cut off and eaten as a vegetable. Boiled banana stem (trunk) with spices, called *ares*, is also served as a vegetable. Young jackfruit braised in coconut sauce, ceremonially transformed into vegetarian jackfruit *lawar* or dressed up into jackfruit curry, and breadfruit, used as a non-ritual *lawar*, are other fruits-cum-vegetables. Young green papayas (*gedang*) gain creative favor as green papaya salad. They are also braised in coconut milk or cream to create a green papaya soup (*gedang mekuah*) or magically mixed into a finely diced *lawar gedang*. The Balinese reinvent their slightly bitter, tangy starfruit leaves as *daun jukut belimbing* (starfruit leaves with spicy sauce). The tropical weather and volcanic soil create pungent, spicy, vegetable varieties compared to produce grown at lower temperatures. The leaves of locally grown greens are fluffier in body and therefore appear larger in size. They are also loaded with more vitamins and nutrients.

Another singular Balinese vegetable dish is *urab bulung*, ocean-fresh green seaweed farmed in Bali's sister island Nusa Lembongan. It is enhanced with sweet roasted coconut, aromatic roasted galangal, fried shallots, lime, kaffir lime leaves, fried *sambal* sauce and (optional) red chilies. The main income for the people of dry, rocky Nusa Lembongan (population 5,000) is seaweed farming. Every family owns approximately 3–5 acres of seaweed farming "bed." One acre produces 150–200 kg of dried seaweed with each harvest. The villagers farm *Euchema cottomi*, a species of ocean algae, by tying the sprouting algae shoots to farming plots with rope and wooden stakes embedded in the seabed. It takes one month to grow to harvest-ready size and then three days to dry in the sun. During the harvest, new sprouts are returned to the seabed to begin the new crop and new sprouts are also collected from the seabed. The dried seaweed is kept in local storehouses, then taken to the mainland to be sold for export to America, Denmark, Japan and Holland. Nusa Lembongan's seaweed is used for medicines, food stabilizers, cosmetics and gelatin for ice cream. The coastal Balinese have collected wild seaweed (*rumput laut* or sea grass in Indonesian, *bulung* in Balinese) for centuries. Only recently has seaweed been treated as a commercial crop, planted, tended and harvested in offshore fields, mainly for export (to make *agar-agar*). On Bali's sister island neighbor, Nusa Ceningan, farmers tend seaweed plantations at the water's edge. Here, seaweed cuttings are tied to plastic frames left to float and sink in the local tides. The seaweed crop harvest supports almost the entire island.

Tofu (*tahu*), a firm, thick block of soybean curd, is the high-fiber protein staple of the Balinese masses. Considered the poor man's meat, tofu costs Rp.1,000 for five pieces in a top-knotted plastic bag at the market or, if bought separately, Rp.250 per piece. Two kinds of soybean (*Glycine max*) are common in Bali. White *tahu Bali* is soft and should sit in clear, not milky water to indicate that it is fresh. *Tahu Jawa* is firmer and mostly used for deep frying or stir-fried dishes. *Tahu takura*, flavored with turmeric and other spices, from Kediri, East Java, is very firm. It is sold in some supermarkets in Bali in a small woven basket. The soybean is one of the most important food sources in Indonesia, serving as the raw material for many traditional soybean-based, fermented and non-fermented foods such as *tempe* and *tahu*. Nutritious and inexpensive, warm, creamy, market-fresh white tofu can be fried (*tahu goreng*), braised into a bean curd stew (*tahu kalas*), skewered on a stick (*saté tahu*) or turned into fritters (*tahu bergedel*), sparingly seasoned and combined with eggs, flour and aromatic spices and fried a golden brown. Most tofu is manufactured in dark, dank factories in back alleys as a family home industry. The Balinese do not know how to do this processing themselves, so it is produced mainly by resident migrants from Java as a cottage industry. Traditional tofu manufacturing is all done by bare hand or foot. More modern factories may use less time-consuming machinery. Hard-working parents and gaggles of smiling children rotate in and out and between the steaming white vats of tofu as blackened pots boil and large flat pans of tofu cool and coagulate on rows of wooden wall shelves. Tofu establishments also typically combine non-vegetarian goat husbandry with tofu production as a second side investment. Furry black and white goats penned in rustic wooden enclosures can often be seen bleating loudly at the side of the sweltering tofu factory production floor.

Tempe (fermented soy bean cake) is another very popular local food. It consists of crunchy, shelled and boiled pale yellow soybeans held together by an introduced yeast culture which forms edible, fungus-like interlacing white (mold) tendrils throughout the cluster host. The *tempe* is imprisoned in a plastic bag or banana leaf to incubate for two or three days until it sets into a small, flat, hard, sliceable block. The Balinese buy labor-intensive eggshell white *tempe* as a thick slab wrapped in banana leaves or in small plastic sealed packages from village market stalls. The Bintang supermarket in Sanggingan-Ubud stocks *tempe daun* (leaf *tempe*), long, rectangular blocks of pale yellow *tempe* double bubble-wrapped inside a green banana leaf roll encased in protective plastic foil. Full of protein and fiber, *tempe* is usually fried with chilies, small dried fish, garlic, peanuts, sugar, spring onions, pepper and salt. *Tempe* also entices the Balinese taste buds as *tempe sambal nyuh* (fermented soy bean cake in turmeric sauce), boiled *tempe* used in a very common spicy hot curry with coconut milk, or grilled into a formidable satay format (*saté tempe*).

Sliced rectangular *tempe* matchsticks are an ever-present feature in *nasi campur* (mixed rice) and *gado-gado* (mixed vegetables). They also metamorphose into common crisp-fried *tempe goreng*. To make very simple *tempe goreng*, the *tempe* block is cut into thin slices, dipped in rice powder mixed with a little water to form a batter and fried. Salt plus a sliced lemon or orange leaf may be added to the rice powder. *Tempe goreng* constitutes a main course, eaten with rice or with *nasi campur* and vegetables. Another very essential sweet *tempe* fantasy is *sambal goreng tempe* (crispy soybean cake in sweet soy sauce). Diced *tempe* are first deep-fried until they are half-cooked and then stir-fried with shallots, garlic, large red Lombok chilies, galangal, brown palm sugar, sweet soy sauce (*kecap manis*), *asam* (tamarind pulp), *salam* leaves, shrimp paste and salt to produce a sticky honey brown caramel-glazed delight. *Tempe* is also mashed and flipped into small round fritters (*tempe bergedel*), revved up with the usual assortment of Balinese condiments: fried shallots, kaffir lime leaves, flour, egg and a roll of spice paste ingredients. *Tempe manis* is Balinese cooking in its purest form. Small strips of *tempe* are mixed with sweet soy sauce, chilies, brown sugar and spices and wok-fried to crispy perfection.

Kangkung Pelecing

(SPICY SPINACH)

Very popular in Balinese villages, spicy kangkung pelecing can be made with kangkung (water spinach) alone or with a mixture of vegetables, including kangkung, long green beans, Chinese bean sprouts, Chinese cabbage leaves or virtually any green vegetable (sayur hijau). Balinese women prepare this dish at home for their families. Pelecing (Balinese) is a way of cooking (chicken, vegetables, etc.) using sambal pelecing (a sauce).

Recipe courtesy of Made Janur and chef Iloh, Janur Dive Inn, Jl. Laviana-Banyualit, Lovina, Singaraja, October 18, 2008.

9 stalks water spinach
long, thin green beans
bean sprouts
Chinese cabbage
6 garlic cloves
2 in (5 cm) fish paste
1½ egg tomato or any other tomato
12 small orange chilies
3 large red Lombok chilies
granulated sugar cane
3 tbs sea salt
dried chicken stock powder or chicken bouillion cube
3 kaffir limes
3 tbs coconut oil

Begin by preparing the *pelecing* sauce. Burn the garlic, tomato and shrimp paste on the grill for 5 minutes.

Wash the water spinach, remove any hard stems and halve lengthwise. Boil the *kangkung* for 2 minutes at a high temperature. Drain and set aside.

Mash the tomato, garlic, shrimp paste and chili peppers in a mortar and pestle.

Add a pinch of salt, a pinch of chicken powder and some granulated sugar cane. Pound all the ingredients finely in the mortar.

Squeeze the juice of a kaffir lime onto the sauce and add the grated rind.

Boil the coconut oil and add to the sauce.

Combine the *pelecing* sauce with the vegetables in the mortar or in a bowl.

Snip the sauce-laden stalks of the pre-cooked *kangkung* into small pieces with a pair of kitchen scissors.

This recipe produces three spoons of sauce to one portion of *kangkung*. Serves 4–6 people.

Urab

(FINELY CUT AND DICED BALINESE VEGETABLE SPECIALTY)

Urab is the premier, most legendary, classic vegetable masterpiece in Bali. Long green beans (kacang panjang) and Chinese bean sprouts are the most commonly used vegetables, as well as paku (fern fiddlehead or leaves). Urab ingredients are always cut into very small, shredded pieces. This is what distinguishes urab from other vegetable creations in both appearance, texture and digestion. Urab is part of the everyday cooking arsenal in the Balinese home kitchen. The wife (ibu) will make this time-consuming dish for the family for lunch or dinner. Beautiful, unusual Balinese urab can also serve as a ceremonial dish for the three-month baby ceremony or a cremation event.

Recipe courtesy of Mr Dolphin (Gede Masda) and Mrs Dolphin (Kadek Astini). Warung Dolphin7 Jl. Laviana-Banyualit, Lovina, Singaraja, Bali. www.dolphinlovina.com, November 12, 2008.

long, thin green beans
bean sprouts
3 cloves garlic
6 pieces lesser galangal
6 pieces turmeric root, chopped
3 candlenuts
9 hot, small red chilies
4½ red Lombok chilies, sliced
3 *salam* leaves
3 tbs sea salt
¾ small coconut, freshly grated
6 tbs coconut oil

Cut the long green beans into ¼–½ inches (1 cm–1.5 cm) pieces, boil for 10 minutes and set aside.

Cut the bean sprouts into small pieces with kitchen scissors, blanche in hot water for 5 minutes and set aside.

Place the ingredients for the spice paste (*bumbu*), except for the coconut, in a stone mortar and pound into a soft, wet, orange-red paste.

Fry the *bumbu* in 6 tablespoons of oil in a frying pan.

Add the freshly grated coconut and a little water to the frying pan and simmer for 5 minutes.

Put the pre-cooked beans and sprouts in the frying pan or a large bowl and mix in the spice sauce using a spatula or bare hands.

Place on a plate and garnish with small fried onions. Drizzle the juice of half a kaffir lime on top and decorate with lime fruit rind.

Serves 4–6 people.

Gado-Gado
(MIXED STEAMED VEGETABLES IN PEANUT SAUCE)

Gado-gado (jukut mesantok in Balinese) is found all over Indonesia in many different versions that vary from island to island. Gado-gado (in Bahasa Indonesia) means "mixed" or consisting of many elements. The dish contains an assorted potpourri of lightly steamed fresh vegetables served with a tangy peanut sauce. It is normally eaten lukewarm or cold, with white rice (nasi putih) as an accompaniment.

Recipe courtesy of Ni Wayan Murni, Campuhan-Ubud, Bali.

½ lb (250 g) cabbage, sliced
½ lb (250 g) carrots, sliced
½ lb (250 g) green beans, halved
½ lb (250 g) Chinese cabbage, sliced
½ lb (250 g) bean sprouts
½ lb (250 g) water spinach or spinach
cauliflower florets
5 boiled eggs, sliced or quartered
30 bite-sized pieces fried tofu
30 bite-sized pieces fried *tempe*
20 slices cucumber
shrimp crackers

fried shallots, handful
sliced tomatoes, to garnish

Steam the cabbage, carrots, green beans, Chinese cabbage, spinach and cauliflower lightly and set aside.

Fry the tofu (bean curd) in a little oil.

On a serving plate, layer the steamed vegetables with the tofu, raw bean sprouts, *tempe* and cucumber. Decorate with eggs and sliced tomatoes.

Sprinkle fried shallots on top and garnish with a circle of shrimp crackers.

Serve the fragrant peanut sauce on the side or in a separate bowl.

Serves 4–6.

Bumbu Kacang

(PEANUT SAUCE)

Peanut sauce is one of Bali's favorite condiments. Varying in subtle, gradual degrees of spiciness and sweetness, it routinely accompanies gado-gado and satay stick presentations. The secret is to use the best quality peanuts. One-inch-long kacang tanah (earth beans) grow under the soil, and are used to make peanut sauce. The red-colored beans can also be fried or stir fried and eaten as a snack.

14 oz (400 g) raw unsalted peanuts
1¾ oz (50 g) tomatoes, chopped
4 garlic cloves
2 tsp fermented bean sauce (taucho sauce)
2 tsp fried shallots
lime or lemon juice
1 tsp sea salt
1 tsp black pepper
1 tsp salty soy sauce
1 tsp sweet soy sauce

Fry the peanuts, a handful at a time, until brown.

Place all the ingredients in a blender and pulse until smooth or, for a better taste, grind by hand in a mortar and pestle. The amount of salt, pepper, lime juice and soy sauce can be varied to suit individual taste.

Serves 4–6.

CHAPTER SIXTEEN

The Sweet Life:
The Balinese Palate
Falls in Love

————— ≠ —————

T HE BALINESE SWEET TOOTH needs constant reinforcement and *jaja*, a staple sweet in Indonesian and Balinese culture sends the island's taste buds into a daily feeding frenzy. *Jaja* are traditional Indonesian and Balinese sweets or snacks, sometimes called *jajan pasar* (market cakes). Peckish villagers patronize market stalls, *warung* and mobile carts from early morning to late at night to gorge on *jaja* masquerading as tropical breakfasts, between meal snacks, local desserts or refreshments after a long journey. They serve as a handy treat in the rice fields or as appetizers for guests arriving at a village wedding ceremony. A selection of fresh *jaja* is also always served at family ceremonies, along with tea or coffee. Simple *warung* "*jaja* chefs" and family "*jaja* chocolatiers" never tire of making, eating and comparing the tastes, smells, ingredients and textures of their village *jaja*.

Jaja embrace hundreds of shapes, types and colors of hand-made or mass-produced Balinese rice-based cakes sold at every *warung* and mini-mart in every village in Bali. In fact, *jaja* are so universal that all sweet, or even savory, snacks are loosely referred to as *jaja* on Bali and the term has become synonymous with any kind of food not eaten with rice or a regular meal. *Jaja* on Bali are made out of three basic ingredients— sticky glutinous rice or plain rice flour dough, coconut and brown palm sugar—and can be classified into four categories according to how they are cooked. The first style is cooked or served with sprinklings of fresh coconut shavings, liquid coconut milk or *unti* (grated coconut cooked in brown sugar and pandanus leaves). The second type is typically wrapped in banana, coconut or corn leaves. The third variety is fried, while a fourth brightly colored category is steamed. Color and presentation are very important in both food and art in Bali. *Jaja* come in a geometric wonderland of amazing shapes and sizes (squares, rectangles, triangles, cones, cubes, tubes, roll-ups and bow ties) and an assortment of rainbow colors. *Jaja* also very often contain surprise fillings. Delicious *kelepon* (small olive-colored balls made from boiled glutinous flour dyed with green leaf juice) pack a soft, juicy brown sugar palm syrup center. These bite size green balls made from sticky rice flour contain a sniper's nest of squirting liquid brown sugar. As a finishing touch, they are rolled in grated coconut. One of the most popular and widely available desserts in Bali, *kelepon* are commercially hand-made in small sweet shops in Gianyar. *Jaja ketan kukus* are made with steamed white glutinous rice while *jaja injin kukus* is made with steamed black glutinous rice. These elongated rolled *jajan* typically contain half-steamed rice hand-folded into a long, thin, rectangular log. The log is then wrapped in a heat-wilted banana leaf, folded around to seal it and steamed for thirty minutes to one hour. Banana leaves also moonlight as conical or cylindrical *jaja* molds. The soft paste of the rice dough is pushed into the cone- or cylinder-shaped leaf which is carefully peeled off when the mold is stuffed to capacity. Adorned with grated coconut, fresh fruits, palm sugar syrup, pandanus leaves and sometimes bean or yam treats, *jaja* are always eaten with the fingers.

The Balinese used to make all the ingredients at home for their sweets, cakes, snacks and puddings. They would refine the rice using a large Balinese-style mortar placed on the ground (a *lesung*) and pestle (a six-foot-long pole called a *lu*). All colorings and flavorings were natural. *Suji* leaves would give cakes their green color and pandanus leaves would bestow a delightful aroma. These methods still apply in the villages, but in urban Denpasar, the Balinese now buy ready-made ingredients, colorings and flavorings. Almost every village woman and girl used to know how to make fresh *jaja*. Now even the local village and roadside *warung* mainly offer mass-produced sweet *jaja* snacks wrapped in sheer cellophane envelopes. Few young women can be bothered to make home-made *jaja* today. Each type of cake can take up to two hours to make, they sell very cheaply, which means small profits, and they have a short, one-day shelf life. Women are too busy now, and the compounds have more money from other sources of income since the advent of tourism. *Jaja* used to be a staple treat in the baskets of the wandering, early morning street vendors and at the traditional morning markets. Young girls would make *jaja* with their mothers at 2 a.m. and go out to peddle them at 5 a.m. to neighbors and schoolmates to earn money to buy rice for the family. There is still a market, and a longing for, these authentic home-made *jaja*. Some Balinese women have set themselves up as fresh *jaja* suppliers for parties and ceremonies using traditional utensils, methods and skills.

Sweet *jaja* cakes and fried crackers (sweet *krupuk*) are fabricated in people's houses as home industry products, not in large factories in the capital Denpasar. Families sell them to the traditional central market in their villages. They are then resold at higher prices to local *warung* who charge customers an additional mark-up. Street markets display big round plastic or metal plates of *jajan basah*, also called *jajan Bali* (wet, moist, soft cakes usually steamed or boiled). The evening market at the crossroads of Lovina offers a large variety of sweet *jaja*: *injin* (black rice), *lupis* (a triangular cake with white and black rice inside), *jaja abug* (a cubed, round or triangular pink and white sticky rice layer cake made for rituals), and mysterious piles of unknown green squiggles and green cakes. Bowls of white grated coconut and brown palm sugar sit nearby to be spooned on to the desserts. Family-owned *warung* also cook the desserts and snacks themselves. *Kué* or *kueh* means cake, pastry or cookie in Indonesian. *Kué kukus* refers to steamed cakes made from glutinous rice flour. Many kinds of *jaja* are designated as offerings, and the markets overflow with them during major religious ceremonies. Sacred *jaja* like *kué mangkok* (tiny fluorescent pink or green tulip-shaped offering cakes resembling cupcakes in both size and shape), fill the village market stalls before major religious holidays. A local *warung* in Tebongkang village offers their own white with pink, orange or brown decoration on the trademark split tops. The pink or orange dye is just for aesthetics, while the brown denotes chocolate flavor. Costing Rp.1,000 per piece, Balinese customers look for and select cakes with artistic value, such as those with a nice petal-shaped crown.

Jaja gina (fried white rice grain cakes folded over in the middle like giant, airy sweet tacos) have been very popular in Bali for a long time. People make them at home or buy them in a *warung*. Like almost all sweets, they are primarily made to be used as a ceremonial offering and only secondarily as a snack. They are purchased daily or several times a week. *Jaja gina* come in endless culinary and visual incarnations.

Competing for culinary favor is *dodol,* a small confection presented in a pale tan paper-thin bamboo leaf or corn cob sheath. The cartridge-shaped *dodol*, made of pounded black glutinous rice flour and coconut milk mixed with melted palm sugar, is wrapped and steamed. The ends are knotted with tiny pink plastic ribbons and strung along in ten-piece bundles like a hanging row of Chinese lanterns. *Dodol* is often enriched with in-season fruits like durian, snakeskin fruit, apple or soursop. Used as an offering on the Galungan feast day, the sweet creation is widely sold in both traditional markets and supermarkets. *Satuh*, also encased in a pale tan bamboo leaf wrapper, are perfectly round in shape with a hard melt-in-the-mouth brown palm sugar ball inside. Similar to *dodol*, *satuh* are also strung in a ten-count row with decorative plastic ties. *Jaja gambir* are wrapped in corn leaves, tied up with string and hung up in bunches like grapes. Traditional *jaja* wrappings were always organic and sourced from nature. Today, many commercial *jaja* are wrapped in plastic and equipped with a plastic spoon! Balinese *jaja laklak* (mini-pancakes) are processed in the kitchen (*paon*) on a three-hole cooking range atop a wood-fired stove using a Dutch-style metal *poffertjes* pan with an accompanying high, bell-shaped cover. The batter is poured into shallow, 2-inch (5-cm)-wide round wells (usually seven), injected with sweet interior fillings and then baked. Shredded coconut is prepared simultaneously for the *laklak*. Balinese *laklak bikang* are also baked in the round depressions of the famous *poffertjes* pan. Made with rice flour, sugar, coconut milk and green food coloring, the round, flat, bright green cakes are always strikingly beautiful and are often served nestling astride a square-cut emerald banana leaf.

Striped *jaja lapis*, cubed, triangular or round, commands attention with alternating pink and white, brown and white, yellow and white, green and white, or red and white sticky rice layers (*lapis* means layer or stratum). Made from rice flour, *jaja lapis* is laboriously prepared for both Balinese ritual ceremonies and everyday delight. Another elaborately constructed *jaja* fantasy, gelatinous *kué agar-agar* appears as a shiny, two-layered white (base) and pink-red (top) half moon-shaped inch-thick domed slice. Cooked for ceremonies or weddings, this dessert also has assorted multi-shaped globules inside, resembling embedded kernels of corn. *Agar-agar* is a clear vegetable gel extracted from seaweed (an edible East Indian seaweed, Ceylon moss, or red algae Gelidium), used as a thickening or solidifying agent in Asian cooking. The Balinese can purchase *agar-agar* in powder form in a packet. *Jaja bulung,* a brown jelly-like cake, sometimes sheltering a banana slice, is made from dried seaweed and also contains gelatinous *agar-agar.* Coastal Balinese gather small wild seaweeds to create this popular snack. The algae are dried, washed in lime water and dried again into light brown, lacy mat forms. Able to be stored indefinitely, the algae is shredded into boiling water to produce sweet *jaja bulung,* sold in markets as a brown, firm gel cut into wiggly squares.

Fresh, soft green *dadar gulung* (pancake rolls) are stuffed with an especially sweet and chewy grated coconut and brown palm sugar mixture called *unti.* The Balinese still use their traditional *pandan* and *suji* leaves to color and flavor the green outer wrapping. Glistening mini crepe-like *dadar* are the most commonly available sweet *jaja* of Bali. Some *dadar* have smooth green wrappings while others can have spongier, bubble-pocked, spring green rolled exteriors. They are made at home and presented to the family as something precious after a meal, as companions to tea or coffee. Extremely tasty *jaja onde-onde,* fried to a golden brown color with a chewy, textured interior, are hefty (Chinese-influenced) round, sesame seed-studded balls made of fried, sweetened rice flour, palm sugar, potato, water and oil. A grated yellow coconut filling often awaits the eater. *Onde-onde* can also be filled with green beans and sugar or black bean paste. *Cerorot,* a specialty of the Bali Aga village of Tenganan, Karangasem, is made of rice flour, melted brown palm sugar, coconut milk and salt wrapped and steamed in a long, thin twisting tube of young coconut leaves. To consume, one must unravel the wrapping from the top of the cone downward. *Cerorot* are usually served with coffee or tea. They are prepared fresh in the markets and eaten immediately. The traditional morning markets, which open at

5 a.m., are the best place to purchase such still-warm, dawn-fresh *jaja* snacks as *pancong* (a cake made of grated coconut, rice flour and coconut milk) and *latok* (firm, round, smooth or puckered green "hockey pucks" made of rice flour served with grated white coconut on top).

Steamed *jaja kue wajik* is a very popular triangle-shaped Balinese cake. It is composed of moist, still-visible sticky rice grains, brown palm sugar, pandanus leaves and coconut milk, often with a small embedded piece of yellow jackfruit for contrast. A common recipe for *wajik* utilizes 1 kg glutinous white rice, 800 ml water for boiling the rice, 400 g brown palm sugar, 1 tsp salt, 2 pandanus leaves and 200 g grated, roasted coconut. To make the *wajik*, the rice is processed in four ways. It is first soaked in water for three hours, drained, and then steamed until half done. It is then removed from the steamer and boiled over a low flame until the water is absorbed. The rice is then put back in the steamer and cooked until tender. In the meantime, the brown sugar, salt and pandanus leaves are boiled over a low flame until the sugar is of a hairy texture. The grated coconut and rice are added, the pandanus leaves removed and the mixture left to cool. The *wajik* mixture is spread out flat ¾ inch (2 cm) thick and cut into diamond-shaped pieces. Transformed into irregular, honey brown wedges, the glutinous, sticky cakes are then individually wrapped in protective plastic.

An entire class of *jaja* stem from Bali's vegetarian Garden of Eden. Fruit, gourds, pumpkins and others invade *jaja* with natural, nutritious content and flavor. *Jajan labu*, made with mature gourd, squash or pumpkin mixed with sugar or tapioca, placed inside a banana leaf and steamed, are eaten as a dessert rather than as a vegetable. Sweet *sumping waluh* (steamed pumpkin cake) and *sumping nangka* (steamed jackfruit cake) glisten with coconut milk, rice flour, sugar and a slice of fruit wedged into a sharply cut, folded, oval banana leaf wallet. *Sumping's* bright green banana leaf wrapping often protects a concealed coin of steamed banana in the heart of the dense, sticky dough. *Sumping talas* (taro cake) is made of taro and rice flour, but can also be made of steamed bananas or beans. Banana *sumping* is a thickened, boiled mixture of rice flour, sago flour, pandanus leaves, thick coconut milk, palm sugar, banana and salt steamed for twenty minutes in a folded parcel of layered banana leaves. Its rice flour relative, *pisang rai*, also hides a banana inside, served and topped with shredded coconut. Gluey sago porridge (*bubur sagu*) is made from the starch of a widely distributed regional palm tree and contains soft sago pearls, palm sugar syrup, coconut milk and pandanus leaves. Caramel colored chewy *jaja batu bedil* (rice dumplings in brown palm sugar sauce) is another island favorite and is available in every market. To make *jaja batu bedil*, rice flour and tapioca flour are mixed with water and salt to form a dough. The dough is then shaped into small but firm balls and boiled for eight minutes. A sweet coating of brown palm sugar, pandanus leaf and thick coconut milk is boiled. The dumplings are then drenched in the sauce, simmered together at low heat for ten minutes and crowned with grated coconut flakes. *Pulung ubi* is a small cassava ball filled with shredded palm sugar.

Lempog, made of cassava or sweet potato, is Balinese creativity and beauty at its best. To prepare this marvel of cooking ingenuity and artistry, the tuber is either steamed (dry) or boiled (wet) and mashed (dry technique) like *bubur* (porridge). Brown sugar is added. After the mixture has been mashed, it is shaped like a volcano, with a crater on the top, and crowned with more brown sugar. This is how it is served. *Lempog* is too complicated to make at home. Most local Balinese will buy it at a small *warung* in the morning and have it with tea or coffee. In villages, this eruptive delight will cost Rp.1,000. *Lempog* can also be fashioned into a heavy, jelly-like rectangular attraction with three horizontal, pale-colored layers (green, yellow and orange) embellished with a white coconut shred topping. Because cassava is widely cultivated throughout the island, the Balinese also make sweet, colorful, round balls skewered through a thin bamboo stick. The ingredients for this spherical cake delicacy include 1 kg finely grated cassava, a quarter of a grated coconut, 1 tsp salt, ½ cup of *suji* leaf extract (as a green coloring agent), ½ tsp red coloring agent and sugar. To prepare, salt is added to the grated cassava and mixed thoroughly. The batter is then divided into three equal parts. One batch is colored green, one batch red and the third (yellow-hued) is left uncolored. Meatball-sized balls are fashioned from each of the three batters and steamed until cooked. The grated coconut is mixed with some salt and sugar. One of each of the colorful cassava balls are threaded through each bamboo skewer and rolled on the white grated coconut flakes prior to serving.

Tape is very famous and popular on Bali and everyone makes it for Galungan and Kuningan Day. *Tape* consists of steamed black or white rice (the black rice may also be mixed with *ketan* or sticky white glutinous rice) combined with *ragi* (yeast, a white powder), the critical catalyst. After preparing the concoction, it must be wrapped in a banana leaf or plastic bag and left in a warm place for a few days to ferment. It is then ready to eat as a dessert or given to the gods as an offering. There is also a sweet version of *tape* made with sweet potatoes instead of rice. It is a much-loved secular dessert and is also made for the very important three-month baby ceremony. For this, the *ragi* and sweet potatoes are mixed together and folded in a banana leaf to ferment for two days. If commercially sold in a *warung, tape* is usually packaged in a small plastic cup.

In super sweet Bali, ceremonial *jaja* fashioned from glutinous rice grains or steamed glutinous rice dough instead of the normal rice flour base please the palates and spirits of the Hindu gods at temple anniversaries, tooth filings and weddings. Pillow-shaped *jaja bantal* (*bantal* is pillow in Indonesian) are commonly used as a ceremonial offering. Made from sticky rice, grated coconut and either bananas, peanuts, fruits, peas or small green or red beans bound and steamed in a spiral of young coconut leaves, the packets are often tied with thin pink or aqua plastic ribbons. Offering trays (*canang* or *banten*) are assembled for ceremonies, consisting of an assortment of two to six *jaja* desserts: *jaja laklak bikang, jaja bantal, kué mangkok, jaja lapis, jaja ku* (chili red firm round pucks also offered to God by the Chinese), *jaja wajik* and *jaja onde-onde*. When the Balinese purchase these types of sweets, their first thought is, "What do I need for a ceremony?" Their second concern is what food they love to eat, because they will be eating it after the ceremony to avoid wasting the food and the money they have spent buying sweets they dislike. Another important consideration is affordability.

Carefully pre-selected colored rice cakes are also incorporated into enormous, layered, six-foot-tall decorative ceremonial offering towers (*banten tegeh*) consisting of cookies, fruits, parts of roast pigs, grilled chicken, whole ducks, eggs and small but omnipresent pink and green tulip-shaped cakes (*kué mangkok*). The fibrous trunk of a banana plant serves as the central pedestal and support for these temple festival towers. A three to six-foot section of banana stem is thrust onto a long

iron rod column attached to a special offering plate shaped and con-
toured to be carried on a woman's head. The food offerings are affixed
by first inserting a bamboo stick through each one and then firmly
pushing it into the soft, upright, mounted banana stem. The decorators
cover it completely to form a magnificent arrangement of diverse colors
and smells. The Balinese are hereditary artists and masters of the decorative and fine arts of woodcarving, stone sculpture, painting and weaving and this extends to ceremonial food presentation and adornment.
Balinese food craftsmanship reaches its apotheosis in the construction
of these elaborate, weighty *banten tegeh* fruit and cake offering towers.
Built to honor the gods, the colorful pagoda-like pyramids are borne on
the heads of spectacularly costumed village women who walk in single
file street processions to area temples. Blessed by the priest, sprinkled
with holy water and accepted by the deities, the cakes for the gods are
infused with a new sacred energy. The bountiful skyscrapers are then
carried home to be consumed by the family.

Jaja uli is a typical *banten tegeh* offering. Made with steamed glutinous rice dough and palm sugar, it is wrapped in a cylindrical bundle in
coconut leaves. After the *jaja uli* are finished being steamed, the cook
cuts very thin slices off with a thread of bamboo. The large, round, bright
pink and white mottled cracker-cakes are then dried streetside in the sun
in villages like Tegallalang in a huge metal barrel or bamboo basket
before being fried. *Jaja gipang* is also visible on high offerings. These rice
crackers are made of brightly dyed glutinous, stuck together rice grains
molded into various shapes. The ceremonial masterpieces are increasingly being manufactured by professionals because of the time and labor
required to make them at home. Local female offering specialists (*tukang
banten*) produce the ritual *jaja* cakes, imposing offering towers and
meticulously crafted high offerings required for mass celebrations. A
roster of over a hundred different offering designs feeds the rich and
continual ceremonial needs and life of the devout people of Bali.

Jaja sirat visually resembles a coarse bird's nest, hairnet or scouring
pad made of colored flour batter. (The word *sirat* means the mesh of
a net, to weave, be intertwined.) Circular, soft and sweet, the Bali-
Hindu people use it as an offering for Galungan and other rituals. *Sirat*
is composed of a mixture of rice flour, starch, sugar, salt and a small

amount of water. The mixture is placed in a mold, usually half a coconut shell with small holes in the bottom. The slightly thick batter falls through the holes into a frying pan and the cake's lacy, web-like pattern is formed by moving the dripping coconut shell in a circular motion over the pan. The batter is deep-fried until it is very crispy and then stored in a spacious container. It is exposed to the air for a while to soften it. *Sirat* is served in elongated rolls, folded taco shell shapes or rolled up like a parchment scroll with a banana inside and tied with a thin banana leaf ribbon. Red and white *jaja matahari* (sun cake) is another arresting offering cake, which is fried, decorated and cut out to resemble the sun. Simpler, less sweet versions of *matahari* are cooked fresh at home or purchased in the traditional market in plastic packets as snacks. The crispy non-greasy confectionary crackers are white with red and white squiggly stripes.

Even more eye-catching are the elaborate *sarad* (*bregembal* in Balinese) offerings made of dyed rice dough. Hard-fried, vividly colored (pinks, greens, yellows) rice dough cookies are shaped into little models of humans, animals and abstracts and are then attached to a nine-foot-high framework of bamboo and cloth stationed by the central shrine during *odalan* temple celebrations. The Balinese also artistically and reverentially etch the fresh rice dough into brilliantly colored faces and figures representing the deities using natural leaf food dyes. Painstakingly decorated with hundreds of these differently sculptured figures along with small fried rice cakes in pink, yellow, orange and green, the *sarad* offering constructions symbolically depict and represent the entire form and content of the Balinese religious universe. The spirit world is both densely populated and close at hand in Bali, as fully alive as the rice fields that cover much of the island. The intricate mandala-quality *sarad* always depicts the earth balanced on the back of the cosmic turtle (Bedawang Nala), supported by the cosmic dragon (Naga Basuki) and surrounded by the skies and heaven. Boma, a ferocious spirit, is also frequently included in the *sarad*. He is enshrined in magnificent, detailed carvings over doorways all over Bali for the protection of the people. These sacred *sarad* arrangements are specially made as decorative representative offerings. They are never eaten because they remain on display in the temple for many days.

Jaja Gina
(WHITE RICE GRAIN CAKES)

Recipe thanks to and courtesy of Wayan Sarma, the very best driver in Ubud. e-mail:sarmananda@hotmail.com. Wayan grew up on these jaja gina cakes, bringing back very fond memories.

Steam the rice.
Add food coloring.
Prepare a round bamboo mold.
Put the steamed rice inside the mold
Dry the rice in the sun (on the grass) until it gets really dry.
Fry until very crisp. The rice expands when you cook it.

Jaja Lapis
(LAYERED RICE FLOUR CAKES)

The food that was cooked on this day was wonderful because it was made by beautiful women who really wanted to make the food beautiful. The Balinese are skilled cooking artists. To anticipate, enthuse over, buy and eat traditional morning market fresh jaja is to fall madly in love all over again. Jaja lapis is eagerly consumed for morning breakfast with coffee or tea or for dessert. As it is very long, hard work to make, jaja lapis is usually only prepared at home for the three-month baby ceremony, cremations and weddings. It is easier to buy it at a warung. Bigger pieces cost Rp.3,000–4,000, smaller pieces Rp.1,000.

Recipe courtesy of Mr Dolphin (Gede Masda) and Mrs Dolphin (Kadek Astini). Mrs Dolphin assembled a hard-working village team comprising herself, her sister as well as a warung employee) to create the jaja lapis. It was my privilege to witness the preparation of this traditional, time- and labor-intensive jaja lapis specialty. Warung Dolphin. Jl. Laviana-Banyualit, Lovina, Singaraja, Bali. www.dolphinlovina.com, November 2008.

1 lb (500 g) rice flour
1 lb (500 g) corn flour
½ lb (250 g) tapioca flour

1½ lb (750 g) granulated white sugar
½ a coconut to yield two 8 ounce glasses of coconut milk
1 tbs salt
1 packet vanilla powder
1 tsp chocolate sauce

Put the rice flour, ¾ of a glass of corn flour, 5 heaped tablespoons of tapioca flour, salt, vanilla powder and 2½ glasses of granulated white sugar (less if preferred) into a large mixing bowl and mix together by hand.

Pour in 2 glasses of coconut milk and continue mixing by hand. Add 2 cups of hot water and mix for 30 minutes or until the consistency resembles a thick, silky pudding. Check for sweetness and consistency.

Transfer half the batter to a second bowl and add 1 teaspoon chocolate sauce to create the brown layer.

Smear a little oil on a shallow pie dish. Put the dish on the steamer for a few minutes to heat it.

Slowly and carefully pour one cup of the white batter in the dish to form a flat layer, then steam for 5 minutes.

Then pour in one cup of the chocolate batter and steam for 5 minutes.

Add alternating colors (white, chocolate, white, chocolate) cup by cup, layer by layer until the two batters are used up. Steam each layer for 5 minutes.

Loosen the edges of the cooked mixture with the top of a spoon, then slice it on the diagonal both ways to form diamond shapes. When lifted from the dish, the brown and white layers will be revealed.

Makes 20–25 pieces.

Jaja Bantal Pisang
(PILLOW-SHAPED RICE CAKES)

There are many types of bantal, ranging from banana to red bean. Mrs Dolphin learned this age-old recipe from her grandmother. Jaja bantal are prepared and eaten for ceremonies, dessert or breakfast. To cook jaja lapis, jaja bantal and tape together for a large ceremony (100 people), the Balinese must spend Rp.2,000,000.

Recipe courtesy of Mr Dolphin (Gede Masda) and Mrs Dolphin (Kadek Astini). Mrs Dolphin and her two female helpers created little packages of

intense beauty as they brought legendary Balinese jaja bantal pisang to life.
Warung Dolphin, Jl. Laviana-Banyualit, Lovina, Singaraja, Bali. www.
dolphinlovina.com, November 2008.

1 lb (500 g) glutinous white rice
½ a coconut to yield 2 glasses grated fresh coconut
1½ glasses granulated white sugar
1½ tsp salt
2 bananas, each 8 in (20 cm) long
strips of young coconut leaf for weaving into baskets 1¼ in (3 cm)
**　　　by 2¼ in (5.5 cm)**
bamboo toothpicks for securing the baskets

Place the glutinous white rice inside a black hairnet, steam for 30 minutes, remove from the heat and place in a bowl.

Add the shredded coconut, sugar and salt to the bowl and mix by hand for 15 minutes.

Slice the bananas diagonally.

Stuff the coconut leaf baskets, alternating one layer of rice with a slice of banana. Tampen down the layers.

Fold the top and the sides over like a purse to seal the rice and banana package. Twine black plastic string around the packages to secure and keep them shut. Steam the packages for 30 minutes.

To eat, remove the black plastic bindings and unravel the coconut leaf casings. Makes 20 packages.

Tape

(SWEET FERMENTED RICE CAKE)

Tape is traditionally made for such major religious ceremonies and events as Galungan and Kuningan. True art requires passion, creativity and blessings from the gods, as does cooking. A Balinese chef is always a master craftsman, but if the chef puts his heart and soul into a complex foodwork like tape, then he is truly a dedicated artist.

Recipe courtesy of Mr Dolphin (Gede Masda) and Mrs Dolphin (Kadek Astini). I stood in awe of Mrs Dolphin and her village ladies as they brought the tape—one of Bali's best loved and exotic creations—into existence. When the fabulous tape was fully fermented and ready to eat three days later, Mr Dolphin brought a tub of it over to my hotel for me to enjoy. I ate every last rare, home-made drop of it with divine reverence and forbidden pleasure. Warung Dolphin, Jl. Laviana-Banyualit, Lovina, Singaraja, Bali. www. dolphinlovina.com, November 2008.

2 lb (1 kg) glutinous white rice or glutinous black rice (or a combination of both)
liquid from an edible green leaf, e.g. *kayu manis*
yeast

Soak the glutinous rice for 2 hours in water in a large bowl. Use a two to one ratio of water to rice.

Squeeze the leaf with for 5 minutes. Mix the extract with one glass of water. Set aside.

Place the rice in a black mesh hairnet and steam for 20 minutes.

Pour the green liquid into the steaming rice encased in the net (making it easier to lift out of the pot later). Stir to mix.

Steam another 10 minutes to saturate the rice with the green liquid.

Lift the rice out of the pot and lay the mixture on a banana leaf on a rectangular platter to cool down, approximately 1 hour.

When cool, sprinkle the yeast powder on top of the rice.

Wrap the rice in a banana leaf and place inside a box. Seal the box so that it is completely airtight.

Leave for 2–3 days to ferment. It will turn into a soft, sweet, porridge-like consistency. (If left longer than 2–3 days, it will become Balinese wine, called *brem*.)

CHAPTER SEVENTEEN

Fruits of Bali:
Nectar from the Trees

---- ≠ ----

THE WARM TROPICAL CLIMATE OF BALI provides a sanctuary for over fifty mouth-watering, sugar-charged species of tropical fruit (*buah*), many of them unfamiliar to the Western diet, palate and supermarket. In Bali, there are no regimented rows of fruit trees or prosperous orchards. Nor do the Balinese scientifically breed, spray, fertilize, cultivate or nurse fruit along to a high-yield Western peak of market-driven, blemish-free, transport-hardy perfection. Instead, most of Bali's edible delights grow prolifically on unattended wild native trees planted by individual landowners in their yards for extra income. Villagers shake down and harvest the fruits to sell in the market. Professional, communal fruit collectors also harvest these natural crops from scattered premises and farms throughout the island and deliver the freshly picked bounty to local village markets where the Balinese go early in the morning to bargain for and buy produce by the piece, bunch or kilogram. There are noticeable annual differences from regency to regency in the taste, appearance and quality of particular fruits according to local soil conditions, the season and regional climate and rain patterns.

At the markets, fruit vendors (*penjual buah*) pile a mesmerizing array of in-season local fruits (*buah-buahan*) on stall counters in brimming blue plastic tubs or high, round bamboo baskets or spread them out on plaited straw or plastic mats on the floor. Local varieties of mango, guava, durian, jackfruit, pomegranate, tangerine (thin, green-skinned oranges) and mangosteen compete with large red-fleshed papayas, watermelons, honeydew melons, many types of banana, Java plums and sweet wild pineapples. Unorthodox pleasures include spiky, scarlet red rambutan, wild, blood red Balinese strawberries (*glungung*) which grow in the cooler mountainous regions around Bedugul, *jeruk* (citrus fruits) and *kecapi* (santol in English), a sweet-sour fruit grown commercially in some areas. *Kecapi*, a slightly flattened, roundish, green-skinned fruit (golden yellow when ripe), has a thick skin that is very hard to open; locals throw it against the floor to gain entry! The handball-sized fruit has a segmented, white, translucent, juicy pulp with a slightly acidic and sweet taste like mangosteen. It is produced by a Malaysian tree in the mahogany family. Bali's *jambu air* (pear-shaped rose apple or water apple) is a shiny, waxy, pink or lime green with a puckered base and an edible exterior. *Jambu air merah* is red water apple. Small, round, green (unripe) *jambu biji* (stone or seed) is guava, and is very popular with the Balinese, picked right off the tree and eaten in the hand. Watery, thirst-quenching, five-pointed star fruit (*belimbing*), also known as carombola, is widely found in Bali as well as other parts of Southeast Asia. *Belimbing* has a slightly waxy skin and the flesh is crunchy, firm, and extremely juicy: when ripe, it is sweet with a slight sour or tart undertone. It is shaped like a star when sliced.

Bali's markets also stock a colorful array of snakeskin fruit, local green oranges (from Bedugul), small yellow bananas, black grapes (from north coast Seririt) and small green kaffir limes (*jeruk purut*; *limo* in Balinese, *lemo* in Indonesian). A local favorite and only found on Bali, the *wani* is shaped like an oversized avocado with a slightly rough and gritty brownish-green skin. Harder than a mango even when ripe, its overwhelmingly sweet white flesh surrounding one large seed is sliced and then eaten. On larger, circulating, major market days (scheduled every third day), the most exciting fruits appear in a kaleidoscope of configurations, textures, flavors and sizes: thick green bananas, avocados (grown on tall, spindly, spare-leafed trees), brown coconuts, passionfruit (a marble-sized version grows wild in the lanes), *sawo* (sapodilla), and pale brown langsat (*Lansium domesticum*). The Indonesian variety of langsat is *duku*, with clear white, translucent, sweet-sour juicy flesh. Sweetsop and soursop (*sirsak* in Dutch), a large, green, 10-inch-long lumpy, spiky fruit), and *calamansi*, also spelled *kalamansi* (*Citrofortunella microcarpa*), native to the Philippines, are among the offerings on sale. *Calamansi* (*jeruk kesturi*) is a small, bright green citrus fruit that is a cross between a kumquat and a Mandarin orange. The thin-skinned green orb can be mistaken for a little kaffir lime but the flesh inside is orange. It is too sour to eat as a fruit and is used as a mixed fruit juice drink ingredient or as part of a cooking sauce. Tropical *srikaya* or annona, in the same family as soursop, resembles a small custard apple with a green exterior and sweet white meat with a sour-bitter tinge. Starchy, bowling ball-sized yellow-green breadfruit (*timbul*) hangs down heavy and noticeable from tall trees. Steamed, crushed, mixed with grated coconut and palm sugar, the fruit is mainly used to make traditional local bread. The sugar palm tree (*punyan jaka*) produces a white fruit (*beluluk*) which is mixed with syrup and other fruits and served on ice as a dessert or snack. The lontar palm also provides fruit in season from December to January. The flesh resembles a young coconut but is tougher and not as sweet.

One of Bali's most distinctive fruits is the spiky-haired, scarlet red rambutan (*rambut* means hair in Indonesian), a bizarre 1–2 inch long round-oval fruit. Its thin red skin bears a network of soft, brush-like lime green cilia concealing translucent, sweet-tart, juicy but firm white pulp around an attached central seed. Native to Southeast Asia, the evergreen rambutan (*Nephelium lappaceum*), which can grow up to 60 feet, produces 5,000–6,000 fruits a year in two seasons: September and from January to March. The Balinese climb up their garden trees to cut down branchloads of the conspicuous globes which are sold fresh in the markets with their twiggy stems still attached.

Delicately sweet mangosteens (*Garcinia mangostana*; *manggis* or *menggusta*) are another notable fruit. The mangosteen is a round, magenta-skinned ball, its thick, fibrous shell concealing six or seven segments of soft, translucent white flesh. Mangosteen must be eaten with care, as the red wine-colored juice from the inner rind leaves an indelible, brownish or deep purple-hued stain on clothing. Bali's mangosteen season runs from November to March.

Bali is also celebrated for its mangoes (*mangga*), the fleshy fruit of the *Mangifera indica* tree, cultivated in India and other tropical countries. (Indonesia, which harvests half a million tons of mangoes during its limited annual season, is the fourth largest mango producer in the world, and Java's plantations alone boast 35 species and 208 varieties). December to February is mango season on Bali. The rainy season (*musim hujan*) brings many varieties of mango to Bali: large, very sweet *mangga mana lagi* (meaning "Where is more of the fruit?"), and deliciously sweet-fleshed *mangga madu* (honey mango, medium small, rounded and green when ripe). *Mangga gedong* and (more acidic) *mangga golek* are both from Cirebon. *Mangga gedong* is a medium small, round mango with orange skin when ripe and a distinctive odor. *Mangga golek* is long and yellowish green with orange meat. Plump *mangga harum manis* or *arumanis* (*harum* means fragrance or smell, and *manis* is sweet) is medium sized, dull deep green, and reddish or yellowish in color when ripe, and very sweet). *Mangga podang* (small and yellow-red), *mangga manis*, white mango, and *lali jiwo* are other notable Balinese beauties. *Lali* (numb, insensitive to pain, forgetful) *jiwo or jiwa* (soul or spirit) means to "forget the spirit." According to the Balinese, after you eat a *lali jiwo* mango, you are "like drunk" and "forget everything" because it is so nice! Aside from the rare international import (*mangga Bangkok*), one must travel beyond Bali to South Kalimantan for the famous dark purple-skinned *katsuri* mango (*Mangifera casturi*) with its legendary sweet aroma. Green unripe fruit is popular in Bali (and throughout Indonesia), and small sour mangoes are simply sliced and eaten, dipped in a mixture of crushed chili and salt, or recruited for *rujak*, a sweet and sour pickled fresh fruit salad.

Known throughout Southeast Asia as the king of fruits, the durian (from *duri*, Malay for thorn; *Durio zibethinus*) is easily recognized by its massive size, menacing armor of thorns, unforgettable aroma and rich, sweet, creamy fruit. Revered, reviled, adored, maligned—and embargoed in hotels and planes—throughout Southeast Asia, the eight pound durian grows abundantly on Bali where it is allowed to fully ripen naturally on the tree for optimal quality. Experienced durian growers wait until their mature fruiting trees, which can grow to a height of 200 feet, spontaneously drop their ripe cargo to the ground, village boys standing by to warn innocent passersby of the danger of the falling fruit. They collect the precious durian several times a day (large safety nets are placed under the trees to intercept the fruit and prevent impact damage). Workers may also climb the trees early in the season to attach a long pulley system to each developing fruit looped over a higher branch and extending to the ground. When the ripe fruits drop, they are caught and lowered to safety. The rich and powerfully fragrant durian is highly perishable and deteriorates quickly. Thus those that have fallen within the past twelve hours command very high prices in the markets. To savor this infamous fruit, the thorny skin must be cut open with a machete and the stiff outer rind pressed to expose the rows of cream-colored, custardy fruit flesh.

The durian is a special but expensive treat for the Balinese. In rural areas, large heaps of the luscious treasures are sold directly from roadside market stands and flatbed trucks on the main roads from Ubud to Ponggang and from Mengwi to Munduk, as well as in traditional markets and modern Denpasar supermarkets at the beginning of the rainy season in November. The very best durian is said to grow in east Bali. Buyers inspect each fruit and sniff the odor to ascertain freshness before making a purchase. Durian is used in a variety of local dishes, especially in sweets, although in many rural areas the durian pits (washed, sliced finely and sun-dried) are preferred over the flesh. Ground in a traditional mortar to a fine texture, the resulting meal is used for making sweets like durian *dodol*. The flesh—reputed to be an aphrodisiac and dangerous to imbibe along with alcohol—is also available in packaged, dried and candied forms.

Salak is the unofficial mascot fruit of Bali. Shaped like an oversized garlic clove, the fruit has one large, inedible internal seed and the flesh consists of very firm, tightly compacted pale yellow lobes which taste like crisp, sweet-tart apples. Salak is referred to as the snakeskin fruit because of its tough, brittle, dark brown skin covered with coarse, triangular, lizard-like scales. Local farmers produce salak on low, almost stemless *Zalacca amboinensis* fruit palms bristling with very sharp, dangerous thorns. The fruits grow in clusters at the base, springing forth in bunches near the bottom of the trunk. The epicenter of salak cultivation and of Bali's snakeskin fruit industry is the cool, mountainous area of Selat (Karangasem regency) in eastern Bali, which benefited from the volcanic ash from Mount Agung's powerful 1963 eruption. Employing age-old methods of growing and picking, salak's fourteen species are most commonly cultivated on small family-owned plantations. Subdivided plots on large tracts of land owned by customary villages are also rented out to sharecroppers. The salak season coincides with the rainy season (January to February), when the well-watered trees produce abundant, bigger, sweeter fruit at peak flavor. There is a second July to August dry season when the fruit is smaller, the trees less prolific and the fruit has a different taste. Professional fruit collectors make the long trip to salak country in trucks, stopping to stock up at different farms.

Salak are consumed either fresh or candied when fully ripe. The Balinese eat the crunchy salak snake by peeling away its papery, reticulated bark and consuming it whole like a water chestnut. Newly picked salak is good to eat and keeps for ten to fifteen days before spoilage sets in. Unripe salak fruits are sour and astringent and are used for pickles or in *rujak* salad. The post-harvest fruit is also processed and packaged into dried snakeskin fruit, crackers or taffy and sold to local markets and supermarkets across Bali. The bark of the petioles may be used for matting and the leaflets for thatching. There is also a fledgling snakeskin fruit wine cottage industry in the village of Dukuh Sibetan.

A perennial favorite, jackfruit (*Artocarpus heterophyllus*; *nangka*) is widely grown in home gardens in Bali. The tree, native to India, bears enormous green football-shaped knobby fruit weighing up to 110 pounds (often wrapped in large, protective plastic bags while ripening). Jackfruit flesh is eaten raw, chilled, battered and deep-fried like a banana, or cooked as a vegetable in a curry; sometimes the seeds are also cooked. To get at the sweet, sticky flesh, the corpulent fruit is hacked open and the hard inner spine pushed back to reveal some twenty nut-like brown seeds surrounded by slightly rubbery, strong-flavored edible pods nestled between fleshy yellow fibers. The fruit lasts well without refrigeration a day or more after being opened. Roadside produce stands near the Jatiluweh rice fields and Tabanan vend jackfruit by the convenient half, quarter or piece. Individual segmented chunks, packed and ready to eat in small, saleable plastic bags are available at village markets.

Cempedak (*Artocarpus integer*), a much smaller cousin of jackfruit, has a thin greenish-brown knobby outer skin with an intriguing hexagonal pattern. It has round, pocketed interior pods of soft, sweet, sticky, mushy, golden yellow flesh with a chewy skin—and a strong aroma when ripe. It tastes similar to the related jackfruit, breadfruit, and durian.

Silik (*Annona squamosa*), also called *srikaya* or sugar apple, is native to Bali. It resembles an oversized acorn with a green knobby shell that turns yellow when ripe. One species, which grows in dry Uluwatu, has sweet, slightly grainy white flesh surrounding pockets of hard, black stones. A second type, also black-stoned, grows all over Bali and has bigger, juicier fruit. Once cut open, the black stones need to be plucked from the slippery flaps of soft, sweet white flesh. Closely related custard apples (*Annona reticulata*) make a rare appearance in tropical zones. Resembling a fleshy green artichoke with a malleable fuzzy shell, the creamy custard-like flesh sectioned around large brown pits is much favored when available. Sweet, juicy lychees, originally from China, are grown exclusively in Payangan where the bright red fruit clusters come into season in late November. Lychees (and closely related longan) are available canned in syrup in supermarkets. The Vietnamese dragon fruit (*buah naga*) from the showy dragon fruit tree (*Hylocereus undatus*), has hard, layered, flaming red sheafs and pointy green petals hiding bright white interior meat speckled with black, poppy seed-like dots.

Bananas (*pisang* in Indonesian, *biu* in Balinese) are important crop plants throughout the tropics. Edible bananas and plantains are berries in which the seeds have failed to develop, and largely derive from two species, *Musa acuminata* and *Musa balbisiana*, both native to Southeast Asia. Besides fruit, the banana plant produces edible stems, an edible male inflorescence and leaves that can be used for plates, wrappings and animal food. Over a dozen species, varying in size, shape, color and taste, are grown on a small scale in backyards for local consumption, wending their way into the standard recipes of the village kitchen. They range from the dwarf-sized *biu susu* (milk banana) to the red-peeled *biu udang* (shrimp banana), the small *biu batu* or *biu biji* (a seed-filled plantain species full of small hard seeds whose leaf provides wrappers) and tiny, sweet ladyfinger bananas (popular in offerings). *Biu gadang* (big or great) are still green when ripe and ready to eat, *biu mas* (gold) are deep golden colored and *biu raja* (grand) are large Western-sized specimens. Bananas are also dried and pounded into sweet or starchy flour used as a substitute for rice flour. Bananas also figure very prominently in sweet desserts. Battered, boiled or poached bananas with pandanus leaf (*pisang rai*) are coated with freshly grated young coconut. "Raya" (grand) and

"Raja" (king) bananas transform themselves into succulent green banana pancakes filled with grated coconut and palm sugar. *Pisang goreng* (golden fried banana fritters drizzled with palm sugar syrup and topped with fresh grated coconut) are an afternoon snack staple. *Pange pisang*, a dessert adopted from Sumatra, is made from banana cooked with brown sugar, coconut and coconut milk and served with sticky rice.

Bananas go far beyond food in Bali. Banana leaves are employed everywhere as very effective, disposable, organic plates and food wrappers. Market stalls sell most of their snacks and foods in take-out banana leaf wrappers, and each *warung* or vendor has a neat pile of banana leaf squares at the ready. Supple banana leaf wrappings are folded around meat, fish and sweet rice cakes prior to steaming or grilling. The large, broad leaves (up to six feet in length) of the banana plant are also marshalled into service as impromptu throwaway umbrellas during unpredictable monsoon downpours. The banana trunk (stem) is used as a central support stand or wall for elaborate offering constructions and in cremation rituals.

Culture and cuisine always coincide on Bali-Hindu Bali. Although fresh fruit is extraordinarily abundant, it is not a common, everyday part of the Balinese diet. Fruit grows everywhere and is plentiful, but it is not a reliable village food source, snack or dessert. Except for the odd tempting durian treat, tree-ripened raw fruit is rarely purchased in the market solely to eat. Rather, most people buy a colorful variety of fruit to incorporate into offerings, visible in the massive ceremonial offering towers (*banten tegeh*) and platters brought to the temple to be blessed. Mangosteens, mangoes, rambutan, salak and yellow bananas surmounted by rainbow-hued *jaja* rice cakes are a powerful visual gift to attract good fortune and blessings from, and to offer thanks to, the ever-vigilant gods and goddesses of Bali. After the offerings are consecrated by the priest and the gods inhale their *sari* or essence, they are taken home and eaten. Only then are the Balinese proud to feast on fruits blessed and preconsumed by the gods. In deep contrast, dressed or cooked fruit greatly affects the indigenous cuisine, either as *buah-buahan campur* (various seasonal mixed fruits), fried battered fruits (bananas, sweet potatoes, yams, breadfruit, pineapple and jackfruit) or poached fruits, commonly and happily consumed every day as hot or cold snacks.

Pisang Goreng
(BANANA FRITTERS)

Usually served as a dessert in the West, pisang goreng, accompanied by a cup of strong, rich, aromatic Balinese coffee, is a typical local breakfast in the villages. Murni shares her personal recipe for this classic Indonesian and Balinese sweet fried banana treat.

Recipe courtesy of Ni Wayan Murni, Murni's Warung, Campuhan-Ubud, January 24, 2006.

6 large ripe bananas, king bananas (*pisang raja*) are best
1 cup (100 g) plain flour
1 egg
½ cup (125 ml) milk
1 tsp vanilla essence
coconut oil for deep frying

Mix the flour, egg, milk and vanilla essence to a smooth batter in a bowl. Allow to stand for 1 hour.

Heat the oil gently in a frying pan until it is almost smoking.

Cut each banana in three pieces or to the preferred size.

Dip the banana slices in the batter and carefully drop them into the hot oil. Fry until they are golden brown.

If desired, roll the cooked fritters in a mixture of sugar and cinnamon.

Serves 4–6.

Rujak
(SPICY FRUIT AND VEGETABLE SALAD)

Rujak is a hot, spicy, sweet and sour raw fruit and vegetable salad mostly eaten as a snack between meals throughout Indonesia. There are endless fruit and vegetable variations and regional ingredients and recipes. In Singapore, the freshly chopped bud of the inflorescence of the torch ginger is an obligatory ingredient of "rojak," a local form of fruit salad served with a hot sauce. (I ate a big, wet container of it in rural Pasir Ris!)

Rujak vendors display a colorful assortment of fruits in glass containers to entice customers. Normally available is a rujak of yam beans, cucumber, pineapple, plaintain and guava. Rujak is made or sold in every market, warung and family compound throughout the island of Bali. A favorite dessert or afternoon snack, rujak consists of cut up pieces of raw, unripe (or half ripe) fruit and vegetables tossed with a very spicy, well-combined, multilayered, tamarind-based sauce.

An alternate, simple, popular, widespread Balinese version of rujak consists of only unripe sliced fruit, super scorching chilies (all Balinese insist: "No spicy, no good!"), dried shrimp paste (terasi), gula merah (brown sugar), salt and vinegar (as a substitute for the sour tamarind ingredient).

Rujak has deep roots throughout Indonesia. In the Batak Mandailing region of Sumatra (Tapanuli village district), it is a widespread, mandatory village custom (called mangarabar) to prepare a rujak when the harvest is finished. The obligatory ingredients are red chilies, salt, granulated sugar (to make it more delicious) and unripe or green fruits (plaintain, cempedak and belimbing, which is starfruit). All the ingredients are put into a traditional stamping utensil (lesung) and are coarsely pounded. The mangarabar is arranged by the village elders and the entire village participates, either by contributing the basic ingredients like fruits and vegetables or by doing the stamping labor, to make it a pleasant get together. Young men cut down a banana tree while teenagers clean and cut the fruits and vegetables to put into the lesung. The entire community gathers together to enjoy a portion of the rujak during this satisfying special event. Information credited to Suryatini Ganie, "What Cooking" The Jakarta Post.

Recipe courtesy of Wayan Sarma, driver, Sanggingan-Ubud; Jero, waitress, Melka Hotel, Lovina; Surayasa, reception, Inna Kuta Beach Hotel, Kuta, Bali, 2007.

Any combination of raw fruits and vegetables, e.g. mango, papaya, guava, pomelo, orange, green apple, water apple, pineapple, starfruit, cucumber, carrot and tomato
small red bird's eye chilies
salt
brown sugar
shrimp paste, scorched
tamarind juice, squeezed from pulp (or vinegar as a substitute)

Cut the fruit and vegetables into bite-size pieces and slice the chilies.

Put the fruit and vegetables in a bowl with the salt, brown sugar, shrimp paste, tamarind juice (or vinegar) and mix thoroughly.

Kolak Ubi

(SWEET POTATO KOLAK)

Kolak is fruit, usually bananas, cooked with coconut milk and brown sugar, but sweet potatoes (ubi) or yams are often used instead. A frequent afternoon snack, it marries a choice of sliced finger bananas (kolak pisang), sweet potato (kolak ubi), yam, ripe jackfruit or tapioca with a thick, juicy, poached sauce of coconut milk, palm sugar, vanilla, pandanus leaves and flour. Kolak campur boasts a winning combination of sweet jackfruit, banana, sweet potato, tapioca and palm sugar served with coconut milk. Sweet potato fritters have also stood the test of time in Bali.

Two wonderful female chefs invited me into their well-organized kitchen for a kolak ubi cooking demonstration at the Dolphin Beach Holiday Apartments in Lovina. Australian owners David and Moira also operate the beautifully situated Pacung Indah Hotel and Restaurant in Pacung. This inland oasis boasts unparalleled mountain and valley views, a magnificent panorama of dense tropical rainforests and lush green rice terraces, and is nestled between two high mountain ranges. A refreshing retreat perched along the main road of the peaceful village of Pacung, its popular restaurant offers delicious European and Indonesian fare and cool, clear, invigorating mountain air. www.pacungbali.com. Or treat yourself to the Dolphin Beach's delicious cuisine and accommodation at Jl. Raya Singaraja, Seririt, Kaliasem, Lovina Beach. www.dolphinbeachbali.com.

Recipe courtesy of local cooks Ni Wayan Sulastini of Karangasem Regency and Ayu from Pemaran village, Singaraja, Bali, December 2011.

6 sweet potatoes (*ubi*)
18 cups water
6 pieces brown palm sugar, each 2½ in (6.5 cm) by 1½ in (3.75 cm)
6 tsp sea salt
3 cups thick coconut milk

Peel and cut the sweet potato into cube-shaped pieces. Place in boiling water and cook for 20 minutes.

Add the palm sugar and salt and boil for 10 minutes.

Then add the coconut milk and stir until the mixture is a little bit sticky and has a caramelized taste. Ladle into small bowls.

Serves 4–6.

CHAPTER EIGHTEEN

Sacred Refreshments: Smooth Healing Ambrosia

———— ≠ ————

O F ALL THE DIFFERENT TYPES OF DRINKS (*minuman*) available in the villages of Bali—water (both secular and holy), herbal *jamu*, local coffee, tea, iced drinks and home-brewed alcohol (*arak*, *tuak* and *brem*)—fragrant holy water (*tirta*) is Bali's favorite. Holy water occurs naturally throughout Bali, both inside and outside its 10,000 odd temples (*pura*) and without benediction by priests. It is in the local rivers, springs and *subak* rice field irrigation ditches. The people search for and cling to their holy water for dear life—to remove impurities, perform purification and receive God's blessing. The lives of the Balinese would not be complete, and could not proceed, without *tirta*. The gods are in the water and the people appeal to them for safety and well-being.

Residing in the sacred temples of the island, holy water sustains all physical and spiritual life in Bali. It is usually kept in a small ceramic or silver bowl containing some flowers, which contribute to its fragrance and sense of holiness. Flowers (offerings), fire (incense) and holy water (*tirta*) are essential parts of all Hindu rituals and ceremonies. The holy water, which provides the element of purification, also becomes laced with the sanctified scent and taste of the ritual incense. The Balinese, believing implicitly in the power of holy water, make regular pilgrimages to their temples, the women clad in traditional sarongs, *kebaya* blouses and *selendang* sashes, the men in white front-knotted *udeng* head cloths, "safari" temple shirts, sarongs and sashes of their own, to make offerings to the gods. A bowl filled with holy water is often placed in front of the temple gate, allowing devotees to sprinkle it on their heads to purify their bodies and minds before entering the temple. They must also cleanse their hands using either holy water or incense smoke before commencing their prayers. Holy water is dispensed inside the temple by a corps of white-clad lay village priests (*pemangku*) into expectant, upturned hands after the completion of prayer and gratefully swallowed. During a ceremony, people also enter the inner sanctum of the temple and sprinkle themselves with water from a large vessel. After they finish praying, they are blessed by priests with water from a small metal urn that purifies and heals. Both men and women quench their spiritual thirst as often as they can with this libation from the gods.

It is a Bali-Hindu religious requirement to have holy water available at home for upcoming ceremonies—and for the old grandmother or aunt who is too frail to go to the temple. There are three basic ways for people to obtain it. *Pemangku*, givers of holy water, will travel to individual houses to bless and create the holy water if the occupants are having a small ceremony. *Pedanda* (high Brahman-caste priests) also make holy water, though normally they will officiate only at larger occasions or at important rites of passage such as the three-month baby ceremony or cremations. Devotees can also go to the temple and drink holy water there or carefully convey it back home in a can, plastic bag or special lidded glass for family use. Water that is deemed suitable for making into holy water can be collected from any clean water source: springs, rivers, streams, lakes, the sea and even a faucet (one close to the kitchen or a temple, never the bathroom). Simple holy water can even be made at home by throwing water onto the kitchen roof and catching it with a conical rice steamer basket. The water that drips through is sprinkled on the hair for purification. Holy water will only last one day—after three days the water smells bad and is no good for drinking—and more must be procured from the temple. The Balinese use the holy water in the morning at their family shrines and home compound temples to pray, concentrate and focus on God, to sprinkle on their heads for blessings and to drink before they go to work.

The spiritual power of springs cannot be underestimated in Bali. Holy water is ideally sourced from a holy spring or a temple such as Gunung Kawi (with its sacred springs). The holy water is transported in hollow flower and leaf-decorated bamboo tubes wrapped in sacred white and yellow cloth. It is collected fresh for every ceremony and is not usually kept over for the next day. If there is no sacred spring or water source near their village to obtain holy water, the priest will use a mantra (words of prayer) to forge ordinary water into holy water. People also collect their own holy water in a clay pot or metal urn and a priest or family head (if the holy water is for the family temple) blesses the water by reciting a prayer to purify it and make it ready for use. Different types of rituals require different types of holy water, each with its own function. There is also specific holy water taken from particular temples (family, seaside, lake, mountain), collected by priests or laymen for a particular ceremony. People are always eager to visit special temples or springs to obtain the correct holy water for specific rituals. The bigger the ritual, the more types of holy water are required from different temples. They also take a bath at holy springs, standing in cordoned-off temple pools, or holy rivers.

Traditional Balinese herbal medicine is rooted in the island's formidable rain- and lava-blessed living pharmacy of over 150 species of plants and plant parts (leaves, seeds, bark, roots, rhizomes and stems), which are transformed into revitalizing hot or cold tonics, efficacious herbal cures and poultices. *Jamu*, also called *loloh* or "food or medication," is the generic (Javanese) word for the traditional medicinal potions that are found throughout the whole archipelago. Perfected in the well-cultured royal court of Solo in Central Java in the seventeenth century and passed down through generations of royal palace women, *jamu* vendors and shops all over Indonesia sell a large variety of medicines to treat health ailments ranging from the common cold and flu to impotence and cancer. Related *lulur* cosmetic treatments, externally applied herbal mixtures to beautify the skin, also trace their origins to the daily pampering of the high-born Javanese princesses to maintain their fair natural complexions. (*Lulur* is a yellow rice powder rubbed on the body.)

Jamu is the second most popular drink on Bali. In warm weather, the Balinese seek the cooling properties (and health benefits) of their traditional herbal *jamu* tonics. Many Balinese have a ripe, renewable, always-ready "natural apothecary" growing in their home compounds;

their yards contain the basic healing herbs, leaves and trees for significant levels of plant medicine. In Bali, traditional plant remedies appear in three formats: as an herbal drink (*loloh*), where leaves are crushed and mixed with water, as an externally applied warming paste, cream ointment or poultice (*boreh*) of ground-up herbs and roots that are smeared on the skin, or as *simbur* (meaning to splash, spurt out or spray), a mixture chewed with raw rice and forcefully blown or spat on a patient's affected areas. In the villages, women chew fresh red shallots and spit mouthfuls of them onto the sick. Shallots are also believed to protect young children from black magic, the likely cause of any unidentifiable disease or state of distress. The Balinese, like all Indonesians, believe implicitly, and unwaveringly, in their indigenous *jamu* products and over 80 percent of them take *jamu* every day to stay or become strong, healthy and beautiful, or for sexual prowess. *Jamu* has maintained its popularity because it is cheap, people believe in it and it is a deeply ingrained tradition. Although modern Western medicine is fairly advanced in Indonesian cities, traditional medicine is still popular in both rural and urban areas. Most Balinese rely on the local *balian* (traditional healers) as their primary medical resource. The *balian* routinely prescribe natural *jamu* for their patients, empowered by prayer to the gods and divine magic. Other modalities also heal the sick in Bali: black magic and witch doctor medicine are still found, used and feared, and *dukun* (magicians) can cast many kinds of spells for their clients.

In Java, *jamu* is big business and much of it is produced in huge commercial factories in Central Java. It is either peddled by *gendong* women (*gendong* means to carry on the back) who cruise the streets and back lanes with "magic baskets" of natural cures in bottles on their backs or is sold in shops stacked high with raw ingredients and ready-mixed and pre-packaged *jamu*. In Bali, the *jamu gendong* (also called *mbok jamu ayu bakul*) slowly stroll down the empty, early morning village streets, offering their healthy natural concoctions to local clients. They produce the coveted Javanese *jamu* cures as a home business, waking up well before sunrise to prepare three or four different kinds of potions from ingredients purchased in the local market. They measure out the plant materials, grind them using a stone mortar and pestle and mix them with water. The finished *jamu* drinks are poured into used Aqua bottles and arranged in the basket, carried either on the back or on the head. Many of the medicinal herb mixtures are also sold as powders to be stirred in warm water and imbibed. Each hard-working *jamu gendong* plies a regular route on foot, often several miles long, in competition with small, specialized *jamu warung* and roadside stalls.

Most Balinese prepare their own mystical *jamu* potions for personal use at home. Although urban Balinese in Denpasar can buy the needed raw materials already mixed in the correct proportions and conveniently pre-packaged, village women simply pluck the required leaves and dig up the desired roots in their compounds, grate them into a powder and stir them into a glass of water. If a child has a fever, a Balinese mother will run out into the yard, pick several *daluman* leaves from a carefully nurtured plant and boil them with water and a block of palm sugar. The soft green jello produced by kneading the leaves is also often used as a healing beverage to treat a sore throat.

Men and women both drink *jamu* in Bali. The most popular *jamu* for men is *sehat* (healthy) *laki-laki* (husband or man). Traditionally believed to be an aid to virility, it is usually mixed with the yolk of a chicken, duck or goose egg. Women are also avid *jamu* consumers. They happily swallow endless liquid powders promising beauty, a slim waist, tighter breasts, easy pregnancies, raised energy and alleviation of lactation and menstrual issues. *Jamu Bali* (basic *jamu* plus an egg yolk) is taken regularly, often daily, to give people strength or as a preventative form of medicine. They mix raw egg yolks with honey, freshly grated and strained turmeric juice, lemon or lime juice and salt for an easy pick-me-up or to "get power" when they are sick.

The three main tubers used in making *jamu* are ginger (it warms the body), turmeric (a natural antiseptic and anti-inflammatory) and galangal (a source of strength and vitality). Tamarind is also a great local favorite in herbal concoctions, while coriander is popular as a cooling agent. Garlic is crushed in hot water with lemon juice and honey to treat colds and flu. Lesser galangal or resurrection lily is ground with rice grains and water to make a multi-ailment curative tonic. It is also turned into a paste and applied to the head and body for fever. An infusion of kneaded hibiscus leaves and raw egg is believed to aid fertility. Young cinnamon leaves are good for treating stomach disorders. To retain their youthful beauty, Balinese women like to concoct a complex *jamu*. They grind a mixture of ginger root, *sirih* leaves (*Piper betle*), garlic and *jangu* (a grass-like tree that grows in water), add water, stir well and drink every morning. A mixture of betel leaves and lime, areca nut, gambier (an astringent substance) and tobacco is popularly chewed as an addictive stimulant (betel nut) throughout rural Indonesia.

The Matahari Department Store pharmacies in Kuta and Denpasar carry a large range of well-advertised, commercially manufactured *jamu* products for hilarious, vague, odd ailments and conditions. Each package or can contains a list of ingredients and indications for use. Producers (and enthusiastic users) never claim that *jamu* will provide an instant miracle cure. It needs to be taken over long periods for its effects to become noticeable.

Indonesians have spent thousands of years developing their own medication. In the last decade, the country's traditional healing techniques and native medicines have been elevated into highly sought-after beautification and relaxation rituals promoted at exclusive international spas and well-being centers, including several in Bali. Commercially manufactured *jamu* has evolved into a large, national-scale business for a world market. Over thirty pharmaceutical companies produce traditional drugs and there are hundreds of commercial *jamu* manufacturers. Bali's obsession with *jamu* drinks has spilled over into tourist restaurants, where one can buy a tonic ("Bali Jamu") of cinnamon, cloves, ginger, nutmeg, honey, palm sugar and hot water.

Holy Water

(TIRTA)

Pemangku I Made Arnila, holy man on duty at the Ganesha temple in Lovina, creates holy water fresh every day from regular, safe-to-drink purified Aqua water that he buys in the store. He changes it into holy water by blessing it. (In the villages, the people obtain good, clean water from a sacred river, a holy spring, or sacred lakes like Danau Tamblingan.) Once it is thus blessed by a priest, Bali's humble, secular drinking water is magically and spiritually transformed into holy water for drinking and for purifying the body. The water becomes a blessing from the gods: God blesses you—this is its function. It is dispensed (sprinkled on the devotees) with a special stick for "taking the holy water," called penirtaan in Balinese. At the Ganesha temple, the penirtaan is a metal handle with a fresh white frangipani blossom whisk at the end for conferring a spray of drops on worshippers—scented, sacred, coveted liquid from the gods.

Recipe courtesy of pemangku (village priest) I Made Arnila, Ganesha (Siwa) Temple, Melka Hotel. Lovina, Bali, November 2008.

Holy water from a sacred spring or river or regular purified drinking water (Aqua)

Pour the Aqua into a metal holy water bowl (*sangku*).

Take small, bright pink bougainvillea flower petals from the offering trays around the central Lingga shrine (at a Siwa temple) and drop them into the *sangku*. This means that Siwa gives power. (Fragrant greenish-yellow blossoms from the Ylang-ylang, an East Indian tree (*Cananga odorata*), can be used instead of bougainvillea.)

Light an incense stick (Dupa Harum) and place it upright in the offering tray beneath the Lingga.

The *pemangku* either sits on the floor to pray or stands and recites three holy mantras for holy water:

Mantra Ganesha Mantra

Guru (Gayatri Mantra)

Mantra Durga

The *pemangku* distributes the fresh holy water to worshippers at temple ceremonies.

CHAPTER NINETEEN

Traditional Village Drinks: Creeping Green Vines and Sweet Ginger Tea

———— ǂ ————

THE RURAL VILLAGE REMAINS THE AGE-OLD STRONGHOLD of traditional drinks in Bali and sweet, bright green *daluman* is its quintessential representative. This mysterious green herbal tonic is made from the extract of *daluman* jungle vine leaves. When mixed with water, the leaves become dark green and gelatinous, with a jello-like texture, hence the vernacular name green grass jelly vine (*cincau hijau rambat* in Indonesian, *daluman melilit* in Balinese). The heart-shaped *daluman* leaves grow profusely in jungle areas on long, low vines supported by stakes. To make the popular village drink, the leaves are crushed, left in water to become a viscous, gelatinous mass—the main substance of the drink—strained of leaves and mixed with roasted coconut milk and brown palm sugar syrup. The result is a veritable tripod of sweetness: a dark green jelly-like layer from the leaf, a second caramel honey-hued layer from the coconut milk and a golden brown sediment from the brown sugar.

Because there is a restricted supply of the elusive *daluman* plant—very few people have it growing near their houses and it very seldom appears in the markets—the Balinese usually purchase a glass of *daluman* from a small *warung*, an itinerant seller or a market stall. The always welcomed "*daluman* lady" travels door to door each morning balancing a small wooden table on her head laden with coconut milk, palm sugar and other exotica. Creating a de facto café at each stop on her village itinerary, the *ibu* ladles a little jellified *daluman* into a glass, adds a few spoonfuls of creamy roasted coconut milk, tops it with a generous crown of caramel-brown palm sugar syrup and stirs slowly and triumphantly. (A *daluman*-like grass jelly drink made with water, grass jelly, sugar and honey is available in cans under the Cin Cau brand.)

Ronde (or *wedang ronde*) is another traditional local beverage made by boiling water mixed with ginger, pandanus leaf, lemongrass and sugar and adding *ronde*—small red, green and white glutinous rice flour and tapioca starch balls filled with roasted ground peanuts, sugar and/or palm kernels. *Wedang ronde* is a hot, ginger-flavored drink containing *ronde*. When a cold is nearing or the temperature drops, the Balinese quaff hot *wedang jahe* made with fresh ginger juice (known for its warming properties), palm sugar and often fragrant pandanus leaves.

Fruits, roots and leaves form the basis for other colorful, very popular, local Balinese beverages and specialty "coconut milk dessert drinks" like *es cendol* (green rice flour noodle pellets, coconut milk, sweet palm sugar syrup, ice and (optionally) sliced fruit. *Es campur* (mixed ice) is another obsession on an island gifted with tropical fruits, coconuts, an equatorial climate and an ever-present need to reduce body temperature. To make *es campur, jaja batu bedil* dumplings, a variety of cubed fruits (*lontar* palm fruit, pineapple, mango, avocado, jackfruit and bananas), sweet potato pieces, green tapioca products and pandanus leaf are boiled in red palm sugar syrup and, when cool, served in glasses or bowls. Coconut cream is poured over and the drink is topped with a "mountain" of shaved ice. Other Balinese concoctions include *es kelapa* (iced coconut milk), *es kelapa muda* (young, sweetened coconut juice with shredded soft coconut meat and ice), and an eye-catching color wheel of pink and blue market drinks sold and poured into portable plastic bags with straws.

Because of the time and work required to make these sweet, colorful drinks-cum-desserts, most Balinese now purchase them from local *warung* at Rp.2,000 per glass. Many of these striking, sweet iced drinks are also inexpensively served prêt a porter in a plastic bag with ice by *kaki lima* pushcart vendors who go from one village compound to the other, often giving customers a choice of ingredients.

Water holds great psychological, religious and symbolic importance in Bali, measured by its ancient royal water palace architecture and its many magically charged waters. But while much of the island benefits from ample rainfall and is lush and green, securing a safe, reliable source of potable running water is very difficult everywhere. Local tap water is not safe to drink in Bali, or elsewhere in Indonesia, and people buy water cooler size square plastic or glass tanks of purified drinking water from a local *warung* or from a commercial home delivery service. Others bring home fresh local spring water and then laboriously boil it before consumption. Small plastic cups of *air minum* (drinking water) are always offered to visiting guests at home with a thin, punch-through straw and to customers or clients at business meetings. Ice cubes first arrived in Bali in the 1970s and Balinese *warung* have factory-made ice delivered to them in trucks in big blocks. *The* ice is cut into little cubes for use in cold drinks or shaved using a special piece of equipment. With limited knowledge of proper food preparation techniques, however, the Balinese often place the hygienically prepared ice on the ground or on dirty wooden tables, often leading to contamination.

According to culinary custom and culture, the Balinese do not drink along with their meals. They take either plain water, lukewarm tea or coffee after the meal is finished. Water is nearly always consumed at room temperature. The Balinese believe that cold water or ice water gives them a sore throat and makes them feel bloated. Miguel Covarrubias commented on the ritual and etiquette of drinking water in Bali in the 1930s: "There were no set meal hours and they ate whenever they felt hungry. A little before noon the men returned from work to eat lunch. A *charatan* or *kendi* for drinking water—an exotic, Egyptian, souk-like vessel with a long, Nights of Arabia spout—was passed around after the meal was finished. Each drank in turn and at a distance from it, letting a continuous jet of water fall into the open mouth, the lips never touching the spout. When we tried to drink like the Balinese we succeeded only in choking or drenching ourselves." *Kendi* are ceramic ewers found throughout Southeast Asia and India and function as both ceremonial vessels for sacred water and as common household containers. The vessel is grasped with one hand around the neck and is tilted towards the mouth, allowing the water to flow into the mouth without touching the lips to the spout. The Balinese boil the water first and then leave it to stand in the *caratan* for a day before drinking it. They also use a bamboo drinking bottle or a *labu* (gourd) flask customarily used to hold water and other precious liquids. The traditional *caratan* is still used in the villages but is replaced by glasses in modern Denpasar.

Bali is a wet, fertile land of milk and honey for some Balinese but a dustbowl of despair for others, especially in arid Karangasem regency in eastern Bali. Here, many indigenous Balinese subsist far below the poverty line in isolated, remote hamlets on the steep, infertile, eastern slopes of Mount Agung and Mount Abang, without roads, running water, sanitation, adequate nutrition and health care. Their only water supply is a one-to-six-hour walk to remote mountain springs. In the eight-month-long dry season, there is no water at all—no permanent streams, rivers or springs. The women and children walk 2–5 hours along steep trails in 40 degree heat to the coast or to Lake Batur to collect 25 liters of water. Other villagers traverse up and down the parched mountains three times a day transporting makeshift coconut pails of water to their homes and families. Millions of hours a year are spent solely on desperate journeys to find water. Their only other option is to purchase water from dealers at high prices.

On these arid mountain slopes, the earth is granular volcanic soil, limiting agriculture to cassava and corn. The men coax a few crops from the resistant earth during the short rainy season, but barely enough for their own needs. Chronic dehydration and malnourishment thus go hand in hand. Western-funded non-governmental agencies like the East Bali Poverty Project and other social programs have engaged this daily Balinese battlefront to find sufficient drinking water. Aid workers have built large, covered, communal rainwater tanks in several of the remote villages. The goal is to bring potable or at least enough running water to all remote mountain slope villages for drinking, cooking, washing and small-scale gardening year round. Farmers have also been given goats to provide milk for the children. Even in Bali's capital city Denpasar, running water dwindles to a trickle during the day. Conservationists say that the feeble water pressure is due to the unquenchable thirst of the five-star hotels in Nusa Dua, an elite tourist resort area.

Tea has long been cultivated in Indonesia—it is the "people's drink"— and in Bali leaf- and root-based herbal teas are a potent natural tradition and addition to conventional tea plant leaves. Deep inside Balinese villages, a soothing breed of aromatic hot tea (*teh panas*) has traditionally been made by boiling two fresh pandanus leaves in water for five to ten minutes and then adding them to tea. Another particularly refreshing Balinese drink is water boiled with pandanus leaves alone. Tea made from white hibiscus tree leaves, and blood red tea infused with scarlet hibiscus flowers are other favorites. All Balinese know a traditional village recipe for home-made hot ginger tea (*teh jahe*), ginger being a powerful herbal remedy for colds, flu, fever, to restore energy to tired limbs and to rid oneself of *masuk angin* (windy season) ailments greatly disliked and feared by the heat-loving Balinese. In the villages, women purchase, peel, wash, cut or crush fragrant ginger root, place it in boiling water with a tea bag and sweeten it with generous amounts of *gula merah* (brown sugar). Lemongrass, easily available on Bali and commonly grown in home gardens, is also pounded, placed in a glass of boiling water with a tea bag and sugar. Besides home-made concoctions, a selection of imported Javanese tea products—blackcurrant, ginseng, ginger, jasmine and green teas—are on sale in the fruit, flower, and spice market in Bedugul and in larger local stores and supermarkets.

Ordinary Balinese cannot afford to drink milk (*susu*) and envy those who can. Milk is not commonly sold in rural villages and has to be bought from a larger local store or supermarket at prohibitive prices in cartons, or from a farmer who might have a cow. Before 2005, most milk was either powdered or sweetened condensed milk in tins. Pasteurized milk was rare but is now available in supermarkets in unrefrigerated cardboard cartons for longer shelf life, but it is mainly for tourists.

Natural fruit juice drinks made from papaya, mango, passionfruit or any other local fruit in season are not normally made at home. In an economy of scarcity, cannibalizing an entire expensive fruit to make juice is considered sacrilegious. The Balinese normally buy fruit to use as temple offerings or they eat a ripe treat straight off the tree. The coconut, however, is ubiquitous, and is often procured for free. Fresh, clean coconut water, with its restorative properties, is the standard drink that the Balinese offer to guests at home-based ceremonies.

Although the Balinese like commercially prepared fruit juices, they cannot afford to drink the cardboard packets of fruit juices with embedded straws that are available on their supermarket shelves; these are VIP drinks only for tourists, expats or rich Balinese. Consumption of local, fruit-based juice drinks at Bali's *warung* or market stalls can be a risky affair as vendors often do not boil their own water for long enough or to the correct temperature. The Balinese often suffer from stomach distress. The Balinese only drink soda on rare occasions as it is also too expensive. Canned (more expensive) or old-fashioned (and cheaper) glass-bottled sodas are available in supermarkets, beach bars and convenience shops. Balinese-style village *warung* stock a more notably limited range of drinks for locals: coffee, beer, Indonesian brand soft drinks, bottled water, tea and *arak*.

Visiting tourists to the island are in heaven with fresh juices that range from the truly exotic to the deliciously familiar—orange, pink guava, soursop, lychee, guava, apple, water apple, lemon, pineapple, mango—in plastic bottles or paper cartons. Hotel buffet breakfasts challenge the imagination with Bali's fruits (honeydew melon, guava, yellow mango, watermelon, coconut) and enticing fruit juice selections: carrot, lemon, spinach and apple, orange and papaya with nutmeg and ginger, strawberry and banana with cinnamon, or avocado. Avocado is common in Bali. The Balinese like to eat it Dutch-style with grated coconut (tourists add chocolate sprinkles). Locals also drink avocado juice with ice and palm sugar syrup or with ice and chocolate syrup!

Daluman

(GREEN JELLY, COCONUT AND PALM SUGAR DRINK)

A very beautifully sweet, leaf-laden, bright green drink, daluman can be found in any bustling market in the early morning hours. Gaggles of busy Balinese vendors compete for nasi campur customers, but the daluman lady—the goddess of emerald refreshments—takes center stage among the row of food sellers. She wakes up at 5 a.m. every day to prepare the daily rice for her family and daluman leaves for her market stall business. The ibu knows how to take command of her mysterious leaves. The daluman leaves have to be washed twice, then squeezed and then left to coagulate in water for one hour until they solidify and form a dark green jello. While the leaves undergo their amazing metamorphosis, the vendor prepares the roasted coconut milk and palm sugar syrup which will be mixed with the magical leaf gel. Seated at her small wooden table and white plastic chair, she dispenses the daluman mixture, a few tablespoons of coconut milk and a dollop of palm sugar into a waiting glass with the pride and finesse of a practiced daluman showman. Revered by the Balinese, the drink is a miraculous, artistic, tri-colored tripod of sweetness. One layer shines dark evergreen from the leaf, a second, caramel honey-hued layer (from the coconut milk) tempts the eye, and a golden brown sediment from the brown sugar completes the vision of paradise. After I ate–drank slurped the sweet beauty, I experienced a sugar rush and a flash of clear vision afterwards— like a jolt! Although daluman is supposed to be good for the stomach, 15 minutes later I experienced flu-like cold symptoms and was sick for three days with fever, weakness and stomach pain (raw local water may have been added to the sugar and the coconut milk!).

Recipe courtesy of Luh Samiasih (Jero), Tejakula, Lovina, and Komang Sukahati, Banyualit, Lovina, Ganesha Restaurant, Melka Resort, Lovina, November 20, 2008.

approximately 300 *daluman* leaves
coconut milk made from roasted and grated coconut
brown palm sugar syrup
salt to taste
ice cubes

Wash the *daluman* leaves twice and then tear them into small pieces by hand. Crush the pieces in a mortar and pestle.

Place the crushed leaves in a bowl of water to steep for 30–40 minutes. The liquid will coagulate, forming a green jelly-like mass.

Squeeze the leaves and press the liquid through a sieve to capture any leaf remnants. Allow the liquid to sit for a few minutes.

Prepare the roasted coconut milk and palm sugar syrup.

Ladle some green *daluman* jello into each glass. Add a few spoonfuls of coconut milk, then some brown liquid sugar and a pinch of salt.

Put some ice cubes in each glass.

Serves 6.

Es Cendol

(GREEN FLOUR PELLETS AND ICE DRINK)

Es cendol is a layered, cooling drink of dark brown palm sugar syrup topped with snowy coconut milk and ice. It also classically contains gelatinous mint green shreds and globules made from mung bean flour. It is found all over Indonesia in many different incarnations. Traditional recipes for es cendol (black, green and/or red-colored) require extended preparation time. It is made with thick, wet, jello-like black ocean sea grass sold in plastic packages in the supermarket. The block of cendol is washed first, chopped up into small pieces and served with palm sugar syrup, coconut cream and ice. It can also be mixed with fruit. Devotees consume it as a drink or as a dessert. Flavored with an extract of kneaded kayu sugi leaves, the recipe below is the most popular one found and followed in Bali.

Recipe courtesy of Morny, Murni's Houses, Ubud, April 2, 2007.

1 cup (100 g) rice flour
1 packet mung bean flour
2 tsp tapioca flour
½ glass green water extract from *kayu suji* leaves (or artificial
    green coloring)
2 tsp salt
4 glasses water
coconut milk
palm sugar syrup
shaved ice

Grind the *kayu suji* leaves, add some water, then squeeze or sieve to extract half a glass of green liquid.

Combine the rice flour, mung green flour, tapioca flour and salt and mix into a thick paste with the green *suji* water.

Cook the mixture in a saucepan over a low heat for about 30 minutes, constantly stirring to avoid scorching. Set aside to cool.

Fill a deep pan with ice water. Rub the *cendol* paste through a coarse sieve, allowing the pellets to drop into the water below. Drain.

Add one tablespoon of the pellets to a glass of coconut milk. Sweeten with liquid palm sugar syrup. Stir to combine and top with shaved ice.

CHAPTER TWENTY

Sweet Spirits, Hot Arak Nights and the Gods of Wine

———— ≢ ————

*T*UAK, *ARAK* AND *BREM* ARE THE MOST POPULAR home-brewed alcoholic refreshments on Bali. All three are cheap and the best quality is always home-made. *Tuak* (*sajeng*), a mild palm beer, is made from the juice of palm flowers, harvested by cutting the undeveloped, unopened flower bud of either the coconut, lontar or sugar palm. *Tuak* is produced by fermenting the sap of the flower bud. The coconut palm (*punyan nyuh*) is most often used because the tree is so widespread. In areas where sugar palms (*punyan jaka*) grow, such as the forested highlands en route to Jatiluweh, their juice, extracted from the flower bud at the crown, is used instead. In dry northern Bali, the thorny drought-resistant lontar palm (*punyan ental*) is selected for *tuak*.

Tapping *tuak* is a traditional Balinese art form. While coconut palm and lontar palm owners simply cut steps directly into the trunk, a precarious one-poled ladder comprising a long, thin, strong bamboo tube with foot rests or pedals is affixed to or leaned against the tall sugar palms. A village *tuak* sap harvester climbs the bamboo pole in the afternoon to collect the day's supply of palm sap. He bends the bud so the tip points down and cuts an incision through the sheath directly into the flower stalk. A container is tied to the flower stalk to catch the draining sap. One bud typically fills one full coconut shell with sap per day. In some areas, bamboo sections are used instead to collect the sap. The sugary liquid is suspended overnight in a bamboo container or coconut shell and by next morning is fermented and ready to drink. The *tuak* bubbles, foams and gets stronger as the day goes on as natural fermentation takes place. The fresh *tuak* can be drunk for a maximum of two to three days after production and then it begins to turn into vinegar.

There are three kinds of *tuak* brewed from palm tree sap: *tuak manis* (sweet or young), *tuak wayah* (old) and *tuak wayah baru* (old–new). *Tuak manis* is fresh from the tree and has a fairly high sugar content because the fermentation process has not gone on for very long. People who drink it often suffer from stomach problems. *Tuak wayah*, produced by letting the fresh *tuak manis* age naturally, is stronger and dryer and is preferred as it has a taste of heavily hopped beer. *Tuak wayah baru* is a ready-to-drink variety with a superior taste because the new sap collection vessels are seeded with a little yeast grown in old coconut husks and some already fermented *tuak* to get the brew started quickly. Once yeast is added to the fresh *tuak*, it is left to ferment for four to five days in the shade.

Because of its volatile, time-sensitive composition, *tuak* is not prepared and bottled in factories for commercial sale in stores. All *tuak* is collected and fermented by individuals or small groups of villagers who market it locally. It is available in innumerable small roadside *warung* in every village all over the island. The *warung* owner will line up a couple of dozen bottles on the table, each filled with foaming *tuak wayah baru* right from the tree. The *tuak* is most often displayed, bought and sold in empty beer bottles (a good tree will produce four or five beer bottles of *tuak* per day). Brewed in large earthenware jars, the beer-like beverage is normally consumed the same day it is made by groups of Balinese men who become increasingly good-natured as the evening progresses. It is never imbibed directly from the bottle, but is traditionally drunk from a glass or a *ceret*, a bamboo tube with a spout. To use this, the drinker bends his head back, raises the vessel and tilts it so that a thin stream of liquid flows into his open mouth.

Drinking *tuak* is a popular social pastime among Balinese men. They often form local drinking clubs or groups (*sekaha tuak*) which meet regularly for camaraderie and company. They congregate at the home of the head of the *seka* every evening to squat on woven coconut leaf mats, talk and drink *tuak* purchased in large plastic cans from neighboring villagers. Drunkenness (*mabuk*) is common. There is a double sexual-alcohol standard in Bali. It is not acceptable for Balinese women to drink alcohol at all. They are treated as outcasts and disparaged as crazy if they do. Balinese men say women cannot drink "because they are not as strong as men, and it is not good for the baby when they are pregnant." Balinese men, however, love to drink at home, and if they have some spare cash will go out to the local *warung* to settle on wooden benches, talk, eat a snack and drink with their friends.

Arak, alternately referred to as Balinese palm gin, palm wine, palm brandy or palm spirit, is distilled *tuak*. In Balinese compounds, it is made in small batches at home stills (*bingkil nira*) as a cottage industry. Instead of harvesting sap and producing *tuak* from scratch, the Balinese often buy already fermented and processed bottled *tuak wayah* from a village manufacturer as the raw material to make *arak*. To distill the *tuak* into *arak*, the villagers boil it in large, covered clay pots over a wood and ash fire attached to a diagonally slanted bamboo pole some 20 feet in length. As the boiling *tuak* vapor is cooled down, the condensed drops (distilled *arak*) pass along the bamboo pole towards their final destination, a container (not always clean) sitting on the ground.

Arak or *sajeng rateng* (straight *sajeng*) is a potent 60–100 proof liquor with a much higher alcoholic content than *tuak*, and is colorless although it may have a slight tint from the addition of ginger, ginseng, turmeric or cloves. Burdened with a sharp, biting, unpleasant taste, the Balinese mix *arak* with spices (*arak mabasa*), honey (*arak madu*) or *brem*, or add it to coffee. Since no fermentation process takes place, *arak* keeps indefinitely and can be bottled in discarded beer bottles, capped and sold in village *warung*. Locally produced Karangasem regency *arak* has the reputation of being the best quality local tipple in Bali. The village of Talibeng near Sideman in Karangasem is the center of large-scale *arak* production in Bali, with 500 stills. Here, *tuak* is laboriously sourced from coconut palm trees, fermented and distilled into *arak*, then brought to the big market at Talibeng in large plastic jugs. Villagers from all over Bali travel here to buy *arak* in bulk to rebottle and sell to small, distant local *warung*. The Balinese in Nusa Lembongan brew up *arak* ("bathtub gin") at home and pour it into discarded, often unhygienic water bottles for drinking party consumption. The clear liquid, which is taken straight or mixed with club soda or soda water, is consumed communally. A single glass is passed around and shared between many. The Balinese can also occasionally get their hands on imported snake *arak* brought back from Madura Island. Whole snakes are steeped in the *arak*, reputed to give those who drink it extra power and an alcohol kick. The purchaser will store it in a large glass bottle or jar and dispense individual drinks from it at home to friends, neighbors and customers.

Brem (Balinese rice wine), pronounced "brum," is heavy, naturally sweet, sticky and milky, much like Japanese *saké*. It is coaxed from mildly fermented white glutinous rice (*ketan* in Balinese) mixed with a smaller amount of black rice (*injin*) to achieve the desired color. *Brem* produced with white rice alone is lemon yellow in color, while *brem* produced from black rice alone is brown. A prosperous *brem*-making cottage industry is conducted in the villages where individuals brew small amounts for home consumption, for ceremonial offerings and for local sale. To produce their product, the rice (3.3 pounds each of *ketan* and *injin*) is first soaked in water for two hours until very soft. It is then steamed and re-steamed for a total of two hours. The cooked rice is placed in a shallow woven bamboo box to cool. A critical ingredient, yeast (*ragi*), purchased in tiny breakable cakes, is added by sprinkling it on top of the rice. This moist mixture is then wrapped and sealed in a round bamboo container lined with banana leaves to ferment for three to seven days. The liquid squeezed from it drains through the loosely woven bamboo bottom into a pan, and the new-born *brem* is ready to drink. The remaining solid pieces left in the container are called *tape* and are eaten as a favorite Balinese dessert. Containing only rice, yeast and water, *brem* is a pleasant drink and can be enjoyed over ice or mixed with *arak*. A refreshing drink is made by adding cubed lontar palm flesh to *brem* with drops of honey, a slice of lemon and ice cubes. A favorite Balinese concoction for sexual stamina combines *brem* with two egg yolks, which are left to set for some minutes before consumption.

Besides being a traditional alcoholic beverage enjoyed by the Balinese, cloudy sweet *brem*, like *arak*, is a necessity for many of the island's Bali-Hindu ceremonies. Home-brewed *brem* and *arak* are universally used as offerings in almost all religious rituals and are consumed in conjunction with temple festivals and weddings. Rice wine and palm brandy offerings welcome visiting gods and deified ancestors to their temple shrines during sacred rites and celebrations. Drops of *tuak*, *arak* and *brem* are spilled on the ground from a bottle through an intermediary banana leaf ladle as important offerings (*patabuh*) to appease the *buta kala*, the negative forces or lower spirits of the universe, during temple anniversaries. Very large quantities of *brem*, usually low-grade home-made *brem* mixed with water, are made and mandated for use as a *patabuh* in Bali. Miguel Covarrubias reported on the use of alcoholic brews in Bali in the 1930s: "Leading *banjar* members pour drinks for the guests: *tuak* (palm beer), *brom*, a sweet sherry made from fermented black rice, or more rarely *arak*, distilled rice brandy. More frequently water alone is served; it is only old men who are fond of alcoholic drinks, drinking, however, with moderation and never becoming drunk. During our entire stay in Bali we never saw a man really drunk, perhaps because the Balinese dread the sensation of dizziness and confusion, of losing control over themselves."

There are four commercial *brem* factories in Bali, the largest being in the fishing village of Sanur where the family who own it still use age-old village processes and all-natural ingredients to make their sweet five percent alcohol traditional Balinese rice wine. In Sanur also, another family-run business specializes in fruit-flavored liqueurs, including *tuak jaka*, a pinkish-red *tuak* made from the stems of the *jaka* sugar palm tree (*punyan jaka*) fermented with readily available fresh local fruits. Flavors include banana, coconut, coffee, pineapple, honeydew melon, vanilla, lychee, lemon, blackcurrant and apple and are sold in Balinese culture-inspired ceramic bottles.

Up until the new millennium, wine made from grapes was very rare and expensive in Bali, since wine brought into Indonesia, a predominantly Muslim country, incurs the 300 percent government tax rate levied on all imported alcohol. Today, many places in Bali stock excellent imported wines, including from France and Australia, as well as less expensive Balinese fruit wine from locally grown and harvested wine-quality grapes. Big black table grapes have been growing along the hot, arid northeast coast of the island since the beginning of the twentieth century but it took years of trial, error and experimentation to develop parasite- and vine disease-resistant grapes that could be satisfactorily cultivated for wine on a commercial scale. The grapes have a surprisingly high quality. Abundant sunshine, clear mountain water and mineral-rich soil have proven to be ideal climate conditions for the types of grapes grown and harvested here, which are planted over vast areas from Seririt to Singaraja on overhead trellises. The tropical climate also makes for the unique character of wine making on the island. Most grape vines require a dormant period during cooler months, but Balinese vines produce grapes continuously in 120-day cycles and are harvested every four months, thus yielding up to three crops a year. Production methods have also been adapted to local cultural beliefs, such as machine crushing instead of the traditional stomping with the feet (as the head is considered holy in the Bali-Hindu religion and the feet are deemed profane and thus not suitable for processing food).

International brands of wine and liquor are available in restaurants and hotels where they are transformed into creative Balinese concoctions when combined with *tuak* beer, *arak* palm spirit and *brem* rice wine. New mixtures of *arak* with *brem*, fruit juices, local coffee, imported liqueurs and sodas, such as Bali's classic Arak Attack (*arak* with Sprite), are very popular and retain a Balinese edge. Cheap, local domestic beers are also popular with club goers. But as Indonesian Islamic law increasingly serves as a gatekeeper over the alcoholic affairs of Hindu Bali, the availability of imported Western brands is becoming more restricted. Local Balinese and Indonesian companies are cornering the alcohol market as the banned, blockaded and heavily taxed imported competition dries up. These products, however, are earmarked for tourists and expatriates. The Balinese cannot afford them. Besides, they prefer their traditional village *warung* rice field and palm tree libations—home-made *arak*, *tuak* and *brem*.

CHAPTER TWENTY-ONE
Kopi Bali:
The Heavenly Coffee

———— ≠ ————

COFFEE IS GROWN AND HARVESTED IN THE STEAMY, life-giving equatorial regions of the globe. The charismatic "coffee belt" encompasses Africa, Arabia, the Asia Pacific, Central and South America and Hawaii. Banded by the Tropics of Cancer and Capricorn circling the earth, these tropical and subtropical regions have abundant sunshine, moderate rainfall and year-round warm temperatures with no frost. Two botanical varieties make up the bulk of coffee consumed worldwide: Arabica (*Coffea arabica*) and Robusta (*Coffea canephora*, var. *Robusta*). Arabica accounts for 75 percent of the world's coffee production. The other 25 percent is plucked from Robusta bushes. Plentiful, very low-grade Robusta is primarily grown for the cheap commercial market. It boosts the caffeine content in instant coffees and is used as a filler in institutional and less expensive coffees. Commercially lucrative Arabica is highly prized for its flavor characteristics and is used exclusively in the gourmet coffee trade. The very carefully cultivated beans only grow in particular environments with adequate rain, a temperate climate, rich volcanic soil and sufficient altitude. The choicest Arabica beans grow at the highest elevations. Arabica trees planted at 3,000–6,000 feet in altitude produce a "hard bean" with concentrated flavors. The colder climate and cool air encourage the beans to ripen and mature slowly, yielding very dense, superior quality beans.

The finest coffee beans are always spun from the rich volcanic earth of the world's tropical highlands. The ideal soil for growing coffee consists of leaf mold, organic matter and disintegrated volcanic rock. Coffee has passport-worthy global origins. The world's largest coffee country barons are Brazil, Colombia, Indonesia, Ethiopia, Guatemala, India, Cote d'Ivoire, Uganda, Kenya, Vietnam, Costa Rica, El Salvador, Ecuador, the Philippines, Honduras, Peru, Kenya, Congo, Madagascar, Thailand and Mexico.

Indonesia is the world's fourth largest coffee exporter. Robusta is the dominant crop in Indonesia, constituting 90 percent of the coffee grown and 95 percent of the coffee exported. Indonesia also produces an elite segment of internationally renowned Arabica. Coffee grows all along this brilliantine necklace of bountiful equatorial islands from Sulawesi, Sumatra, Java, Bali, the highlands of Papua New Guinea, Flores and Sumbawa to East Timor. The vast Indonesian archipelago is rich in natural beauty and primeval wildlife. Each sip of its intriguing coffees evokes the lushness of its 17,508 remote, often still-primitive, culturally distinct islands. Seven percent of Indonesia's total coffee production comes from the island of Sulawesi, particularly from the densely forested mountainous areas of Tana Toraja in South Sulawesi. True Toraja coffees (*tana* means land and Toraja means "people of the uplands" in the local Bugis language) come from the mystical Tana Toraja highlands. The highest growing areas are in the extreme north. Farmers bring these coffees down from the mountains to the two local market towns of Sapan and Minanga, the best accumulation points for the highest-grown Toraja lots, to sell to collectors for the larger mills. The high-altitude coffees were formerly heralded as "Celebes Kalossi." Torajaland used to be called Kalossi, the Dutch colonial name for the region, while Sulawesi was formerly called Celebes. South Sulawesi's elevated, inaccessible mountain jungles are a paradise for the production of these extremely fine, hand-picked and sun-dried Arabica coffee beans.

Sumatra is home to wild Asian elephants, endangered orangutans, supercharged jungle soil and full-bore, single-origin "Sumatran" coffee. Arabica coffee production began in Sumatra in the eighteenth century under Dutch colonial domination, introduced first to the northern region of Aceh around Lake Tawar. High-value coffee crops are also cultivated near the southern shores of Lake Toba, around the towns ringing Lintong Nihota. "Sumatra Onan Ganjang Cultivar" coffee comes from this region.

The top-grade, uniquely prepared Lintong coffee, is called "Blue Batak" in honor of the local, indigenous Toba Batak people. Blue Batak is a near zero-defect preparation, without the split beans and broken pieces found in standard Sumatras. It is always carefully density-sorted and triple-sorted by hand. "Sumatra Toba Batak Peaberry" is also a Lintong coffee from the southern area of Lake Toba, the world's largest volcanic crater lake. It is farmed by the Batak people, a tribe of small growers that produce the coffee in this vicinity. Peaberry is a rare, exquisite, high grade of connoisseur coffee. Peaberry occurs when a coffee tree is stressed in its growing environment. This results in an individual coffee cherry producing only one round, very dense bean rather than the usual two beans. Lintong coffee also grows on high plateaus, at 3,000–4,000 feet, in the Lintong mountains to the west of Lake Toba.

Sumatra's coffees are supremely intense, pungent, powerful, brooding and opaque. Sumatras are sold under the general trade name "Mandailing," also spelled Mandheling, referencing an ethnic group of shopkeepers in Central Sumatra that were once involved in coffee production. The Mandheling bean is considered to be the most full-bodied coffee bean in the world. Sumatra's high-quality 100 percent Arabica coffees are known for their forest floor earthiness and deep, husky, aggressive taste. Hailing from the finest coffee growing region in Sumatra, the Mandhelings are at home at an ideal growing altitude in excess of 2,500 feet. "Sumatra Ankola," the cream of the coffee market, is a famous gourmet Arabica, grown near the port of Padang at elevations of 2,500–5,000 feet above sea level. Sumatra is also renowned for its deliberately "aged coffees" using historical Indonesian processing methods. Closely monitored lots are held for three to five years in stainless steel vats to carefully antique and transform their flavors. Aged Sumatra Aceh and Aged Sumatra Lintong are premeditated, absolute geriatric coffee beauties!

Ambitious Dutch colonial administrators turned thousands of hectares of fertile mountainous areas in Java into Arabica coffee plantations for commercial development. Dutch settlers first brought Arabica coffee seeds to Jakarta, then called Batavia, in 1699. The Netherlands became the sole producer-exporter of the world's most sought-after coffee bean. The coffee from this region was so valuable that Java became an active acronym for coffee. The Arabica groves prospered until 1869 when they were decimated by an epidemic of leaf rust. Disease resistance in coffee was later found to be related to the height at which the trees grow. Robusta thrives when cultivated at 1,312–2,624 feet above sea level and is relatively disease-resistant at this altitude. Arabica is much less prone to *Hemileia vastatrix*, the fungus that causes leaf rust, and other diseases when grown at altitudes above 2,624 feet. Coffee growers in Indonesia adapted and learned to plant Robusta at the lower elevations and Arabica at the higher peaks. All of the main coffee estates are located in East Java, clustered in the vicinity of the Kawah Ijen complex, a cauldron or volcanic crater. The most suitable altitude for coffee production here is 3,000–6,000 feet above sea level, with most coffee plants growing in the plateau region at an elevation of 4,500 feet. Coffee also prospers on the volcanic slopes due to the fortuitous altitude (the Kawah Ijen summit is 7,545 feet above sea level) and well-drained soil. The government produces 85 percent of the coffee in East Java. There is also "Private Estate" Java, but Government Estate is preferred as it is a higher quality coffee. Java "Government Estate" coffee comes from four old farms that date back to the Dutch colonial era: Djampit and Blawan (2,268 hectares) are the largest government estates, while Pancoer is 1,110 hectares and Kayumas is 725 hectares in size.

Flores, a former Portuguese colony, is a small, 224-mile-long island in the Indonesian archipelago, the traditional gateway to the fierce, carnivorous Komodo dragons of nearby Komodo and Rinca islands. Mountainous Flores has numerous active and inactive volcanic peaks, including its famous, color-shifting, emerald-green-brown crater lakes (Kelimutu). The relatively undeveloped island of Flores is another player in the rich Indonesian coffee trade. The local "Kopi Flores" brand of plastic packeted coffee is only exported to Surabaya, however; Jakarta forbids Flores to send its coffee overseas. Coffee in Flores grows in mountainous areas near Ruteng and Manggarai. This coffee growing district is farmed by the Manggarai people, an ethnic hilltop tribe. Coffee is also cultivated in the Bajawa highlands in central Flores (the small traditional town of Bajawa is home to the Ngada people). Coffee is grown on this high fertile plateau at between 3,772 and 4,593 feet, a respectable altitude for Indonesian coffee farming. Coffee trees in Flores are not normally pruned, and often reach heights of 25–30 feet. The older trees create virtual coffee forests which provide shade for the younger, still-productive Arabica coffee plants. World-famous "Blue Dragon" coffee is grown in the Bajawa region. Cultivated in volcanic soil at elevations up to 6,000 feet, it is organically grown and processed by the coffee growing families of Flores island. This high mountain grown delicacy has hints of dark chocolate and berries, with a touch of smoke.

Like many other islands throughout Indonesia, Bali is doubly blessed with an ideal environment for both Arabica and Robusta coffee cultivation. Bali's coffee regions and coffee fortresses are all at the higher altitudes. The fortuitous, god-given combination of a moist, cool climate, enriched volcanic soil, frequent rainfall and the gradually sloping terrain give Bali coffee its unique, exclusive, world-envied flavor. Bali's coffees reflect the strength, spirit and spirituality of Bali's majestic holy mountains and abundantly rich, lava-based soils. Bali's farmers use traditional growing and processing techniques to produce the rich tasting coffees. Fresh from the *kampung*, delicious *kopi Bali* (*kopi* is coffee) is famous in Indonesia for quality. The Javanese even prefer it over their own Java coffee. In innocent, peaceful "village Bali," fresh always means newly made. There is still ancient, inherited craftsmanship in both the kitchen and in local hand-wrought and hand-powered coffee making rituals. The very best hand-picked coffee crops come from small family-owned farms and private estates in the northern mountainous regions of Bali. Much of Bali's coffee is single origin "Estate Coffee," meaning that it is grown on a private coffee plantation or on a single estate. Almost all Indonesian coffee comes from small independent farms, often located in the owner's backyard! Bali's 100 percent Arabica coffee is strictly high-grown, high-quality, single bean Estate Coffee (European Preparation). Unroasted green coffee beans are classified according to the number of defective beans. European Preparation only allows three to five defective beans per thousand.

The Mengwi kingdom in old Bali (Badung Regency) enjoyed great riches from the beginning of the nineteenth century because of its great coffee plantations. In Buleleng Regency there are spectacular views of rice fields, coffee plantations and wild dolphin pods in the placid coastal waters. Small farmers here tend their "coffee gardens" on elevated slopes and terraces in the magnificent coffee-forested highlands. These altitudes are so cool that Bali's ultra sweet, blood red strawberries grow here year round, brightening the chilly, rainy market stalls in mountainous, misty Bedugul. The exceptional coffees are grown in opulent volcanic soil using the same traditional methods as those employed in raising pesticide- and herbicide-free organic coffee. They are also carefully shade-grown under an umbrella of fruit and citrus trees: banana, clove, mango, jackfruit and cocoa trees. Shade-grown coffee means that the coffee trees are grown under a dense forest canopy, often interplanted with protective shade trees and windbreak trees. Coffee trees need adequate shade and Balinese farmers plant a bower of shade trees two full years before planting their first coffee seedlings to provide cover and allow air circulation. The dapdap tree, *Erythrina variegate*, also called the Indian coral tree, is commonly used. The deciduous tree reaches up to 49 feet in height with bright red flowers, and is widely distributed in the Philippines and India. A coffee plantation produces a great deal of biodiversity. Shade trees and introduced companion cover trees also add additional color to the natural, bland green visual environment of the coffee farms.

This blessed island is the visible, uplifted summit of a submerged volcano and is one of dozens of islands east of Java with breathtaking mountain terrain, foggy hillsides and deep pockets of rich volcanic soil. Coffee growing (Arabica) began in Bali in the 1750s but the plants succumbed to leaf rust a hundred years later. Coffee production was revived with new Robusta strains in 1912. Bangli, Buleleng and Tabanan regencies are the three main coffee growing areas in Bali. In 2011, 3,080 tons of Arabica beans were harvested in the Kintamani (Bangli Regency) coffee growing district. Coffee plantations in the volcanic highlands of Kintamani now cover a total of 10,485 hectares of cultivated land. Eighty percent of Bali's coffee crops are raised in this mountainous hinterland landscape. Arabica, which commands higher prices, mainly grows near Kintamani village in northeast Bali and in the steep mountain passes south of coastal Singaraja. Robusta coffee production is centered in Pupuan (Tabanan Regency) and Banyuatis (Buleleng Regency). Scattered hillside plantations and coffee groves also spring up along the main roads in most of the upland areas of mountainous Bali. Coffee trees are visible from Mengwi to Bedugul, in Tampaksiring and

Kintamani, and along the zigzag, bone-chilling mountainous decline from lofty Bedugul to coastal Singaraja (Buleleng Regency). Kayu Putih, a small hillside village in northern Bali, is three miles inland from the Singaraja-Seririt main road of Lovina, and is also a fertile plantation area for cacao, coffee, mango, tobacco and cloves. Coffee, clove and rice terraces surround Gitgit Waterfalls, the highest waterfall in Bali.

Dutch colonists conquered Buleleng Regency in 1849 and rapidly introduced the commodity plantation system of agriculture. Arabica coffee was first planted as a cash crop in 1870. The frigid mountainous area around Munduk has numerous coffee (Robusta and Arabica), vanilla, cocoa and clove plantations rooted in its rich, volcanic highland soil. Munduk village, with its gorgeous cascading rice terraces, is located near the center of northern Bali's alpine coffee industry. Hand-made "Coffee Bali Munduk" is prepared and processed traditionally in the clear mountain citadel of Munduk. This traditional small village grown coffee is packaged by Puri Lumbung Cottages in Munduk as part of a sustainable tourism project and training initiative for local villagers.

Coffee begins with and is rooted in the earth. Grown high on lava-enriched slopes, Bali coffee owes its unique taste and quality to both the ancient rich soil and very favorable botanical conditions. A highly specialized, spectacular micro-climate is required to produce these singular Balinese coffees. Each charismatic equatorial cup also bears the unmistakeable imprint of Balinese village culture, where nothing is left to chance. Culture and coffee horticulture coincide and mesh to produce coffees with a true touch of the gods. Protective divine clouds hover over the highland village coffee trees during the hottest parts of the day, and there is just the right amount of rainfall at the right times throughout the growing cycle. Reared and hidden in inaccessible, secret mountain Shangrilas, the gourmet, volcanic-field coffee beans grow on large ever-green bushes and small trees. The coffee growing cycle begins with the first rains of the year, signaling the trees to flower. Flowering is critical to the growing process, as the node where each white flower is formed will produce a single coffee cherry. Each coffee cherry contains two green beans called seeds or stones (coffee beans grow in pairs). The beans (seeds) vary from a pale green to a dull emerald in color. They only turn to a rich coffee brown after roasting. The outer fruits (coffee cherries) are green when first developing and turn a brilliant red when they are completely ripe and ready for harvest. Grown with great care on relatively small, remote family farms, Bali coffee is picked by hand in limited quantities. The pickers come back with only the most perfectly ripened rich red, plump coffee cherries. The beans will then be rigorously hand-sorted with local labor from the community. The premium coffee beans are subsequently hand-roasted to traditional perfection in village compound backyards.

Coffee from the island of the gods basks in the luxury of superior volcanic soil, lavished with generous rain, at the summit of the world in tropical equatorial highlands. A huge amount of care is required to grow, harvest and process this enhanced quality coffee. Decisions, and a passion for perfection, determine which varieties of Coffea Arabica to plant, the quality of the coffee bean and the growing conditions. Coffee crops can differ greatly from year to year due to variables in environment, weather, soil, climate, amount of sunlight, altitude and harvesting. The coffee from the same farm, from the same exact patch of earth, can be excellent one year and mediocre the next year. The taste of a coffee is determined by where and how high it is planted, and how it is processed and prepared, since coffee reflects the qualities and characteristics of the delicate soil in which it is cultivated. Each "coffee region" (the growing region of origin) has a specific character, and cupping (tasting) experts are able to pinpoint and identify a coffee according to the exact height where it grew on the slope of a particular plantation. After the harvest, command decisions dictate when the beans are picked, whether they will be sun-dried, how soon they will be roasted after picking, how long they will be roasted (light, medium or dark), and the temperature of the roasting. Roasting is the carefully orchestrated art, and science, of responding to the coffee throughout the entire roasting process since all batches must have the identical rich aroma and taste. Another variable is how long the finished coffee rests before being shipped and the final blend of the beans.

There are two agricultural demonstration farms in Bali where visitors can see and learn about traditional home coffee roasting processes. One farm is the government-owned Bas Agrotourism Coffee/Tea Plantation located 2,952–3,937 feet above sea level. It is called Buana

Amertha Sari (BAS), Br. Seribatu, Jl. Jurusan, Tampaksiring-Kintamani, Bangli. www.basnaturebali.com. Coffee for the family's domestic needs is roasted on a traditional Balinese wood-fired clay stove in the *paon* (kitchen). Raw, freshly harvested Arabica coffee beans are first placed in a clay frying pan. This is the best type of pan for roasting coffee, the real everyday way it is done at home. Coffee beans are typically roasted in this manner once a month, and this task can be performed by either the man or the woman of the house. Most often, however, the wife usually roasts the coffee while she is cooking the day's meal. Two to four pounds of beans are placed in a pan and roasted at a time. The coffee beans are roasted over the fire for one hour, continuously turned over and over with a coconut shell spoon with a bamboo handle (metal handles are too hot). When done, the still-steaming roasted beans are placed in a bamboo basket to cool down. The final product is fresh, hot, blackened, newly pan-roasted coffee beans.

The other agricultural demonstration farm is Amertha Yoga Agro Wisata, Br. Temen (Jurusan Tampaksiring-Kintamani), Bangli. Amertha Yoga also offers a traditional home coffee making demonstration. The first step is to pick the beans from the Arabica coffee tree. Dry the beans for five days in the sun (the beans look like green-gray hard stones). Clean the beans. Remove the skin by pounding with a traditional, round Balinese *lesung*, a stone mortar on the ground, and a wooden *lu*, a long pole made out of coffee tree wood. Then place two pounds of the beans in a black pot and roast them over a wood fire for one hour until the beans are black. Then pound them into powder using the *lu* and *lesung*. Sift the powder afterwards using a mesh. The final product is *kopi bubuk*. Home family industries sell these prepared coffees to local area people. The Shanti Hotel in Lovina also offers a guest program enabling visitors to see how local people traditionally process Bali coffee. "The raw coffee seeds are displayed under sunshine after few days harvesting. The dry coffee seeds are traditionally baked (*nyahnyah* in Balinese) on the fire of *paon* (Bali kitchen) using fire wood for thirty to forty minutes. Then the baked coffee seeds are processed by chopping the seeds with stick wood (*lu*) on the hole of the old hard volcanic stone (*lesung*). After that, the chopped coffee seeds are concentrated on specified nets (called *sidi* in Balinese) to find the coffee powder."

Most Bali coffee comes from small village-based coffee enterprises. Pak Made Paten (Br. Lungsiakan, Kedewatan, Ubud, Gianyar) runs a small family coffee business from his home in the tiny village of Lungsiakan, just outside Ubud. His grandmother originally started the business fifteen years ago. Made continues to use their age-old, traditional Balinese village methods to produce hand-roasted whole coffee beans (*biji*). Made also processes coffee powder (*bubuk*) two to three times a week. The frequency of roasts and the quantity depend on the size of incoming orders. Made, his teeth stained red from years of chewing betel nut, purchases his fresh, superb quality Robusta (popularly called *kopi Bali* or Bali coffee) beans through suppliers. Sourced from farmers in the coffee growing mecca of Pupuan, the Robusta beans are small compared to the larger Arabica beans. To roast the heavenly coffee beans, Made places them inside a big roaster, a metal drum suspended over a wood-fired stone stove. The roaster is sheltered under a bamboo shed, a small outdoor room in the family compound. Made laboriously revolves the metal roaster drum using a handle for two hours. The drum heats up slowly, so it takes a long time. This equipment is for his home industry business, not for his family's ordinary coffee needs. He does the roasts in large quantities. Some 22–44 pounds of beans are placed in the drum at a time. After two hours, he takes the beans out, now turned an earthy coffee brown, and puts them in a big bamboo basket to cool down for 10–20 minutes. Made next puts the roasted beans in a coffee grinder to make coffee powder. As Made's "coffee factory" is only a very small, traditional home business, he does not have all the necessary equipment, such as the grinding machine. He must either hire a grinder or travel to a friend or relative's house to use their grinder. The grinder works rapidly. It takes 10–15 minutes to produce 2.2 pounds of powdered instant coffee. With the coffee grinding equipment in full swing, the heady aroma of fresh coffee wafts out into the ancient side lane beyond his lava stone compound walls. Made weighs the finished coffee powder, divides it into 1.1 or 2.2 pound piles and packages it Balinese village style in a plain plastic bag tied with a simple knot on top to close it. His customers are local *warung*, neighboring villagers, and some hotels who appreciate and know the good taste of his product. He vends the fragrant, farmer-fresh powder to the *warung* for Rp.35,000 per kilo. The *warung* then sells it to their retail customers for Rp.40,000 per kilo—a Rp.5,000 per kilo profit. There are many other gracious Mades, and other homespun, basic coffee fabricators in countless rural villages in Bali. They patiently produce beautiful, newly home-roasted, home-made bags of real Balinese coffee for local villagers.

Kopi luak (civet coffee), an Indonesian island coffee treasure, is the most expensive, rare and exclusive coffee in the world, highly sought after for its unusual flavor. Valuable small boxes of *kopi luak* beans and powder sell for US$100–600 per pound in Bali. *Kopi luak* is prepared from coffee cherries which have been eaten by and then passed through the digestive tract of the Asian Palm Civet (*Paradoxurus hermaphroditus*), called *luwak* in Indonesia. The *luak* (civet cat) has large brown eyes and coarse, charcoal-grayish hair. A small member of the Viverridae family native to Central, South and Southeast Asia, it weighs from 4.4 to 11 pounds with a body length of 17–28 inches plus a 19-inch-long tail. *Luak* like to eat ripe berries and pulpy fruits, including the fruit of coffee trees. They select the fruit carefully and consume only very ripe red coffee cherries with sweet flesh. They leave the less ripe fruit for a later date. They eat only the outer fleshy fruit, allowing the coffee beans inside to pass sealed through their enzyme-filled digestive tract. The gastric juices extract the proteins and make the beans less bitter. After spending a day and a half in the civet's gastrointestinal system, the "fermented" beans are then discharged in clumps of pale yellow dung. The beans retain their original shape and are still covered with some of the fleshy berry's inner layers. Plantation workers have the unenviable task of retrieving and sifting through the morning feces on the forest floor looking for beans embedded in the 14-carat gold droppings of an extremely fussy civet cat that only eats premier coffee cherries! After they are collected, the "organically processed" beans are thoroughly washed and hygienically processed, and given a gentle medium roast so as not to destroy the complex flavors that develop through this process. *Kopi luak* production takes place in Bali, Java, Sumatra (mainly Arabica beans) and Sulawesi in the Indonesian archipelago, as well as in the Philippines and Vietnam. Only a limited number of pounds per year are produced to be distributed throughout the world.

Consumption of *kopi luak*, considered to be the best coffee in the world, has been going on naturally for ages in Bali, long before it became an expensive gourmet commodity. A nocturnal animal, the *luak* is only active and eats at night. The Balinese would normally never see the *luak*, except at night. Villagers traditionally made traps and hunted them for their meat, which tastes like lamb and is cooked like a beef or chicken curry. The crafty civet cat would walk around the garden or property, climb up the coffee trees, eat the best, choicest beans and defecate them out three to four hours later. The Balinese would observe these animals going around the coffee farm and accidentally discovered their intact, whole coffee bean-filled droppings discharged on the ground the next day. Part of ancient, fortuitously acquired Balinese knowledge and careful husbanding of any and all scarce food resources, the villagers picked up the droppings, dried them on a mat in the sun and discovered that they were still edible. Nowadays, the expensive sun-dried beans must be put in a special place so that no one steals them! The *luak*-processed coffee beans were always obtained randomly and by accident. Villagers would never know when a *luak* would come to their farm. To exploit today's marketplace, the village of Temen, Tampaksiring District, has introduced a small number of these "four-footed coffee filters" into the nearby jungle to increase *kopi luak* production. The very smart animals smell the coffee cherries and other fruits and use instinct to selectively choose only the very finest, superior quality beans on the tree to eat. As a result of the unique coffee cherry voyage, *kopi Bali* is transformed into *kopi luak*, a stronger tasting and lower caffeine content coffee with a different aroma and taste. Caged live civets, the royal kings of coffee, are on display at the Bas Agro plantation as well as at the neighboring Amertha Yoga agricultural farm.

Coffee in Bali is not limited to a beverage. The use of coffee as a body scrub ingredient is famous throughout the island of the gods. A *kopi* scrub is a traditional body cleansing treatment using a combination of aromatic ground coffee beans, fine pumice, volcanic rock, cinnamon powder and red rice flour to exfoliate the skin, soothe and relax the body and remove dead skin cells. Balinese coffee and coconut scrubs contain a mixture of natural Balinese coffee beans, coconut and kaolin clay to stimulate skin circulation. The Spa Factory Bali (www.spafactorybali.

com) in Kedonganan (Jimbaran) has created an enticing line of invigorating coffee-based body treatment rituals (Espresso Massage Oil, Cappuccino Scrub Powder, Mocaccino Body Wash and Cafe Latte Moisturizing Lotion). Spa Factory Bali's stimulating "Bali coffee body scrub" is an aromatic application of rich Balinese coffee powder ground together with rice powder, glutinous rice powder, cinnamon powder and sintok bark powder.

The small Balinese-run Utama Spice factory in Ubud (www.utamaspicebali.com) has also designed a gorgeous hand-mixed and hand-ground Coffee and Spice Body Scrub (the finely powdered ingredients are rice, coffee, cinnamon, cardamom and Alpinia galangal). Utama's luscious, 100 percent natural spa products are made with ancient Balinese herbal knowledge, plus love, passion and compassion for the earth. Many of the natural healing ingredients grow in the nearby macrobiotic hills of Ubud. (Ubud comes from the Balinese word *obat*, which means medicine). Rub, exfoliate and smell the coffee plantations!

Bali coffee is always a strong coffee. That is its trademark. The coffees have a thick, big, rich, soupy, earthy textured taste. The Balinese are devoted coffee drinkers. They prepare their coffee at home by putting a heaped spoonful of finely ground roasted coffee powder (*bubuk*) in a cup or glass to which they add boiling water and one or two ample spoonfuls of sugar. The Balinese love everything they drink to be super sweet. Bali coffee powder is ideal for use as an instant coffee. Like most Indonesian coffees, however, the *bubuk* leaves very fine grinds, a powdery, floating residue, throughout the suspension. There is grittiness to the coffee all the way through. You can taste the coffee flecks in the liquid, giving it a full-bodied, full-flavored taste. The grinds settle on the tongue and go down the throat. You can feel a difference in your throat from all the particles for the first week after you begin to drink Bali coffee. Some coffees leave less residue in the cup than others. The grinds sink to the bottom quickly, so you can drink it as an instant coffee. You should never drink the cup all the way down to the bottom, however, as you risk swallowing a mouthful of debris! With other brands, the grinds linger on top creating a halo around the perimeter of the cup. You must stir frequently to keep the powder distributed throughout the liquid. The cheapest brands are more muddy and less soluble. They leave considerable flotsam and jetsam on the sides of the cup. It is like sipping a mouthful of dirt! If you spend time in Bali, you will learn the hereditary tricks that only the Balinese know about coaxing the particles of roasted rice flour mixed in with many coffees to sink to the bottom of the glass so they don't get caught between your teeth as you drink!

Balinese coffee drinking customs are ancient and complex and offer great relaxation. Bali's people understand their great cup of coffee. It is their deepest, darkest act of meditation. Drinking and using coffee is a big part of life in Bali. The men will consume several, often 2–3 cups of *kopi Bali* a day, usually at a local *warung*. If a driver has had a long, difficult day taking guests around the island, he very much wants to go back home to a hot cup of coffee and a *kretek* (clove) cigarette! It is mostly Balinese men who drink coffee, but women enjoy 1–2 cups a day and almost always at home. To the Balinese, coffee is an occasion and a personal ritual, and the Balinese always like it piping hot. The joy of Bali's freshly roasted coffee beans graces and refreshes every rural village and every impromptu, simple wooden *warung*. The Balinese love to drink coffee, either at home or at small coffee stall *warung* in the villages, often with only a long, rough wooden bench to sit on. A cup of *kopi Bali* is usually served with a piece or two of sweet *pisang goreng* at these innumerable little *warung kopi*.

My friend and driver, Wayan Sarma, eats breakfast at home at 8 a.m. and usually drinks 4–5 cups of black coffee with sugar a day. He usually does not add milk because *susu* is costly and would make drinking coffee too expensive. The Balinese usually never use milk. My good friend Kasena does not like *susu* in his coffee. The Balinese want to drink it black. He will use one or two spoons of coffee and one or two spoons of sugar in equal proportions. Most often, however, it will be one spoon of coffee and one spoon of sugar. *Kopi tok* is black coffee without sugar and milk (*tok* means pure, without anything added). Kasena buys his coffee in the local market for Rp.50,000 per kilo (good coffee would be even more expensive). At this price, it is adulterated with rice or corn, but he likes it best this way. I saw bags of Ginseng coffee for sale in the glass display case of a local *warung* on Kusamba beach across from Goa Lawah bat cave though Kasena did not recommend the taste. My royal (Satria caste) friend Surayasa said that the Balinese prefer to buy local coffee mixed with either corn or rice rather than the original (100 percent pure coffee) because it has a better smell. Small Balinese coffee mills produce three grades of *kopi bubuk*: Grade A is pure coffee, Grade B contains 50 percent corn by weight and Grade C (bulk coffee) contains 70 percent corn. The corn is boiled and roasted separately from the coffee and is then added to the coffee before it is ground. The coffees, with or without corn, visually look the same.

Most of the coffee consumed in Bali is Robusta because the Balinese say that the taste of Robusta is more *pahit* (has more bite) and is stronger. The Balinese are not used to the taste of Arabica and consider it to be coarse and bitter. On other Indonesian islands, people still commonly buy green coffee beans, roast them in a frying pan and pound them into a powder by hand. In Bali, however, almost all of the coffee sold to villagers has already been roasted and ground into a ready-to-drink powder (*kopi bubuk*). *Kopi Bali* (Balinese coffee) is dark and thick and is usually served in a manner similar to Turkish coffee. To prepare Turkish coffee, very finely ground coffee powder is boiled in a pot with sugar and then served in a cup. The visible grounds are allowed to settle to the bottom. A proverb about Turkish coffee says that "coffee should be as black as hell, as strong as death and as sweet as love." Much the same can be said of, and is demanded of, Bali coffee! *Kopi tubruk* is hand-pounded coffee produced using age-old village equipment—the *lu* (a long pole) and the *lesung* (an oversized round or square-bottomed stone mortar). This ancient, traditional coffee processing method is also called *kopi tubruk*. *Tubruk* means to lunge, collide with, crash into, slam against, or an impact, referencing the slamming action of the *lu* into the *lesung* as it breaks up the roasted coffee beans. After the beans are hand-pounded into powder, they are then sifted through a sieve or strainer. *Kopi tubruk* also entered the lexicon as strong coffee made by pouring boiling water over coffee grounds, usually in a glass.

Wayan Sarma's parents grow coffee in the mountains near Bedugul in the small village of Bukian-Pelaga (pop. 500 people), Petang district, Badung Regency. Here they grow coffee trees, vanilla beans, cloves, sweet potatoes, rice, taro, corn and chilies. Wayan's father owns 100 coffee trees, both Robusta and Arabica. The beans are nurtured in rich volcanic soil using age-old, traditional mountain village methods. The coffee's captivating taste reflects the romance, power and divine energy of Bali, situated eight secluded, precious degrees south of the equator. The family produces 100 percent pure coffee that is not mixed with corn or rice, a cheaper coffee with a worse taste. The father tends the trees and the mother picks the beans and dries them on the compound floor in the sun. Then she takes them to another man in the village who has the processing machinery. He roasts the beans and then grinds them for her into *bubuk*. She takes back the *bubuk*, buys plastic bags in the market and packages the coffee, tying the bags with a knot on top. Professional packaging is rare. This is normal packaging for locals. She has an agreement to supply *bubuk* powder to a local market seller and can produce 11–22 pounds per week. She also buys beans from other villagers who have only a few trees and beans. They do not want the expense of transporting their beans to the processor and to the market, so they sell them to her instead.

Coffee runs in the veins of the people of Pelaga. High in the clouds, nearby Kiadan-Pelaga is another coffee growing village. The forest gardens around the village are extensive and drip with coffee beans, vanilla pods, cocoa, chili and a myriad of other crops springing up amid native wild species. Journey to this small *kampung* set amidst rice fields, bamboo thickets, native forest and jungle-like gardens, where local farmers will take you on a tour through the coffee gardens and demonstrate the organic coffee making process.

Coffee plays a central role in Balinese society. It is commonly used as a gift or as a form of payment. Coffee is also a village social lubricant. The Balinese will carry a present of coffee to a wedding and it is served to guests at home ceremonies or on special ritual occasions. My friend Ari at the Grand Inna Kuta hotel went to a faith healer in Java to fix his broken pinky bones after a *sepeda motor* accident. Balinese patients normally only pay Rp.10,000 to a local *balian* for this type of medical-spiritual treatment or offer some gift, like coffee. An essential food commodity, fresh *kopi bubuk* is available and circulates quickly, throughout all parts of the island. Most of it is low-grade Robusta, sometimes mixed with low-grade Arabica. Local *warung* in isolated, mountainous Pacung stock and sell supplies of coffee from both distant Singaraja and nearby Baturiti, hot off the local coffee trees in unmarked plastic bags.

Cok Oka's mother from Guwang fuels the inter-Regency coffee supply chain via her *warung* in the main market in Denpasar. She sells coffee *bubuk* and coffee beans by the pound to Balinese customers. Rural suppliers come and deliver the coffee to her at the market. My long-time friend Nyoman (Mr Black)'s family owns many hectares of coffee trees. They sell their home-made powdered coffee loose and unpackaged, simply piled up in a bin at the local market. Surayasa's wife's family runs a small coffee business from their ancestral village of Perean, Tegal Jadi, near Bedugul (Tabanan Regency). They do not grow the coffee. They buy the raw coffee beans from a nearby village, roast them on a grill and grind the beans by hand. Everything is done traditionally without technology. After the processing (the roasting and grinding), they wrap the soft aromatic *bubuk* powder in very thin plastic bags at home. They then seal the bags in the traditional way by running a hot wax candle along the top seam of the plastic. The coffee is vended in the nearby markets in unmarked, plain plastic bags with no brand name because it is not licensed. To get a license costs money and they would then have to pay taxes on the earnings. It must remain only a home enterprise. They sell three kinds of coffee: original (100 percent coffee), coffee mixed with corn and coffee mixed with rice. The unmistakable, delicious smell of original coffee, without corn or rice fillers, oozes out through the sheer plastic case. Bali coffee is often adulterated with rice because rice is cheaper. You can tell there is rice in it because the coffee is not as strong. It contains less pure coffee beans. The family produces 22 pounds a day and they sell it to local market stalls frequented by the Balinese. Surayasa's family also acts as a distributor. They buy coffee in sealed plastic bags from another family to sell to the market vendors.

A large proportion of Balinese families are involved with coffee beans. It is a critical agricultural resource and many Balinese earn at least part of their cash income from coffee. Aliastrawan's family near Singaraja owns two hectares of coffee trees (around 1,000 trees) and produces professionally packaged bags of coffee. They also have a grinding machine to process the beans whereas most local families do not have this capability. Their coffee plantation is in the village of Lemukih, near Singaraja, Buleleng Regency. They grow both Arabica and Robusta but mainly Robusta. The trees yield one crop a year. The harvest is in July and August, and by September the coffee is all processed. The beans are still green at the beginning of the harvest and turn red by the end of the harvest. The red beans are picked as the choice crop. By late August, they take all the beans, good and bad quality together. The cheaper quality coffee would be made from broken beans. After picking, they dry the beans in the sun. The family then does the processing at home. They first clean their machine in order to roast the beans and then grind them into *bubuk*. This is the typical way that coffee is produced in Bali in the villages. The next stage is to put the coffee in locally made plastic bags. The family does their own packaging right in the village. They pay Rp.2 million for the plastic, yielding 10,000 double- and single-wrapped bags. The labels and outer pouches are made in Surabaya. Aliastrawan's brother lives there and takes care of this part of the family business. They produce 88 pounds of coffee during each processing interval, totalling 2,204 pounds during the three-month-long coffee season. This is their annual capacity. What they don't sell immediately, they keep in stock in the house all year long. The family sells the coffee in the local market at Singaraja, in traditional village *warung* and in some small stores in Kuta. Enterprising Aliastrawan also runs an on-premises drugstore for the Grand Inna Kuta employees out back and sells coffee to them in the canteen. His brother sells 55–110 pounds a week to a hotel in Surabaya, depending on occupancy rates and the number of guests. He also has a fish business. The Balinese like to have more than one often food or art-related business at the same time. A hotel bellboy may have a home wood sculpture gallery, while a sun-bronzed poolboy might raise cere-monial pigs at home or give tennis lessons to tourists!

Coffee from Bali—from the morning of the world—is grown at high elevations on sacred magic mountains, on the sides of rasping, restless, turbulent volcanoes. The coffee beans are picked and then wet-processed (washed) like neighboring coffees from Java, East Timor and Papua New Guinea. Securing enough water to do this is difficult. Bali's steep slopes and coarse volcanic soil makes surface water non-existent during the dry season, and wells must be hand-dug hundreds of feet deep to reach fresh water. Due to this water deficit, the *subak* (small-scale coffee farmer cooperatives) are unable to produce sufficient traditional washed Indo-nesian style beans. (*Subak* or *subak abian* are close-knit communal associations formed for agricultural, social or religious activities. They are governed by *adat*, local, customary village law. "Abian" means an equal share of the crop between the owner and workers of the land.) Coffee cultivation is a prime agricultural industry in Bali but individual farmers still produce and process beans using traditional, rudimentary, generations-old methods. It is difficult to get small farmers in remote hinterland areas to process coffee carefully. Under the best conditions, unprotected green coffee is laid out to dry on raised beds or clean concrete patios. In smaller mills and with home processing, it is simply laid on driveways, on dirty tarpaulins or directly on hard dirt plots of land. Visiting Western coffee importers/advisors persuaded the coffee farmer organizations to use raised-net drying racks instead. "Bali Kintamani Natural," a premier product, is now sun-dried on these protective racks, keeping the beans free of dirt, musk and mildew from contact with the ground and humidity. Traditional organic agricultural techniques have also been reintroduced to farm Bali's older heirloom Arabica coffees, botanical varieties or cultivars such as Typica and Bourbon. Indigenous Arabica varietals include Ateng-type coffee shrubs, a Catimor cultivar, predominant in the Kintamani co-operative areas.

A group of Balinese coffee experts launched a campaign in 2012 to teach local farmers throughout the island how to retrieve their long-lost legacy of high quality coffee production. Coffee specialist Pak Rai Bangsawan trained Balinese coffee farmers in the villages of Tamblingan, Pupuan, Kintamani and Pengotan (Bangli Regency, near Kintamani) to improve their skills in harvesting and processing coffee. Only a small number of coffee farmers remain in Tamblingan (Buleleng Regency), where coffee cultivation is an almost forgotten art; it was the first Balinese territory to be given coffee seeds by the Dutch. "We are training our fellow farmers in the villages to produce better coffee, half to be sold as raw beans, with the remainder sold as premium coffee powder. Farmers can get 300 percent higher prices when they are able to sell processed (ground) coffee instead of whole coffee beans." Tamblingan and Pupuan are among the best spots for coffee cultivation as they are located 3,937–4,265 feet above sea level. Farmers, often highly skilled moonlighting artisans and craftsmen, are being taught about "the importance of pruning the coffee plants, the perfect harvesting time (when the beans turn red), and to use a medium roast, which is healthier than dark-roasted coffee beans."

Most coffee in Bali is spawned on small farms. The average farm in Bali is five acres in size. The coffee farmers, or *tani* (*tani* means a farmer, tiller of the soil or peasant) sell their fresh bean crops to visiting professional collectors called *tengkulak* (broker or middleman). Other collectors, often families, also gather picked coffee beans directly from these small local producers. The gatherers then take the beans to the brokers, where they are carefully sampled, hand-sorted into grades and paid for on the spot. The large coffee brokers, buyers, roasters and exporters are all headquartered in Singaraja, the commercial center for coffee in Bali. Once the coffee is purchased, it is conveyed by large, hurtling, overloaded trucks from Singaraja to the port of Gilimanuk. From there, it will be shipped by boat and then overland to the sweltering port of Surabaya for export to Jakarta. Only the lowest quality coffees remain in Bali. All of the coffee is exported as raw green beans. The roasting is done after arrival.

Magical cups of local Balinese coffee start the morning off at tables decorated with precious-scented, yellow-magenta-striped frangipani flowers for the gods. Packaged *Kopi Bali* appears in many tempting brands and formats in large supermarkets like Matahari. Singa brand offers Robusta, Arabica and Toraja coffees from Indonesia. The coffee brands available in Bali (*kopi bubuk* powder) are Setia Bali, Kopi ABC (ABC Central Food Industry, Jakarta) and Kapal Api (Kapal Api Group, Jakarta). Good Day brand provides you with a complete three-in-one coffee experience: *kopi*, *gula* and *krim* packets. Kopi Banyuatis is a well-known Balinese coffee manufacturer in Buleleng Regency (Desa Banyuatis, Pemaron village, Jalan Singaraja-Seririt, near Lovina Beach). Coffee is a very familiar drink for the Balinese community: Banyuatis brand coffee is sold locally in sealed plastic bags of *bubuk* with their trademark yellow print design on the package front. Coffee trees are widely distributed throughout much of Buleleng Regency in northern Bali where both Arabica and Robusta are planted, tended and cultivated. Buleleng has long been one of the biggest coffee producers in Bali. People from the south of Bali used to flock here to work as coffee harvesters. As a supplier of both coffee beans and ready-to-use powder,

Buleleng boasts several coffee mills, managed either traditionally or by means of sophisticated, modern machinery.

Kopi Banyuatis, founded by Ketut England in 1976, processes coffee beans grown by local farmers in the village of Banyuatis into ready-to-use coffee powder. Raw materials (Robusta) are also supplied by coffee growers in Pupuan village (Tabanan). The journey to turn the dry and therefore easily processed coffee beans into powder begins in the oven. The company still uses firewood to fuel the oven baking journey. An oven tube containing 165 pounds of coffee beans is baked for one hour, then milled for an hour and then packaged. The company employs 27 workers consisting of six people in charge of the baking (roasting) phase, three people at the milling division to turn the coffee into powder and nine others at the packaging division to make the coffee ready for sale. The Banyuatis company processes 30 tons of coffee per month. Its first-class coffee line consists of a combination of Arabica and Robusta, yielding the typical, distinguished aroma and superior flavor of Banyuatis coffee. The second-class coffee line consists of Arabica mixed with a different percentage of Robusta and blended with a mixture of corn powder.

P.T. Bersama is another professional coffee manufacturer in Bali, owned by a resident Italian expatriate Guido Beretta. ("Bersama" means "together, joint, or collective": the spirit is to "join together" to produce fine Balinese-Italian coffees.) A combined coffee business and dairy, the Bersama coffee plant is located in the small rural village of Sideman in Karangasem Regency (the separate cheese operation is in Bangli). The up-to-date facility produces three distinctive lines of tropical gourmet Bali coffees. Kopi Bali Bersama (Bali coffee) is a very finely ground Robusta powder (*kopi bubuk*) used as an instant coffee, similar to home-grown Balinese village coffee. Pour hot boiling water into a cup with a spoonful of the fine powder, watch the flavorful grinds sink and settle to the bottom, a traditional Asian way of preparing and drinking coffee, and experience a strong, full-bodied, sensual cup of 100 percent pure Balinese coffee. Bersama sources high-quality Robusta and Arabica coffee beans grown in the northern mountain regions from local suppliers. Collectors visit village coffee farms to acquire newly picked crops and then transport the beans to buyers like Bersama. The coffee beans are roasted, ground and packaged on-site using roasting machines and other equipment imported from Italy. The coffee factory produces 10–12 tons of coffee per month, employing seven workers who do seven-hour work shifts, five days a week. The coffee is roasted at 180 degrees Celsius over an open coconut-wood fire. Roasting time varies according to sight and sound. Balinese workers use personal judgment and experience to know when it is done.

Bali's largest coffee manufacturing business, P.T. Putra Bhineka Perkasa (Kopi Bali The Butterfly Globe Brand), was started by the Chinese-Indonesian Tjahjadi family in 1935. They bought coffee beans from farmers, processed them and sold them at their coffee outlet (Bhineka Jaya) on Jalan Gajah Mada in Denpasar. *Bhineka* in Sanskrit means various types or many, while *perkasa* (Sanskrit) is powerful, courageous or mighty. *Jaya* means successful, prosperous or victorious. Using modern processing machines, the family began to manufacture fine coffees using hygienic techniques in their clean, efficient factory in Denpasar. Putra Bhineka Perkasa uses premium high-grade beans cultivated either in the lush highlands of Bali or sourced throughout the volcanic islands of Indonesia. Once the coffee seeds are purchased from the growers, they are meticulously sorted and graded by hand at Kopi Bali's Denpasar factory. The traditional way to produce coffee is to lay the freshly hand-picked beans out in the sun to dry. After two weeks, the outer shells turn dark brown and brittle. The beans are then pounded by hand to remove the dried husks, and are stored in the warehouse in large burlap bags or huge plastic sacks for at least one year to mature. The beans will then be roasted at 370–450 F degrees for 15–30 minutes by machine and quickly ground into different textures, either into a powder-like consistency for instant coffee or a coarser grind for percolator preparation. The whole roasted beans and ground coffees are then packaged by hand for local distribution or export. Ladies in shower caps wearing neat clean uniforms pour the *bubuk* into plastic bags, while others seal the packets with a clamp press (no traditional village wax seals here). The bags are stacked into cartons for shipping. Almost everything at each step is done by hand. The coffee will be sold in Bali's larger convenience stores and supermarkets, or exclusively packaged for hotels and duty free shops. It is not for the local Balinese population.

Lofty, rich Putra Bhineka Perkasa looks down on and dismisses the Balinese and their coffee drinking habits and preferences and the inexpensive class of village coffees that they buy packaged only in plain plastic bags. Bhineka manufactures separate, thin, utilitarian, plastic-encased lines for the Balinese using local Robusta, the low-grade coffee relegated to the Balinese. Putra Bhineka's three Balinese-oriented brands include Cap Kupu 2 Bola Dunia brand (Kupu Kupu Bola Dunia), which is Bali Robusta powder in a sheer, plastic, village-style bag. Warung Pojok, in a basic plastic bag, is a simple Balinese all-Robusta coffee powder (Kopi Bubuk Kopi Bali). Ikan Bola Dunia coffee, encased in another rectangular plastic bag, is local Robusta coffee mixed with 5–10 percent corn. Bhineka's better coffees are packaged instead in attractive, artistically designed, elegant containers. Putra Bhineka Perkasa buys their coffee from local Balinese farmers and then produces beautifully presented upmarket lines of coffee geared only for tourists. The Balinese cannot afford to purchase their own island-grown coffee in this format. Local villagers participate in an entirely different village coffee economy and coffee buying strategy. They buy their coffee in the local markets. The Balinese are very happy to enjoy their favorite, fragrant, corn- or rice-adulterated coffee and there is a thriving exchange in the villages involving the production and sale of local coffee for local people. The children of the gods produce coffee mainly for each other, for consumption in their own or in nearby villages. Putra Bhineka Perkasa is one of only two companies on the island that have a coffee export license and they carefully control, block and thwart the export of almost all Bali coffee from Bali. Very little coffee leaves the island. They maintain a tight stranglehold on the shipping companies and on the struggling farmers who grow the coffee and cannot afford to buy their own export license. As a result of their domination, most of the world has never had the joy of drinking indigenous, mountain-born Balinese coffee.

Putra Bhineka Perkasa produces thirteen lines of coffee under the Cap Kupu Kupu Bola Dunia, The Butterfly Globe Brand label. (*Cap* means brand or trademark, *kupu-kupu* means butterfly, *bola* is globe and *dunia* means the world.) The series includes the Best of Bali 3-pack, Best of Indonesia 3-pack, Nubby Burlap Bag, Pemandangan Pack, Decorative Can, Miniature 3.3-ounce, Foil-Pack Brickettes, Brown Paper

Bag Satchels, Kopi Kotak Janger, Bali Gold Special (Gold Foil Pack), Kopi Bubuk (Brown Aluminum Foil Pack), Cap Kupu2 Bola Dunia (Kupu Kupu Bola Dunia), Warung Pojok and Ikan Bola Dunia. Almost all of the coffees come in a choice of either aromatic, whole roasted coffee beans; a flavorful, medium fine grind for percolators and coffee machines; or soft Bali coffee powder (*bubuk*) for instant coffee. The Best of Bali 3-pack sampler contains three brightly colored, shiny, foil-wrapped 2.82-ounce mini-bricks of *kristal* ground Bali coffee, a rougher, medium grind crystal powder. The rich-tasting coffee powder treasures are premium blends of Bali's finest Arabica beans from the various growing regions of the island. The Best of Indonesia 3-pack boasts a classic trio of high-quality Indonesian coffees born, bred and nurtured in the rich volatile soil of the Ring of Fire! It includes two 100 percent pure Arabicas: Toraja Coffee from the finest coffee plantations in the fertile region of Tana Toraja in South Sulawesi, and Sumatra Mandailing from the mysterious fastness of Sumatra's jungle-veiled mountain passes. Sumatra Mandailing is fuel-injected with all of the cultural mystique and ancient white magic of the brooding, barely explored Indonesian island chain. The world's most full-bodied Arabica, it has a vibrant, concentrated flavor and pungent aroma reminiscent.

The fiber-textured chubby Burlap Bag model is stuffed with either mountain peak grown whole roasted coffee beans or luscious ground coffees. These Old World tropical sacks are eye-catching colonial reminders of the way that coffee was traditionally stored and transshipped. Decorative Pemandangan (panorama scenery) packs have a peek-a-boo plastic window for a teasing glimpse of their superb smelling dark brown powders and beans. An elegantly designed landscape view canister of 100 percent pure Bali coffee, a premium food gift, bears museum quality painted images of the island. The "boutique" rope-handled brown paper bag packaging series houses the most sacred coffee keepsakes of the gods (spectacular instant coffee powders or densely textured grounds for a powerful roller coaster coffee ride). Its superstar is the very rare, elegant Bali Kintamani Arabica coffee. This top-grade "aged" Kintamani coffee blessed with divine mountain highlights has a devout flavor fit for the ancient *cokorda* (kings) of Bali. But Bali Kintamani can seldom be savored outside of Bali due to the small quantity harvested annually.

The Balinese Paon Meets the Western Kitchen

Traditional cooking equipment and materials in the Balinese kitchen (*paon*) can be easily and satisfactorily substituted by modern Western cooking utensils and accessories. These are available in most homeware stores and bigger department stores as well as in Asian stores in urban Chinatowns.

Stove Most Balinese women use an age-old wood-fired, mud-brick stove with three holes in the top, as well as a more modern two-burner stove or gas cooker (*kompor gas*) for home cooking. A modern baking oven and gas or electric stove top is the logical replacement in Western kitchens.

Grill The Balinese love to grill (burn) chili peppers and other vegetables directly on a raised, round, slotted metal grill placed atop one of the stovetop's side burners. They also use this technique to char garlic cloves, whole spices and banana leaf-wrapped food parcels. A 12-inch-square cast-iron grill pan or skillet grill is the ideal Western equivalent for such searing, frying or browning. It is very heavy and provides even heat distribution.

Rice cooker The combination *kran-dangdang-kukusan-kekeban* is a traditional Balinese village rice steamer using four separate multilevel pieces of equipment. An iron brazier (*kran*) to boil the water sits at the base surmounted by a *dangdang*, an hourglass-shaped water-filled gray sheet iron pot. Above it rests the *kukusan*, a cone-shaped woven bamboo basket to hold the steaming rice, covered with a *kekeban*, a heavy clay bowl. Laboriously cooked steamed rice is at the very core of all secular and religious cuisine on Bali and is eaten at every single meal. Many Balinese in the villages are now beginning to substitute an automatic electric rice cooker. You may do the same, or boil rice using a stove top pot with a lid.

Mortar and pestle The heart and soul of the busy Balinese kitchen is the indispensable, incredibly heavy stone mortar and pestle (*batu base* or *cobek*). The Balinese *batu base* is a shallow, round stone mortar made of local black volcanic rock with low sides and a flat bottom, accompanied by a sturdy stone pestle. Modern granite mortar and pestle sets, in a variety of sizes, are readily available in the West. A mortar and pestle is perfect for crushing herbs and for combining, bruising and grinding whole spices, dry spices, aromatic seasonings, dried or fresh chili peppers, leaves, shallots, garlic cloves, ginger, fish and chicken. It is a terrific way to infuse flavor, Balinese style, into meats, fish and vegetables. You can also create and blend home-made *bumbu* (coarse or fine spice pastes), *sambal* (sauces), marinades and dressings. As a last resort, you can use a blender to pulverize your ingredients but the taste will not be as vibrant.

The Balinese also traditionally use a *lu*, a six-foot-long wooden pole to crush, pound and grind newly harvested rice grains, spices, meat and village coffee beans by hand. The foods are placed in the *lesung*, a large stone mortar set on the ground. Instead, you can buy already processed rice in a bag, powdered spices, coffee in jars and butchered, packaged meat as an alternative, available everywhere in Western supermarkets.

Chopping board Bali's thick, high, round chopping board (*talenan*), cut straight out of a tree trunk, serves as a durable, heavily used, organic cutting block. It can give way in the West to a universally available simple wooden chopping board. There is always a plain, square-edged kitchen-tile chopping bench surface along the wall in every Balinese kitchen. Granite or marble counter tops in Western homes serve the same purpose.

Cleaver The very sharp, weighty *belakas* is a hand-crafted axe-like Balinese cleaver used for chopping ingredients. The *belakas* comes into play during mass ritual ceremonial cooking done by men as well as in everyday home cooking done by women. Broad, heavy, sharp cleavers are readily available in Western stores.

Rolling pin Softer ingredients will bend to the will of a wooden chopping board, rolling pin and kitchen (tea) towel. Fold the towel in half. Put chili peppers and other soft ingredients on top of the towel. Fold the towel once more over the ingredients. Roll over it very hard with a rolling pin to crush the imprisoned ingredients. Tap the rolling pin along the length of the towel.

Grater The hand-held *parutan* is wielded every day to scrape and grate and shred the ubiquitous Balinese coconut. The wooden paddle bristles with rows of small, sharp iron nails to scrape coconuts and fine-grate vegetables. It gives way to the modern stainless steel grater.

Potato ricer A flat, broad, round potato ricer is perfect for mashing potatoes, root vegetables, root spices and selected fruits in place of a mortar and pestle.

Nut cracker A nutcracker will crack open and deconstruct hard ingredients like candlenuts and gingers.

Seafood cracker A cracker designed for crab and lobster claws can also be used to crack open and pulverize hard spices. Grip it to apply pressure on the spice item.

Garlic crusher or garlic Press Place the garlic in the garlic chamber, one clove at a time. Squeeze and squash the clove, which will emerge as strings out of the little holes. Scrape the ends off with a knife. Or you can place peeled garlic or shallots on a wooden chopping board and press down using the flat side of a large knife.

Egg beater or whisk A stainless steel egg beater with round, rotating blades or a metal wire whisk can be used to blend ingredients.

Colander A conventional colander can assist in squeezing out grated coconut flesh or leaves that are used for coloring and fragrance.

Poultry equipment Poultry shears are useful to cut through raw or cooked chicken or duck. Use a poultry lacer, a thin metal rod with a loop on the end with strings, to sew up the cavities of both small and large poultry. When stringing pieces of chicken along a stick, switch to a metal skewer instead of a Balinese-style hand-whittled bamboo stick.

Meat tenderizer A meat tenderizer, composed of a metal block at the end of a hammer-like handle, is ideal for hammering meat on a wooden board to spread it out while simultaneously removing the toughness. A stone pestle can also be used to hammer the meat.

Sausage stuffer To stuff pork sausages, the Balinese construct a hand-held funnel carved out of bamboo and insert a coconut leaf spine in the middle as the tube. They then squeeze the pork meat through it into the attached intestinal pig casing below. You may prefer to use a simple stainless steel or plastic funnel or invest in a professional restaurant stainless steel sausage stuffer.

Flavor injector Resembling a hypodermic needle, a flavor injector is ideal for inserting melted brown palm sugar (*gula merah*) into small *jaja* dough balls.

Poffertjes pan The Dutch-origin metal *poffertjes* pan is a shallow round pan with several two-inch-wide round wells. The Balinese use it to make small pancakes (*jaja laklak*), often injected with sweet interior fillings just prior to baking. A muffin pan with small round holes conveniently replaces the bell-lidded *poffertjes* pan.

Bamboo rice basket In a world without refrigeration, a bamboo rice basket (*sok asi*) is used in Bali to store freshly steamed rice. Westerners love bamboo baskets for their beauty and artistic merit, but it is best to place leftover rice in a covered glass bowl in the refrigerator.

Molds The Balinese normally use banana leaves as their molds, folded into a beautiful array of shapes and sizes. You can substitute a variety of common metal or plastic cookie cutters to fashion perfectly uniform rice cake treats and cookies.

Bamboo and coconut holders Young bamboo nodes and tubes as well as empty coconut shells are used as food molds, storage vessels and food packaging in Bali. They also serve as traditional containers for cooking food over fires and grills. Cast-iron and stainless steel cookware, bakeware, pots and pans are the main alternatives in Western countries.

Coconut palm leaves Young pale green coconut palm leaves are used for weaving *ketipat* rice baskets in Bali. It may be possible to source long thin coconut or pandanus leaves in urban Chinatowns.

BALINESE INGREDIENTS
Western Substitutes or Equivalents for Classic Balinese Foodstuffs

Most of the spices and ingredients for the Balinese recipes featured in this book can be easily purchased in Western supermarkets or health food stores. These include, for example, garlic cloves, hot chilies, shallots, raw ginger, turmeric, nutmeg, sea salt, white pepper, black pepper, coriander seeds, coconut oil, bananas, mung beans, lemongrass stalks, chicken bouillon powder, chicken, tuna steaks, white snapper, mackerel, anchovies, sardines, tempe, tofu and rice. The more exotic ingredients are listed below with suggested substitutes and alternatives. Almost all of the specialty items can be sourced at a reasonable price in your local Asian supermarket, Chinatown precincts, Indonesian grocery stores, Indian spice shops and from online food sites that will ship right to your door.

Banana leaf squares Fresh banana leaf squares are used as organic food plates, portable food holders, food-shaping molds and wrappers for steaming minced food parcels. A dinner plate for eating or aluminum foil for cooking and wrapping can serve as substitutes but banana leaves impart a nice scent to the food. Try local Asian or Latin-American supermarkets. Corn husks, properly cooked taro leaves and vine leaves are possible substitutes. If you live in California, Florida or Hawaii, you can plant your own backyard banana tree for a permanent supply. If using aluminum foil, use either a grill or barbecue or bake the parcel in the oven. Add a little extra water to the package to compensate for the reduced moisture normally provided by the banana leaf insulation.

Banana tree trunk stem *Jukut ares* recipe. Substitute fresh (or canned) pieces of whole bamboo for a similar look and consistency.

Bulan baon leaves *Bubur mebasa* recipe. Obtained from the Cabbage tree, *bulan baon* leaves can be substituted with *salam* or spinach leaves.

Candlenut (kemiri) Employed as a thickening agent in Balinese cuisine, candlenuts must be cooked prior to consumption. They are toxic when raw. Candlenuts are easy to procure via web-based Indonesian stores. Macadamia nuts and cashews are viable alternatives.

Cassava (*ketala*) leaf and root Cassava, also called yucca, is a tuberous, starchy root vegetable three inches round and eight inches long. The root has a brown fibrous skin and white interior flesh. Look for it in Hispanic food markets or greengrocers.

Chilies You will find a vast array of different chili peppers in Western supermarkets and even more in vegetable stores. You need not search for the exact name or type of chili used in Bali. In general, one-inch-long orange or red chilies pack the most heat, while large chili peppers are relatively mild. Be mindful of "the scorch factor" at your family dinner table. Sometimes less is more!

Cinnamon leaves (*daun kayu manis*) *Tape* recipe. Fresh cinnamon leaves can be replaced with ground cinnamon.

Coconut milk (*santen*) Coconut cream or coconut milk hand-squeezed from a newly grated, fully matured coconut, is a staple in Balinese cooking. Canned or packaged coconut milk or cream can be substituted.

Coconut oil (*minyak kelapa*) Coconut oil is used for cooking virtually everything in Bali. It is the daily home cooking oil of choice, and of necessity. It is high in saturated fat, however, so it is best to select a lighter, more heart-friendly vegetable oil.

Daluman leaf Also called *daun cincau*, the vine leaf may be hard to find even in Bali but is worth searching for. Use it to create the village drink *daluman*, one of the most sensational beverages in the world. There are no real substitutes.

Dragonflies (*capung*) There is no easy equivalent for a freshly caught dragonfly flitting freely through the rice fields.

Fern tips (*paku tanjung*) The Balinese use fiddlehead fern or bracken, an edible, non-decorative species of marsh fern, as a vegetable. Some greengrocers may be willing to source it for you.

Frilly winged beans (*kacang botor*) These amazing looking four-angled beans are plentiful in Chinatown vegetable markets in Honolulu, Hawaii. The shape, taste and texture is clean, crisp and crunchy. They can be eaten raw as well as cooked.

Grated coconut (*kelapa*) Whole mature coconuts are frequently found in the fruit section of large supermarkets. If you have no inclination, or time, to hand-grate the meat, you can substitute a package of grated coconut flakes.

Greater galangal (*isen* or *laos*) A member of the ginger family, this aromatic pinky-yellow rhizome is available in spice stores and through online Asian food sellers.

Jackfruit (*nangka*) This sweet Asian heavyweight has wended its way into many supermarket fruit sections and specialty fruit stores. Canned jackfruit is not a suitable substitute.

Kaffir lime (*jeruk purut*) Small, round, green kaffir limes (colloquially called *limo* in Balinese) are available in many Chinese markets. You can use regular green limes instead, but the taste and scent will not be as fragrant.

Kaffir lime leaves These bright green delicious-smelling leaves are available fresh in plastic packets in Chinatown stores and as dried leaves through online Indonesian food vendors. It is well worth the effort to locate kaffir limes and leaves for the difference they make to Balinese cooking.

Krupuk Crunchy, deep-fried shrimp, fish, cassava, banana, tapioca with embedded peanuts (*rempeyek*) or sweet potato crackers are used to garnish almost all Balinese (and Indonesian) meals and are also eaten as snacks. Unfried crackers are commonly carried by online Indonesian grocers. Airy Chinese shrimp crackers or crunchy Mexican tortilla chips are poor substitutes for Indonesian *krupuk*.

Lemongrass (*sereh*) Fresh stalks of lemongrass are available in more up-market supermarkets and vegetable stores.

Lesser galangal (*cekuh* or *kencur*) Resurrection lily is available in spice stores and through online Asian (often Thai) food merchants. Always use fresh galangal if it is available as its unique taste cannot easily be replicated or replaced. Powdered galangal does not offer the same taste as fresh galangal, but for convenience, cooks can use dried slivers or galangal powder instead.

Long green beans (*kacang panjang*) These extra long green beans are becoming increasingly available in both Western and Chinese supermarkets. Fresh green string beans are a fine substitute.

Palm sugar (*gula merah* or *gula Bali*) Solidified, hard chunks of brown palm sugar, shaped like a half-coconut or bamboo tube, can be substituted with raw brown sugar.

Pandanus leaf (*daun pandan harum*) Distinctive, scent-laden, spear-like pandanus (screwpine) leaves, usually tied together in a knot, are used to add green color and a sweet flavor to cakes, porridges, rice and tea. They can also be ground to a paste and added to desserts and drinks. The leaves are best but pandanus paste, spread and jam are available in packages in Chinese shops in Chinatown.

Roast pig *Babi guling* recipe. If you are not in Puerto Rico or the Philippines, a whole roast suckling pig turning on a spit by the side of the road may be hard to come by. You may substitute a smaller section of pork, grill the meat instead of rotating it over a fire, and adjust the spices accordingly.

Salam leaves Referred to as Indonesian bay leaves, aromatic *salam* leaves, either fresh or dried (brown in color), are used as an ingredient in many Balinese dishes. They can be purchased at online Indonesian food markets.

Sea eels Seafood stores should carry a selection of imported or locally available eels.

Sea salt Although widely available in better supermarkets and organic food stores, table salt can also be used as an alternative.

Shrimp paste (*terasi*) String-smelling dried shrimp paste is an indispensable element in Balinese and Indonesian cooking. It is listed by virtually every online Indonesian food supplier.

Soy sauce (*kecap asin*) Salty sour soy sauce is available in Indonesian or Chinese grocery stores and in larger supermarkets in the Asian condiments aisle. Regular soy sauce can also be of service but has a somewhat different tang and bite.

Soy sauce (*kecap manis*) Sweet thick soy sauce, an Indonesian mainstay, is widely available through online Indonesian stores and in the Asian section of well-stocked supermarkets.

Suji leaves Derived from the plant *kayu sugih*, suji leaves are a useful green food coloring agent for dyeing traditional cakes and drinks. There is no equivalent in the West. You may substitute an artificial green food coloring.

Tamarind pulp (*asam*) This hovers between a sweet and sour taste. Try obtaining it at Indian grocery stores and online Asian supermarkets.

Taro (*keladi*) root, leaves and stem Fresh taro roots and dried taro leaves are available on Amazon at www.amazon.com through the Namaste India Storefront and Moondish Storefront. Taro grows in California, Florida, and Hawaii, and can be found in local markets and Asian supermarkets.

Tempe A completely different soybean-based product from tofu, *tempe* is available in organic or whole health food stores in a block or as single pieces.

Water spinach (*kangkung*) grows prolifically in Florida and Texas, where it has been declared a noxious weed, so it should be available in vegetable stores and markets in the US. You may substitute spinach but you will not get the same crunch, taste and consistency.

BALINESE RESOURCE GUIDE
Where to Buy Balinese and Indonesian Food Ingredients and Spices

UNITED STATES OF AMERICA

Indo Food Store www.indofoodstore.com e-mail: info@worldtohome.com or info@indofoodstore.com. Based in Los Angeles, California, they have warehouses around the US and ship US-wide. They carry over 500 Indonesian food products and are listed on the LA Indonesian Consulate website. They stock a large number of the recipe ingredients mentioned in this book: dried packaged *salam* leaves, blocks of *terasi* (shrimp paste), candlenuts, light coconut milk, kaffir limes, *pandan* coconut paste, *agar-agar* powder, greater galangal (*laos*) in a spice jar, many kinds of *krupuk* crackers, *kecap manis* (sweet soy sauce), salty soy sauce (*kecap asin*) and stone mortar and pestle sets. They do not sell banana leaves as these spoil during shipping.

Indo Kiosk www.indokiosk.com e-mail: info@indokiosk.com P.O. Box 5696, Hacienda Heights, California 91745 (tel. 626-377-0996.) Mails all over the USA. Go online to purchase such treats as frozen *tempe*, *daun salam* (dried leaves), *kemiri* (candlenuts), Sri Kaya brand pandan jam, *kecap manis*, *krupuk* crackers, tofu, *ikan bilis*, cassava and dark caramel brown palm sugar chunks.

Toko Gembira www.tokogembira.com e-mail: help@tokogembira.com 3011 Kaiser Drive, Ste. A, Santa Clara, California 95051 (tel. 408-260-1394). Ships everywhere in the US. E-mail them for additional products and special requests. They stock *laos* galangal roots, *daun salam*, *gula Jawa* palm sugar, *belacan* (shrimp paste block), *sambal taucho*, *krupuk* (*tempe, shrimp, rempeyek*), *agar-agar* powder and modern mortar and pestle grinding sets.

Amazon www.amazon.com Amazon sells gelatinous Bubble Tea (a cousin to *es cendol*) through Asian Foods Stop Storefront (www.asianfoodstop.com), and packaged cassava and tapioca flour via The Barry Farm (www.barryfarm.com). Amazon even has ABC brand *kecap manis* (sweet soy sauce) from Indonesia, pandanus tea, tamarind pulp and dried kaffir lime leaves. The Grocery and Gourmet Food Department, International Market, also has many other hard-to-find goodies.

NEW YORK RESOURCES

Indo Java 8512 Queens Boulevard, Ste. 1, Elmhurst, New York 11373 (tel. 718-779-2241). A small, well-stocked, crowded Indonesian grocery for intrepid New Yorkers and fearless food fighters. Highlights include *tempe, dodol, onde-onde* and *krupuk*.

Chinatowns are the ultimate Asian food pantries of America. New York's Chinatown, south of Canal Street, is big, bustling and bold. It is filled with every spice, fresh squirming commodity and food specialty imaginable.

Indian spice stores and grocery stores are redolent with luscious smelling powders and mysterious imported pieces of the Indian subcontinent. A supplementary resource for Balinese ingredients, these businesses are clustered together in Little India (East 6th Street from First to Second Avenue), and on Lexington Avenue from 26 to 28th Streets in Manhattan. Try Kalustyans and Foods of India.

CANADA (TORONTO)

Oey Trading Co. www.oeytrading.com e-mail: oeytrad@yahoo.com 3241 Kennedy Road, Unit 12, Scarborough, Ontario M1V 2J8 (tel. 416-6091201). Products are imported from Indonesia. Ships all over Canada and to US For ingredient-shopping fun, browse the website for packaged *ketupat* rice cakes, candlenuts, palm sugar tubes, *pandan* aroma paste, shrimp paste (*terasi*), taucho sauce, frozen *tempe, krupuk* crackers, *kaffir* lime leaves, *salam* leaves (green), greater galangal powder, sweet soy sauce, *agar-agar* powder and *kelepon*.

AUSTRALIA (NEW SOUTH WALES)

Asian Grocery Store www.asiangrocerystore.com.au e-mail or admin@asian-grocerystore.com.au 45/51 Leighton Place. Hornsby, NSW 2077, Australia (tel. 0294460170). The Asian Grocery Store is ready, willing and able to ship all over Australia and is a treasure trove of all foods Indonesian (Australia's closest neighbor). They carry many of the important recipe fixings: Ayam brand pourable palm sugar, ABC brand *kecap manis, terasi udang* (shrimp paste or *belachan*), coconut cream, tamarind purée, *daun salam, krupuk* crackers and Bunga Janggelan brand *bunga cincau powder* (grass jelly powder). This is the closest that you are going to get to creating the pleasure rush of the *daluman* drink.

NEW ZEALAND (AUCKLAND)

Auckland is extremely well-endowed with Asian foodstuffs due to its large Indian and Chinese immigrant communities. Many New Zealand expatriates grow their own chilies, tomatoes and leafy edible plants. Fijian Indians cultivate red cherry tomato-size super hot chili peppers and giant taro leaves in their back yards (essential for rolling up and then steaming or frying food parcels). Local Indonesian grocery stores have most of the more esoteric Indonesian ingredients, including frozen banana leaves and canned *daun cincau* (green *daluman* jelly. The best places to buy Balinese Indonesian ingredients are at the Tofu Shop and the Tai Ping Supermarket; this is where Auckland's Indonesian restaurant owners go to purchase their own food supplies.

Tofu Shop www.tofushop.co.nz Nine store branches include Mt Albert, 955 New North Road, Shop 3 (tel. 09-8453050) and Mount Eden, 89 Dominion Road (tel. 09-6310016).

Tai Ping Trading Co. Ltd 911 Dominion Road, Sandringham 1041 (tel. 09-6290340).

Fern tips (*paku* or *pakis* in Bali, *pikopiko* in the Maori language) are readily available in New Zealand, where seven edible species of native ferns grow wild in the damp areas of New Zealand's regional forests. The most commonly eaten species is a pale green fern with brown speckles. The *pikopiko* is picked before the fiddlehead emerges and unfolds to a full fern frond. A traditional Maori food, the very young fern fronds (called bush asparagus) are gathered when they are 4–6 inches high and cooked in a *hangi* with kumara (sweet potato). The fiddleheads are as tender as asparagus, and resemble it in taste. Paku, a common vegetable in Bali, is considered a delicacy in New Zealand or is used as a food garnish.

GREAT BRITAIN (LONDON)

East West www.eastwestoriental.com e-mail: tokoeastwest@yahoo.co.uk 57 Charing Cross Road, London, WC2H One (tel. 07531378329). East West is an Indonesian-style *warung* run by an Indonesian expat from Bandung, a grocery store and an online food-selling business. The range of Indonesian foods available online is staggering: *kecap manis*, *pandan* paste, *krupuk*, fresh *tempe* blocks, fresh *dadar gulung pandan*, packaged *kue mangkok*, *daun kering salam* (packaged dried *salam* leaves), *kemiri* (candlenuts), seedless tamarind and *gula Jawa* (palm sugar chunks). The list of fresh leave, fruits and vegetables is also amazing: *daun kunyit* (turmeric), *daun pandan*, *daun pisang* (fresh banana leaves), *daun singkong* (cassava), *daun salam* (*salam* leaf), *daun jeruk purut* (kaffir lime leaves), *kangkung*, *kemangi plant*, *kencur* (lesser galangal), *laos* (greater galangal), lemongrass stalks, *salak*, *rambutan* and *ketupat* baskets.

Index

The Tuttle Story "Books to Span the East and West"

Many people are surprised to learn that the world's largest publisher of books on Asia had its humble beginnings in the tiny American state of Vermont. The company's founder, Charles E. Tuttle, belonged to a New England family steeped in publishing.

Immediately after World War II, Tuttle served in Tokyo under General Douglas MacArthur and was tasked with reviving the Japanese publishing industry. He later founded the Charles E. Tuttle Publishing Company, which thrives today as one of the world's leading independent publishers.

Though a Westerner, Tuttle was hugely instrumental in bringing a knowledge of Japan and Asia to a world hungry for information about the East. By the time of his death in 1993, Tuttle had published over 6,000 books on Asian culture, history and art—a legacy honored by the Japanese emperor with the "Order of the Sacred Treasure," the highest tribute Japan can bestow upon a non-Japanese.

With a backlist of 1,500 titles, Tuttle Publishing is more active today than at any time in its past—inspired by Charles Tuttle's core mission to publish fine books to span the East and West and provide a greater understanding of each.